W9-DFD-799

Cultural Diversity

A Primer for the Human Services

Cultural Diversity
A Primer for the Human Services

Jerry V. Diller

Brooks/Cole • Wadsworth

I(T)P® *An International Thomson Publishing Company*

Belmont • Albany • Boston • Cincinnati • Detroit • Johannesburg • London
Madrid • Melbourne • Mexico City • New York • Pacific Grove
Paris • Singapore • Tokyo • Toronto • Washington

Property of AERL Library
Wilfrid Laurier University

Property of
Social Work Library

DISCARD DISCARD

Sponsoring Editor: *Eileen Murphy*
Editorial Assistant: *Julie Martinez*
Marketing Team: *Steve Catalano,*
 Margaret Parks, and Aaron Eden
Sales Representative: *Carla Lennox*
Permissions Editor: *Connie Dowcett*

Interior and Cover Designer: *Christine Garrigan*
Production Editor: *Mary Anne Shahidi*
Copy Editor: *Frank Hubert*
Compositor: *The Cowans*
Interior and Cover Printer: *Webcom*

COPYRIGHT © 1999 by Wadsworth Publishing Company
A division of International Thomson Publishing Inc.
I(T)P The ITP logo is a registered trademark used herein under license.

For more information, contact Wadsworth Publishing Company, 10 Davis Drive, Belmont, CA 94002, or
electronically at http://www.wadsworth.com

International Thomson Publishing Europe
Berkshire House
168-173 High Holborn
London, WC1V 7AA, United Kingdom

International Thomson Editores
Seneca, 53
Colonia Polanco
11560 México, D.F. México

Nelson ITP, Australia
102 Dodds Street
South Melbourne
Victoria 3205 Australia

International Thomson Publishing Asia
60 Albert Street
#15-01 Albert Complex
Singapore 189969

Nelson Canada
1120 Birchmount Road
Scarborough, Ontario
Canada M1K 5G4

International Thomson Publishing Japan
Hirakawa-cho Kyowa Building, 3F
2-2-1 Hirakawa-cho, Chiyoda-ku
Tokyo 102, Japan

International Thomson Publishing Southern Africa
Building 18, Constantia Square
138 Sixteenth Road, P.O. Box 2459
Halfway House, 1685 South Africa

All rights reserved. No part of this work covered by the copyright hereon may be reproduced or
used in any form or by any means—graphic, electronic, or mechanical, including photocopying,
recording, taping, or information storage and retrieval systems—without the written permission
of the publisher.

Printed in Canada

10 9 8 7 6 5 4 3 2 1

Library of Congress Cataloging-in-Publication Data
Diller, Jerry V.
 Cultural diversity : a primer for the human services / Jerry
V. Diller.
 p. cm.
 Includes bibliographical references and index.
 ISBN 0-534-35584-6 (pbk.)
 1. Minorities—Services for. 2. Social work with minorities.
3. Social service and race relations. 4. Cross-cultural counseling.
5. Multiculturalism. I. Title.
HV3176.D55 1999
362.84—dc21   98-37384
                                                          CIP

Contents

Preface

Cultural Diversity: A Primer for the Human Services is a comprehensive textbook for students in the human services. It is about how to most effectively and competently provide services cross-culturally. It presents a clear understanding of how a complex variety of social and psychological factors come together to shape a provider's ability to work with those who are culturally different. Included are chapters on cultural competence; racism; culture and ethnocentricity; ethnic children, parenting, and families; ethnic mental health issues; bias in mental health service delivery; and the clinical dynamics of getting started. There are, in addition, chapters focusing specifically on working with African Americans, Latinos/as, Asian Americans, and Native Americans, written by expert providers from those communities, as well as a final chapter on Whites and White ethnics.

The book can be used as a primary text for multicultural issues and cultural diversity courses in counseling, psychology, social work, and human services programs in community colleges, 4-year colleges, and beginning graduate programs. It can also be used as a supplementary text in basic counseling and clinical courses where the intent is to sensitize students to the cultural dimensions of treatment and service provision. Finally, it can be a valuable asset in the continuing education of professionals interested in broadening their theoretical and clinical knowledge of what has become the fastest growing content area in the helping professions.

The book is unique in its breadth of coverage as well as its organization and style. It integrates theoretical with hands-on clinical knowledge and does so from the perspective of asking specifically what kinds of information a student needs to grasp the essentials of cross-cultural helping. Its treatment of topics is comprehensive. For example, racism, a vital issue seldom addressed in most multicultural texts, is explored from a variety of perspectives. What is it? How does it operate in the individual and in society's institutions to oppress People of Color? Why is it so hard for mainstream Whites to acknowledge it and their own privilege? How do the prejudices of providers compromise the helping process? How does one become aware of and alter negative racial attitudes? What are the psychological consequences of racism and oppression on People of Color, especially for the developing child? And how does it operate both within agencies and the helping professions themselves? To assist the student in personalizing these questions, a series of self-awareness exercises are provided at the end of Chapter Three.

A second unique feature of the book is its accessibility. Though it is rich in theoretical and clinical material, it is not overly academic. For example, rather than exhaustively reviewing all studies within a given subject area, it succinctly surveys critical questions and issues and supports this with detailed descriptions of exemplary research. In addition, anecdotes, personal clinical experiences, and real-world examples are generously included. It is easy to read and written for and to the student, anticipating questions, concerns, and anxieties that the topic has regularly elicited from course participants during over 20 years of my teaching experience. For most students, cultural diversity is a "loaded" topic, and the more roadblocks that can be removed, making it more accessible, the more likely significant learning will occur. It is important, for example, to acknowledge White students' concerns over being called racists and to normalize their anxieties over cultural differences as well as to acknowledge the enormous frustration People of Color feel at the denial of racism by Whites. Part of the motivation for writing this text comes from my experience of never having found a textbook on cultural diversity that truly engaged students while educating them. The vast majority of books on the topic are overly academic and hard for the average student to "wade through." Such engagement is imperative, however, if students are not only to grasp a body of knowledge, but also to become sensitized to their own biases, discomforts with difference, and other transferential material. All efforts to define cultural competence to date begin with acknowledging the importance of self-awareness in the provider.

A third unique feature of the book is its treatment of clients of Color and the presentation of specific cultural knowledge about working with African Americans, Latinos/as, Asian Americans, and Native Americans. Four providers of Color, each with extensive clinical experience working with clients from their respective groups, were interviewed and asked to discuss the following topics: professional and ethnic autobiographical material, demographics and shared characteristics of their community, group names, history in a nutshell, help seeking behavior, family and community characteristics, cultural style, values and worldview, common presenting problems, socioeconomic issues, important assessment questions, subpopulations at risk or experiencing transition, tips for developing rapport, optimal therapeutic style, and a short case study. The result is four highly informative and engaging chapters, each filled with rich cultural material and hands-on clinical suggestions and cautions, relayed with passion by four professionals strongly committed to working with clients from their communities. The interviews are only lightly edited to retain their personal and cultural flavor.

Acknowledgments

A book like this is not written in a vacuum. I would first like to thank my daughters, the lights of my life, Becca and Rachel, whose support kept me going and whose encouragment allowed me to complete the dream of writing this book. And to Carole Diller, for her help in supporting my escape to Berkeley where this book was written. Also, special thanks to my colleagues at Lane Community College—Garry Oldham, Ruth Bichsel, and especially, Barbara Thorson—who believed in what I was doing and willingly took on extra work to cover my courses while I was on leave.

A number of indispensable people made writing this book possible. Stuart W. Cook, Tom Vernon, Harrie Hess, Gil Davis, Zalman Schachter-Shalomi, Ed Diller, and Nevitt Sanford were early teachers who taught me about race, ethnicity, and my own Jewish tradition. More recent teachers include Bob Cohen, Manny Foreman, Martin Acker, Reuben Cota, Jack Lawson, and Guadalupe Quinn. In particular, Leland Robison shared with me the richness of his Rom tradition. Saul Siegel, Myrna Holden, Deb Johnson and Carol Stone provided helpful feedback on early drafts of the work. Shuly Plaves, Cynthia Colvin, Esther Wright, Alan Briskin, and Dan Hocoy are friends who gave me support, encouragement, and listened as I ranted and raved about this or that aspect of the book. Brooks/Cole editor Eileen Murphy was indispensable in her clear information, direction, encouragement, and support in all aspects of the book's development and production. Julie Martinez, also of Brooks/Cole, was of enormous help in taking care of a variety of details and small but necessary tasks. Special thanks to the following people who served as readers and reviewers of the text: Sherlon P. Brown, Bowling Green State University; Susan Marcus-Mendoza, University of Oklahoma; Arthur Sanchez, California State University-Chico; Saundra Tomlinson-Clarke, Rutgers University; and Elizabeth Wosley-George, Portland State University. Their comments and suggestions were invaluable and truly challenged my thinking. And finally, special thanks to my colleagues Jimmie Turner, Inez Souza, Dan Hocoy, and Jack Lawson. They generously took time out from very busy schedules and lives to share their expertise as interviewees in the chapters on working with clients of Color. I chose them as much for their very special human qualities as for their expert knowledge.

Jerry V. Diller

Chapter One

Introduction

I once worked at a university counseling center which was baffled by the fact that very few of the university's rather sizable Asian student population ever sought treatment. In the hope of remedying the situation, they invited Asian student leaders to visit the counseling center to learn about available services. After a very polite but unproductive meeting, I overheard one of the students commenting to another, "This place looks like a hospital. Why would anyone want to come here? This is where people come to die." No one on the staff had ever considered that the remodeled health center with its hospitallike rooms might deter clients from seeking help or that in some cultures hospitals are places one goes to die and are thus to be avoided.

Contained in this simple scenario is the crux of a serious problem currently facing human services providers. How can one hope to offer competent services cross-culturally when one lacks basic knowledge about the people one hopes to serve? Ethical guidelines of all human services professions expressly forbid discriminating against clients on the basis of race and ethnicity. However, these organizations are only now beginning to define what culturally competent services might look like and to censure those who provide such services without the requisite skills. The reality is that most service providers regularly, though unknowingly, discriminate against culturally different clients by lacking the skills and knowledge necessary to serve them properly.

This fact is reflected in research that repeatedly shows that community facilities and services are underused by culturally different clients, especially those of Color. There are a number of reasons for this. Mainstream agencies, as in the opening scenario, may inadvertently make clients feel uncomfortable or unwelcome. Clients may not trust the motives or abilities of providers because of past experiences with the system. They may, in addition, believe they will not be understood culturally or have their needs met in a helpful manner. Or they may be unfamiliar with the kinds of services available or come from a culture in which such services are very differently conceived. Each of these possibilities is, in itself, sufficient to deter culturally different clients, who as a group tend to have especially high mental health needs, from seeking treatment or help.

The purpose of this book is to sensitize providers and those learning to be providers to the complex issues involved in cross-cultural service delivery. Only when culturally sensitive services are routinely available will utilization rates of public facilities among culturally different clients begin to approach those of mainstream groups. Providers, as professionals, are expected to demonstrate expertise and competence in the services they offer. Cross-cultural service delivery should be no less an area to be mastered. Only by gaining the requisite knowledge and skills necessary to become "culturally competent" can human service providers hope to actualize their professional commitment to nondiscrimination and equal access for all clients.

Discrimination in this context involves more than merely refusing to offer services to those who are racially or ethnically different. It includes all of the following. Being unaware of one's own prejudices and how they may be inadvertently communicated to clients. Being unaware of differences in cultural style, interactive patterns and values, and how these can lead to miscommunication. Being unaware that many of the theories taught during training are culture-bound. Being unaware of differences in cultural definitions of health and illness as well as the existence of traditional cultural healing methods. And being unaware of the necessity of matching treatment modalities to the cultural style of clients or of adapting practices to the specific cultural needs of clients.

Of equal importance is developing empathy and an appreciation for the life experience of those who are culturally different in America. Why do so many culturally different clients harbor fears and mistrust of providers and others who represent the system? Why are so many angry and frustrated? Why do many culturally different people tend to feel tenuous and conflicted about their traditional identities? Why is parenting for these clients such a major challenge? What is the source of the enormous stress that is the ongoing experience of many culturally different clients? And why do they so often feel that majority group members have very little awareness or concern for the often harsh realities of their daily lives? Without keen insight into the complex answers to these questions, helping professionals cannot hope to serve their clients sensitively.

Providers are by training familiar with the inner workings of the system and thus able to gain access to it on behalf of clients. But special care must be taken in this regard. First, there is the danger that culturally different clients may, as a result of interacting with providers and the system, be unintentionally socialized into the ways of the dominant culture. For example, in working with women from traditional cultures, it is important for them to understand that becoming more independent and assertive, a frequent outcome of counseling with mainstream women, can prove highly problematic when reentering the traditional world. Culturally competent providers educate their clients as to the service alternatives available, as well as the possible consequences, and then allow them to make their own informed choices. A second danger is dependence. Culturally different clients are especially susceptible due to their more limited knowledge of mainstream culture. As their conduit to the system, providers may unknowingly perpetuate dependence rather than help them learn to function independently. Often, for example, it is easier and more expedient to arrange referrals for clients rather than teach them how to do it for themselves. Helping is most useful, however, when it facilitates clients' own interaction with the system on their own terms and in light of their own cultural values and needs. In the literature, this is called "empowerment" and involves supporting and encouraging clients to become their own advocates.

Providers and clients from culturally different backgrounds do not come together in a vacuum. Rather, each brings a certain amount of baggage about the ethnicity of the other. Clients, for example, may initially feel mistrust, anger, fear, suspicion, or deference in the presence of the provider. Providers, in turn, may respond with feelings of superiority, condescension, discomfort, fear, or inadequacy. Each may also perceive the other in terms of cultural stereotypes. Such reactions may be subtle or covered up, but one can be sure they will be there and, for a time at least, get in the way of forming a working alliance. Projections such as these fade with time as client and provider come to know each other as individuals instead of stereotypes. The least helpful thing that a provider can do at this point, however, is to take these reactions personally and respond defensively. A much better strategy is to acknowledge their existence and raise them as a topic for discussion. Research shows that clients of all backgrounds are most comfortable with professionals from their own culture. Unfortunately, there is a serious shortage of non-White providers, and clients of Color will more than likely find themselves working with dominant group professionals. This is where cultural competence comes in. It is my belief and experience that basic trust can develop cross-culturally. But it is not easy. It requires the right skills, a sincere desire to help, a willingness to openly acknowledge and discuss racial and ethnic differences, and a healthy tolerance for being tested.

This book focuses on working with clients from different cultures. Its principles, however, are applicable in a variety of helping situations where provider and client come from qualitatively different backgrounds. This is even true for members of the same cultural group. Differences in class, gender, age, geography, and social and political leanings can lead to such diverse life experiences that members of the same group may feel they have little in common. A middle-class White provider, for example, growing up in a major Eastern city may experience difficulties similar to those just described when working with poor Whites from the rural South. Likewise, providers and clients from different cultural backgrounds who share similar demographics of class, gender, geography, and so forth may feel that they have much in common from which to build a working relationship.

I have used a number of different terms in referring to culturally different clients and have done so consciously. Anyone familiar with this field is aware of the power of such terms. They possess, first of all, subtle connotations and at times implicit value judgments. They have often been used as means of oppressing and demeaning devalued groups. But they can also serve as powerful sources of empowerment and pride. It is not surprising that ethnic group members pay such serious attention to the ways in which they label themselves and are labeled by others. Finding out what term is preferable is a matter of respect, and if providers are in doubt, they should just ask clients what name they prefer. I have never seen anyone offended by that question. I have, however, repeatedly watched providers unintentionally alienate clients through their use of outdated and demeaning terms like "Orientals" or insensitive general references such as "you people."

The general term *cultural diversity* refers to the array of differences that exist among groups of people with definable and unique cultural backgrounds. When I use the term *culturally different*, it is synonymous with cross-cultural and implies that the client comes from a different culture than the provider. It suggests no value judgment as to the superiority of one culture over the other, only that the two have been socialized in very different ways and may likely find communication problematic. It is useful to think of culture as a lens through which life is perceived. Each culture, through its differences (in language, values, personality and family patterns, worldview, sense of time and space, and rules of interaction), generates a phenomenologically different experience of reality. Thus, the same situation, (e.g., an initial counseling session at a community mental health center) may be experienced and interpreted very differently depending on the cultural background of individual clients and providers.

An *ethnic group* is any distinguishable people whose members share a common culture and see themselves as separate and different from the cultural majority. Their observable differences, whether physical, cultural, or geographic, frequently serve as a basis for discrimination and unequal treatment within the larger society. In general, I avoid the concept of race as a definer of group differences. For purposes of this book, I refer to non-White clients as People of Color or clients of Color, to White clients whose origins are not Northern European as White ethnics, and to those whose origins derive from Northern Europe as Whites, dominant group members, or majority providers. The term culturally different is for all practical purposes synonymous with ethnic. In naming specific ethnic groups, I try to use the term or referent that is most current and acceptable to members of that group (although there is always some debate within communities about what names are most acceptable). In relation to clients of Color, I generally use the following: African Americans, Latinas/os, Native Americans, and Asian Americans or Asians.

This book is written from a perspective that assumes that there are certain psychological characteristics and experiences that all ethnic or culturally different clients share. First is the experience of belonging to a group that is socially stigmatized and the object of regular discrimination and derision. Second is the stress and harm this causes to the psyche and the resulting adaptations, some healthy and empowering and others unhealthy and dysfunctional, that ethnic individuals and families must make to survive. Third is the stress and harm that result from problems regularly associated with prejudice and racism (e.g., poverty, insufficient health care, crime, and drug abuse). Not all cultures or individuals within cultures, however, experience these factors with equal intensity. Each society, in its inner workings, designates certain groups as primary scapegoats and others as secondary. In America, for example, People of Color have traditionally been the primary object of derision. In Europe, on the other hand, it has been Jews and the Rom (Gypsies). In one form or another, most ethnic clients exhibit some modicum of these factors and thus share in their dynamics.

It is also important that providers be aware of the diversity that exists both across and within ethnic groups. Each group, first of all, has its own unique history in America. As a result, somewhat different problems have emerged for each around its status as a culturally different group. People of Color, for example, are set apart by the color of their skin and different racial features. As a consequence, they may struggle with concerns over body image and the possibility of "passing" for White. Many Latinas/os and Asians have immigrated from traditional homelands and face ongoing dilemmas around assimilation, bilingualism, and the destruction of traditional family roles and values. Native Americans, as victims of colonization in their own land, have experienced destruction of traditional ways and identities and struggle to come to grips with these losses. African Americans have faced a similar psychological dislocation due to slavery. White ethnics, in turn, find themselves suspended between worlds: They are culturally different, yet perceived, and often wish to be perceived, as part of the majority. These ethnically specific circumstances shape and determine the kinds of problems for which clients seek help.

Differences among clients from the same group can also be extensive. The surest indicator of cultural insensitivity is the belief that all members of a particular group share similar characteristics and circumstances. A recently arrived migrant worker from central Mexico, poor and barely able to speak English, faces very different life challenges than a similarly aged man from a wealthy Chilean family, born in the States, well educated, and working as a banker. The first task of any cross-cultural worker is to carefully assess the client's demographic and cultural situation. Some of the following information may be critical in determining the situation and needs of a culturally different client.: place of birth, number of generations in America, family roles and structure, language spoken at home, English fluency, economic situation and status, amount and type of education, amount of acculturation, traditions still practiced in the home, familiarity and comfort with Northern European lifestyle, religious affiliation, and community and friendship patterns.

The culturally competent provider not only seeks such information, but is also aware of its possible meaning. The migrant worker just described may be in need of financial help, unfamiliar with the system, homesick, fearful of authorities, traditional and macho in his attitudes, and possibly abusing drugs or alcohol. His Chilean counterpart is more likely to be concerned with issues of cultural as opposed to economic survival: how ethnicity is impacting him in the workplace, parental concern over his acculturation, changing roles with his wife and children, and balancing success with retaining traditional ways.

I bring to this text both my own perspective on ethnicity and my experience as an American Jew and White ethnic. The autobiographical material in Chapter 13 should make it quite clear that these are not merely academic issues for me. Like so many other racial and ethnic group members, I have struggled personally with conflicts over group belonging and identity. This has taught me both the complexity of the kinds of issues that are the focus of this book and the fact that becoming culturally competent is indeed a lifelong process that needs constant monitoring. It is important for you to know, as someone beginning to learn in this field, that even those of us who have gained some competence in working cross-culturally never stop struggling with these issues. It is just part and parcel of the process of becoming culturally competent.

I have worked in intergroup relations for over 20 years: teaching courses on multicultural issues in counseling, consulting with various public and private agencies and institutions, and doing clinical work with a wide range of ethnic populations. Yet, I still grow uneasy when I am put in the position of speaking about those who are culturally different from me. To this end, I have written the chapters dealing with the broader conceptual issues, drawing on research as well as examples from my own experience, and have invited experts from the four communities of Color to speak about working with clients from their respective groups. I am still learning about my own culture and heritage. How can I presume to speak authoritatively about the culture of others? Finally, I take very seriously the proposition put forth by many professionals of Color regarding the role of Whites in teaching about multiculturalism and altering racism. It requires educating and transforming the consciousness of other Whites about issues of race and ethnicity. This is my overriding goal in this book.

I have called this work a "primer." According to Webster, a primer is a book of elementary or basic principles. This book's intention is to provide the reader with basic principles, sensitivities, and knowledge that will lay a foundation for becoming a culturally competent professional. The chapters that follow explore different aspects of cultural diversity. Chapter 2, What It Means to Be Culturally Competent, discusses the need for cultural competence, the skill areas it comprises, and the kind of benefits gained by providers who choose to pursue it. In Chapter 3, Understanding Racism and Prejudice, I describe the dynamics of racism and prejudice as they operate at individual, institutional, and cultural levels and how they may impinge on the helping relationship. Chapter 4, Understanding Culture and Cultural Differences, in turn, focuses on the elusive concept of "culture"—its various dimensions, how to make sense of and deal with cultural differences, and the meaning of multiculturalism. With Chapter 5, Ethnic Children, Parenting, and Families, we begin exploring some of the issues involved in ethnic psychology. This chapter discusses developmental issues peculiar to children from racial and ethnic backgrounds, the challenges to parenting these children, differences in family structure across cultures, and issues related to biracial and bicultural families. Chapter 6, Mental Health Issues, deals with mental health issues that have particular relevance for culturally different clients. Included are discussions of group identity conflict, stress, acculturation, unresolved historic grief, and substance abuse. In Chapter 7, Bias in Service Delivery, we explore various factors that lead to bias in service delivery and discuss ways of adapting human services to varied cultural needs. Chapter 8, Critical Issues in Working With Culturally Different Clients, directs attention to the process of actually working with culturally different clients and provides certain guidelines and specific hands-on information. The next four chapters focus specifically on working with clients of Color. In each, an expert from one of the four communities of Color in America—Latinos/as (Chapter 9), Native Americans (Chapter 10), African Americans (Chapter 11), and Asian Americans (Chapter 12)—highlights key issues and differences of which providers working with clients from their culture should be aware. The final chapter, Chapter 13, Working With White and White Ethnic Clients, highlights ways in which Whites structure and protect their racial attitudes and unique issues in working with White ethnics.

Chapter Two

What It Means to Be Culturally Competent

The demographics of the United States are dramatically changing, and central to these changes is a significant increase in non-White populations. Atkinson, Morten, and Sue (1993) refer to this as the "diversification" of America. The statistics speak for themselves. Look first at the relative percentages of population increases for ethnic groups between 1980 and 1992: Asians and Pacific Islanders 123.5%, Hispanics 65.3%, Native American/Eskimo/Aleut 30.7%, African Americans 16.4%, and non-Hispanic White 5.5%. These percentages not only represent sizable increases in actual numbers of Asian Americans, Latinos/as, Native Americans, and African Americans, but also a serious decline in the relative percentage of Whites in America from almost 80% to less than 75%. As Healey (1995) points out, "If this trend continues, it will not take many generations before 'non-Hispanic whites' are a numerical minority of the population" (p. 12).

In the 1990 census, for instance, People of Color made up approximately 40% of California's population, with one out of four school-age children coming from a home where English was not the primary language and one out of six being born outside of the United States. It is projected that by the year 2000, California will be the first "minority majority" state in the country. Texas and New Mexico will not be far behind. In addition, in several major cities, Whites are no longer a majority. Other projections hold that by the year 2050, one out of three residents of the United States will be non-White. These changes are largely due to two factors: immigration and birthrates. The last 30 years have seen an unprecedented wave of immigration to the United States, with yearly numbers rising to 1 million. Unlike earlier immigration patterns, however, the new arrivals are primarily non-European: approximately a third from Asia and a third from South and Central America. Differential birthrates of ethnic groups in the United States are equally skewed. Birthrates of Hispanic populations tend to be approximately 1.7 times that of Whites, and Asian Americans anywhere from 3 to 7 times greater depending on the specific subpopulation.

Opportunity 2000, a study of projections for the work force in the year 2000, commissioned by the U.S. Department of Labor and carried out by the Hudson Institute (1988), shows similar trends. Over the next 10 to 15 years, it is estimated that the labor market will become smaller, older, and most interestingly for our purposes, significantly more diverse. Only 15% of new entrants into the job market will be native-born White males, although this group has traditionally accounted for 47%. People of Color will constitute 29% of this future work force, women 42%, and immigrants 22%. The projected percentage for People of Color represents a twofold increase compared to their current share of the work force. Unfortunately, projections suggest that these growing numbers will be of little help to urban, African American, and Latino males, who may actually experience a decline in available jobs if work-related skills do not keep up with the growing demand for increased technical knowledge.

Reactions to the Changing Demographics

What has been the reaction to this growing diversification? First, White America has clearly felt threatened by these changes. The sheer increase in numbers has stimulated a widespread political backlash. Most prominent has been a rise in anti-immigrant sentiment and legislation and a strong push to repeal affirmative action practices, which were instituted over the last several decades to level out the economic and social playing fields for People of Color. As economic times have worsened for White working and middle classes, frustration has increasingly been directed at non-White newcomers who have been blamed for "taking our jobs" and told to "go back to where you came from if you're not willing to speak English." In a similar vein, White supremacist, militia, and antigovernment groups, playing on racial hatred and a return to "traditional values" and "law and order," have attracted growing numbers. The result has been a society even further polarized along Color lines. People of Color, in turn, have sensed in their growing numbers an ultimatum to White America: "Soon you won't even be the numerical majority. How can you possibly continue to justify the enormous injustice and disparity?"

For those in the helping professions, a major implication of these new demographics is a radically different client base. More and more, providers will be called on to serve clients from diverse cultures. Job announcements increasing state: "bilingual and bicultural professionals preferred" and "cross-cultural experience and sensitivity a requirement." There is, at the same time, a growing awareness that it is not sufficient to merely channel these new clients into the same old structures and programs or to hire a few token professionals of Color. Rather, a radical reconceptualization of effective helping vis-à-vis those who are culturally different and how it occurs is needed. At the center of such a renewed vision is the notion of *cultural competence.*

A Model of Cultural Competence

In its broadest context, cultural competence is the ability to effectively provide services cross-culturally. According to Cross (1989), it is a "set of congruent behaviors, attitudes, and policies that come together in a system, agency, or among professionals and enable that system, agency, or those professionals to work effectively in cross-cultural situations" (p. 13). It is not a new idea. It has been called "ethnic sensitive practice" (Devore & Schlesinger, 1981), "cross-cultural awareness practice" (Green, 1982), "ethnic competence" (Green, 1982), and "ethnic minority practice" (Lum, 1986) by human service providers. It has been referred to as "intercultural communication" (Hoopes, 1972) by those working in international relations and "cross-cultural counseling" (Petersen, Draguns, Lonner, & Trimble, 1989) and "multicultural counseling" (Ponterotto, Casas, Suzuki, & Alexander, 1995) in the field of counseling psychology. What is new, however, is the projected demand for such services and the urgent need for a comprehensive model of effective service delivery.

The work of Cross, Bazron, Dennis, and Isaac (1989) on cultural competence offers a good example of such an evolving model. Cross is the executive director of the National Indian Child Welfare Association in Portland, Oregon. For over a decade, he and his associates have attempted to articulate an effective and comprehensive approach to cross-cultural service delivery (i.e., one that works in the real world).

Basic Assumptions

Cross et al. (1989) begin by asserting that cultural competence, whether in a system, agency, or individual professional, is an ideal goal toward which to strive. It does not occur as the result of a single day of training, a few consultations with experts, reading a book, or even taking a course. Rather, it is a developmental process that depends on the continual acquisition of knowledge, the development of new and more advanced skills, and an ongoing self-evaluation of progress. Cross et al. further believe that a culturally competent care system must rest on a set of unifying values, or what might be called "assumptions," about how services are best delivered to People of Color. These values share the notions that being different is positive, that services must be responsive to specific cultural needs, and that they be delivered in a way that empowers the client. Specifically, the system of care Cross et al. (1989) envision:

- Respects the unique, culturally defined needs of various client populations.

- Acknowledges culture as a predominant force in shaping behaviors, values, and institutions.
- Views natural systems (family, community, church, healers, etc.) as primary mechanisms of support for minority populations.
- Starts with the "family," as defined by each culture, as the primary and preferred point of intervention.
- Acknowledges that minority people are served in varying degrees by the natural system.
- Recognizes that the concepts of "family," "community," etc. are different for various cultures and even for subgroups within cultures.
- Believes that diversity within cultures is as important as diversity between cultures.
- Functions with the awareness that the dignity of the person is not guaranteed unless the dignity of his/her people is preserved.
- Understands that minority clients are usually best served by persons who are part of or in tune with their culture.
- Acknowledges and accepts that cultural differences exist and have an impact on service delivery.
- Treats clients in the context of their minority status, which creates unique mental health issues for minority individuals, including issues related to self-esteem, identity formation, isolation, and role assumption.
- Advocates for effective services on the basis that the absence of cultural competence anywhere is a threat to competent services everywhere.
- Respects the family as indispensable to understanding the individual, because the family provides the context within which the person functions and is the primary support network of its members.
- Recognizes that the thought patterns of non-Western peoples, though different, are equally valid and influence how clients view problems and solutions.
- Respects cultural preferences which value process rather than product and harmony or balance within one's life rather than achievement.
- Acknowledges that when working with minority clients process is as important as product.
- Recognizes that taking the best of both worlds enhances the capacity of all.
- Recognizes that minority people have to be at least bicultural, which in turn creates its own set of mental health issues such as identity conflicts resulting from assimilation, etc.
- Functions with the knowledge that behaviors exist which are adjustments to being different.
- Understands when values of minority groups are in conflict with dominant society values. (pp. 22–24)

(From *Toward a Culturally Competent System of Care,* by T. L. Cross, B. J. Bazron, K. W. Dennis, & M. R. Isaacs. Georgetown University Development Center, Washington, DC. Reprinted by permission of the author.)

Taken together, these assumptions provide the psychological underpinnings for a truly cross-cultural model. First, they are based on the experience of People of Color and those who have worked intimately with them. Second, they take seriously notions that are not typically included in dominant culture service models. These include the impact of cultural differences on mental health, the family and community as a beginning point for treatment, agency accountability to its constituent community, and biculturalism as an ongoing life experience for People of Color. Third, they provide a yardstick against which existing agencies can measure their own treatment philosophy and assumptions.

Assessing Agency Cultural Competence

Cross et al. (1989) have also defined a developmental continuum along which agencies can be assessed according to their ability to deal effectively with cultural differences in their clients. At one extreme is *cultural destructiveness.* Included here are agencies whose policies and practices are actively destructive to cultures and the people who are a part of them. Although it is difficult to find examples of such blatant practices today, it is important to realize that "historically, some agencies have been actively involved in services that have denied people of color access to their natural helpers and healers, removed children of color from their families on the basis of race, or purposely risked the well-being of minority individuals in social and medical experiments without their knowledge or consent" (Cross et al., 1989, p. 14).

Cultural incapacity is the designation given to the next set of agencies along the continuum. These providers, although not intentionally destructive, lack the capacity to help People of Color and their communities. In the process of doing their work, they routinely perpetuate societal biases, beliefs in racial inferiority, and paternalism. In addition, they tend to discriminate in their hiring practices, send messages that People of Color are not valued or welcome, and usually have lower expectations for these clients.

Agencies exhibiting *cultural blindness,* the third group of providers, try to be unbiased in their approach, but do so by asserting that race and culture make no difference in how they provide services and then proceed to apply a dominant cultural approach to all clients. They routinely ignore the cultural strengths and uniquenesses of People of Color, encourage assimilation, and tend to blame victims rather than society for their problems.

More to the positive end of the continuum, providers move into a phase Cross et al. (1989) call *cultural precompetence.* Such agencies are sincere in their efforts to become more multicultural but have had difficulty in making progress. They realize they have problems in serving ethnic group clients and have discovered this fact through ineffectual efforts at better serving a single ethnic population. They tend to lack a realistic picture of all that is involved in becoming culturally competent and often succumb to either a false sense of accomplishment or a particularly difficult failure. In addition, they tend to fall prey to tokenism and put unrealistic hopes in the hiring of one or two professionals of Color whose cultural competence they tend to overestimate. It is probably fair to say that the majority of human service agencies today are culturally precompetent, with some still functioning at a level of cultural incapacity.

The last two points on the continuum, which are still probably more hypothetical than real in today's service world, represent increasing levels of cultural competence. Agencies that possess *basic cultural competence* are well versed in the five skill areas believed to be essential to competent cross-cultural service delivery (to be described shortly). Such agencies also "work to hire unbiased employees, seek advice and consultation from the minority community, and actively decide what they are and are not capable of providing minority clients" (Cross et al., 1989, p. 17). Finally, *cultural proficiency* the positive endpoint of the continuum refers to providers who in addition to those qualities exhibited in basic cultural competence, advocate more broadly for multiculturalism within the general health care system and are engaged in original research on how to better serve culturally different clients and its dissemination.

Having defined this continuum, Cross et al. are quick to point out that movement from one stage to the next takes significant effort. It requires a determined reshuffling of agency attitudes, policies, and practices, the implementation of skill development for all staff, and the serious involvement of all agency personnel: board members, policymakers, administrators, practitioners, and consumers alike. Readers may find it useful to consider where agencies with which they are familiar might be placed on this continuum and why.

Individual Cultural Competence Skill Areas

Turning their attention to the development of cultural competence in individual practitioners, Cross et al. (1989) define five basic skill areas necessary for effective cross-cultural service delivery. Each can be assessed on a continuum of its own, although growth in one tends to support positive movement in the others. It is believed that these skills must infuse not only the provider's work, but also the general climate of agencies and the health care system as a whole. They must be taught, supported, and even more basically, introduced as underlying dimensions of everyday functioning within agencies. One of the skill areas, for example, involves being aware of and accepting differences. For providers, this means respecting differences in their clients. At an agency level, however, a similar commitment to accepting and valuing diversity must also be evident in the clinical practices that are adopted, in the philosophy that is shared, and in the relationship between colleagues and with associates from other parts of the system.

Awareness and Acceptance of Differences.   A first step toward cultural competence involves developing an awareness of the ways in which cultures differ and realizing that these differences may affect the helping process. While all trive to meet the same basic psychological needs, they differ greatly in how they have learned to do so. Cultural differences exist in values, styles of communication, the perception of time, the meaning of health, community, and so on. In attuning one's helping efforts to work with clients from other cultures, acknowledging and looking at differences are as important as highlighting similarities. The discovery of exactly what dimensions of living vary with culture is an ever-evolving drama. Each individual begins life with a singular experience of culture which is taken for reality itself. Only with exposure to additional and differing cultural realities does one begin to develop an appreciation for the diversity that is possible in human behavior.

Equally critical to becoming aware of differences is accepting them. Rokeach (1960), in his analysis of the sources of prejudice, goes so far as to suggest that differences in beliefs and cultural views, rather than a reaction to race per se, are at the heart of racial antipathy. Most difficult is accepting cultural ways and values that are at odds with our own. For instance, as a success-oriented, hyperpunctual individual of Northern European ancestry, I might find it very difficult to accept the perpetual "lateness" of individuals who belong to cultures where time is viewed as flexible and inexact. What eventually emerges in providers who are moving toward cultural competence, however, is a broadening of perspective that acknowledges the simultaneous existence of differing realities that requires neither comparison nor judgment. All exist in their own right and are different. Further along the continuum is a position where differences are not merely accepted but are truly valued for the richness, perspective, and complexity they offer. A culturally competent practitioner actively and creatively uses these differences in the service of the helping process.

Self-Awareness. It is impossible to appreciate the impact of culture on the lives of others, particularly clients, if one is out of touch with his or her own cultural background. Culture is a glue that gives shape to life experience, promoting certain values and experiences as optimal and defining what is possible. As a skill area, self-awareness involves understanding the myriad ways that culture impacts human behavior. "Many people never acknowledge how their day-to-day behaviors have been shaped by cultural norms and values and reinforced by families, peers, and social institutions. How one defines 'family,' identifies desirable life goals, views problems, and even says hello are all influenced by the culture in which one functions" (Cross, 1988, p. 2).

In addition, the skill of self-awareness requires sufficient self-knowledge to anticipate when one's own cultural limits are likely to be pushed, foreseeing potential areas of tension and conflict with specific client groups, and accommodating them. If I am hung up on time and it is in the nature of my clients' culture to be late, I must find a strategy for meeting with them that allows me to remain true to my own cultural values and concurrently allows them to do the same. Cultural self-awareness is an especially difficult task for many White providers, who grew up in households where intact cultural pasts have been lost. What remains instead are bits and pieces of cultural identity and personal history that were long ago cut loose from extended family, traditions, and community, and as a result, lack meaning. Without such a felt sense of the role of culture in the lives of People of Color, certain areas of client experience become difficult to empathize with and understand.

Dynamics of Difference.   Related to self-awareness is what Cross et al. (1989) call the "dynamics of difference." When client and provider come from different cultures, there is a strong likelihood that sooner or later they will miscommunicate by misinterpreting or misjudging the behavior of the other. An awareness of the dynamics of difference involves knowing what can go wrong in cross-cultural communication and knowing how to set it right. Cultural miscommunication has two general sources. The first relates to past experiences either client or practitioner has had with members of the other's group or the nature of current political relations between groups. Mexican immigrants, for example, tend to be hypervigilant in relation to anyone who is perceived as either White or authoritative. Or given recent tensions between African Americans and Jews in the United States, a helping relationship between an African American provider and Jewish client, or vice versa, might prove initially problematic. Dynamics of difference also involve differences in cultural style. If a teacher from a culture that interprets direct eye contact as a sign of respect works with a student who has been taught culturally to avert eye contact as a sign of deference, there is a good chance that the teacher will come away from their interaction with erroneous impressions of the student. If providers are prepared for the possibility of such cross-cultural miscommunication, they are better able to immediately diagnose a problem and more quickly set things back on track.

Knowledge of the Client's Culture.   Cross et al. (1989) also believe that it is critical for providers to familiarize themselves with a client's culture so that behavior may be understood within its own cultural context. Many serious mistakes can be avoided if only one would preface each attempt at analyzing client motivation or behavior by considering what it might mean within the context of the client's cultural group. Similarly, other kinds of cultural information can be clinically useful. "Workers must know what symbols are meaningful, how health is defined and how primary support networks are configured" (Cross, 1988, p. 4). Interpreting the behavior of someone who is culturally different without considering cultural context or ethnocentricity (i.e., from one's own cultural perspective) is fraught with danger as the following anecdote amply demonstrates.

Several years ago, during a period of particularly heavy immigration from Southeast Asia, Children's Protective Services received a rash of abuse reports on Vietnamese parents whose children had come to school with red marks all over their bodies. A bit of cultural detective work quickly turned up the fact that the children had been given an ancient remedy for colds called "cupping," which involves placing heated glass cups on the skin, leaving harmless red marks for about a day. The resulting fallout was a group of irate Vietnamese parents, always hyperattentive to the needs of their children, deeply insulted by accusations of bad parenting, and several workers feeling rather foolish about their cultural ignorance.

Given the variety of populations that must be served and the diversity that exists within each of these, it is not reasonable to expect any single provider to be conversant in the ways of all cultures and subcultures. However, it is possible to learn to identify the kind of information that is required to understand what is going on in the helping situation and have available the use of cultural experts with whom one can consult.

Adaptation of Skills.   The fifth skill area involves adapting and adjusting generic helping practices (that in reality, as we shall see, have their roots in the dominant cultural paradigm) to accommodate cultural differences. Such adaptations can take a variety of forms. Treatment goals can be altered to better fit cultural values. For example, a Chinese family may not feel comfortable working toward an outcome that involves greater assertiveness in their children. The style of interaction in which the helping process is carried out can be adjusted to something that is more familiar to the client. In many cultures, for instance, healing practices are highly authoritative and directive, with advice freely given by experts. Some clients only respond to healers by showing deference. The definition of who is a family member, and thus should be included in treatment, can also vary greatly from culture to culture. Family therapy with African Americans, for instance, usually involves the inclusion of multiple generations as well as nonbiological family members, such as good friends and neighbors. Time and place of meeting can be modified to fit the needs of those who could not ordinarily be available during traditional hours or would find it difficult or threatening to come to a professional office far from their community. Finally, treatment topics can be expanded to include issues that are unique to culturally different clients. Dealing with racism, resolving conflicts around assimilation and acculturation, and clarifying issues of ethnic identity are three examples.

Defining Professional Standards

Sue, Arredondo, and McDavis (1992) offer a somewhat different approach to defining individual cultural competence. Their efforts have as an ultimate goal the enumeration of a set of professional multicultural competencies that will "become a standard for curriculum reform and training of helping professionals" (p. 477). As yet, however, none of the major helping professions' associations has seen fit to develop and/or accept such a standard that would serve to define competent cross-cultural work. What practitioners have been left with are professional codes such as that of the American Association of Counseling and Development, which warn against counselors "claiming professional qualifications exceeding those they possess and recognizing their boundaries of competence" (AACD, p. 481). But without specific guidelines as to what competence looks like, how is one to either achieve or assess it? Sue et al. (1992) believe that this problem "represents one of the major shortcomings of our profession" (p. 481). The framework they offer defines three areas of characteristics of culturally skilled counselors, borrowed from Sue and Sue (1992). First, such counselors "understand their own worldviews, how they are the product of their cultural conditioning, and how it may be reflected in their counseling and work with racial and ethnic minorities" (p. 481). Second, they "understand and share the worldviews of their culturally different clients with respect and appreciation" (p. 481). Third, they "use modalities and define goals consistent with the life experiences and cultural values of clients" (p. 481). Next, each of these three general characteristics—counselor awareness of own assumptions, values, and biases; understanding the worldview of the culturally different client; and developing appropriate intervention strategies and techniques—is broken down into three dimensions that underlie them: attitudes and beliefs, knowledge, and skills. Thus, the following nine competence areas (three characteristics by three dimensions) are defined as basic to a culturally skilled counselor or helper.

Counselor Awareness of Own Assumptions, Values, and Biases

Beliefs and Attitudes

1. Culturally skilled counselors have moved from being culturally unaware to being aware and sensitive to their cultural heritage and to valuing and respecting differences.
2. Culturally skilled counselors are aware of how their own cultural background and experiences, attitudes, and values and biases influence psychological processes.
3. Culturally skilled counselors are able to recognize the limits of their competencies and expertise.
4. Culturally skilled counselors are comfortable with differences that exist between themselves and clients in terms of race, ethnicity, culture, and beliefs.

Knowledge

1. Culturally skilled counselors have specific knowledge about their own racial and cultural heritage and how it personally and professionally affects their definitions and biases of normality-abnormality and the process of counseling.
2. Culturally skilled counselors possess knowledge and understanding about how oppression, racism, discrimination, and stereotyping affect them personally and in their work. This allows them to acknowledge their own racial attitudes, beliefs, and feelings. Although this standard applies to all groups, for White counselors it may mean that they understand how they may have directly or indirectly benefited from individual, institutional, and cultural racism (White identity development models).
3. Culturally skilled counselors possess knowledge about their social impact upon others. They are knowledgeable about communication style differences, how their style may clash or facilitate the counseling

process with minority clients, and how to anticipate the impact it may have on others.

Skills

1. Culturally skilled counselors seek out educational, consultative, and training experiences to enrich their understanding and effectiveness in working with culturally different populations. Being able to recognize the limits of their competencies, they (a) seek consultation, (b) seek further training or education, (c) refer out to more qualified individuals or resources, or (d) engage in a combination of the three.
2. Culturally skilled counselors are constantly seeking to understand themselves as racial and cultural beings and are actively seeking a non-racist identity.

Understanding the Worldview of the Culturally Different Client

Beliefs and Attitudes

1. Culturally skilled counselors are aware of their negative emotional reactions toward other racial and ethnic groups that may prove detrimental to their clients in counseling. They are willing to contrast their own beliefs and attitudes with those of their culturally different clients in a nonjudgmental fashion.
2. Culturally skilled counselors are aware of the stereotypes and preconceived notions that they may hold toward other racial and ethnic minority groups.

Knowledge

1. Culturally skilled counselors possess specific knowledge and information about the particular group that they are working with. They are aware of the life experiences, cultural heritage, and historical background of their culturally different clients. This particular competency is strongly linked to the "minority identity development models" available in the literature.
2. Culturally skilled counselors understand how race, culture, ethnicity, and so forth may affect personality formation, vocational choices, manifestation of psychological disorders, help-seeking behavior, and the appropriateness or inappropriateness of counseling approaches.
3. Culturally skilled counselors understand and have knowledge about sociopolitical influences that impinge upon the life of racial and ethnic minorities. Integration issues, poverty, racism, stereotyping, and powerlessness all leave major scars that may influence the counseling process.

Skills

1. Culturally skilled counselors should familiarize themselves with relevant research and the latest findings regarding mental health and mental disorders of various ethnic and racial groups. They should actively seek out educational experiences that enrich their knowledge, understanding, and cross-cultural skills.
2. Culturally skilled counselors become actively involved with minority individuals outside the counseling setting (community events, social

and political functions, celebrations, friendships, neighborhood groups, and so forth) so that their perspective of minorities is more than an academic or helping exercise.

Developing Appropriate Intervention Strategies and Techniques

Attitudes and Beliefs

1. Culturally skilled counselors respect clients' religious and/or spiritual beliefs and values about physical and mental functioning.
2. Culturally skilled counselors respect indigenous helping practices and respect minority community intrinsic help-giving networks.
3. Culturally skilled counselors value bilingualism and do not view another language as an impediment to counseling (monolingualism may be the culprit).

Knowledge

1. Culturally skilled counselors have a clear and explicit knowledge and understanding of the generic characteristics of counseling and therapy (culture-bound, class-bound, and monolingual) and how they may clash with the cultural values of various minority groups.
2. Culturally skilled counselors are aware of institutional barriers that prevent minorities from using mental health services.
3. Culturally skilled counselors have knowledge of the potential bias in assessment instruments and use procedures and interpret findings keeping in mind the cultural and linguistic characteristics of the clients.
4. Culturally skilled counselors have knowledge of minority family structures, hierarchies, values, and beliefs. They are knowledgeable about the community characteristics and the resources in the community as well as the family.
5. Culturally skilled counselors should be aware of relevant discriminatory practices at the social and community level that may be affecting the psychological welfare of the population being served.

Skills

1. Culturally skilled counselors are able to engage in a variety of verbal and nonverbal helping responses. They are able to send and receive both verbal and nonverbal messages accurately and appropriately. They are not tied down to only one method or approach to helping but recognize that helping styles and approaches may be culture-bound. When they sense that their helping style is limited and potentially inappropriate, they can anticipate and ameliorate its negative effects.
2. Culturally skilled counselors are able to exercise institutional skills on behalf of their clients. They can help clients determine whether a "problem" stems from racism or bias in others (the concept of healthy paranoia) so that clients do not inappropriately blame themselves.
3. Culturally skilled counselors are not averse to seeking consultation with traditional healers or religious and spiritual leaders and practitioners in the treatment of culturally different clients when appropriate.

4. Culturally skilled counselors take responsibility for interacting in the language requested by the client; this may mean appropriate referral to outside resources. A serious problem arises when the linguistic skills of the counselor do not match the language of the client. This being the case, counselors should (a) seek a translator with cultural knowledge and appropriate professional background or (b) refer to a knowledge-able and competent bilingual counselor.

5. Culturally skilled counselors have training and expertise in the use of traditional assessment and testing instruments. They not only under-stand the technical aspects of the instruments but are also aware of the cultural limitations. This allows them to use test instruments for the welfare of the diverse clients.

6. Culturally skilled counselors should attend to as well as work to elimi-nate biases, prejudices, and discriminatory practices. They should be cognizant of sociopolitical contexts in conducting evaluations and pro-viding interventions, and should develop sensitivity to issues of op-pression, sexism, and racism.

7. Culturally skilled counselors take responsibility in educating their clients to the processes of psychological intervention, such as goals, expectations, legal rights, and the counselor's orientation.

A comparison of the models of Cross et al. (1989) and Sue et al. (1992) shows significant overlap in the kinds of development and learning essential for those who hope to move toward cultural competence. The reader may find it valuable to consider the specific categories of both models and assess where he or she might currently fall. Of late, there has been an increase in the availabil-ity of good training programs and courses designed to develop such skill areas. These learning experiences use a variety of process and interactive techniques including self-exploratory and self-assessment exercises (such as those included at the end of Chapter 3), immersion in alternative cultural environments, and observation and on-the-job training in culturally competent agencies.

(From "The Conceptual Framework" by D. W. Sue, P. Arredondo, & R. J. McDavis, *Journal of Counseling and Development*, Vol. 70, pp. 477–486. Copyright © 1992 American Counseling Association. Reprinted with permission.)

Why Become Culturally Competent?

In the past, gaining what is now called cultural competence was an ethical decision undertaken by practitioners with a particularly strong moral sense of what was right and fair. Usually, such individuals sought training with the express purpose of working with specific cultural groups, and they gravitated to minority agencies. Mainstream providers, with their predominantly White client base had little reason to pursue cultural competence. But today, the pic-ture is quite different. All agencies are seeing more culturally diverse clients walking through their doors, and it may not be long before cultural competence becomes a professional imperative. In time, cultural competence may be a routine requirement for all jobs, not just those in the helping professions. If the Opportunity 2000 projections are correct and over 50% of the new entrants into the job market will be People of Color, most Americans will find themselves in close working relationships with colleagues who are culturally different. Whether it is a matter of working under a superior who is a Person of Color, supervising others from different backgrounds, or just retaining good relations with colleagues who are culturally different, being skilled in cross-cultural communication will increasingly be an asset. Given the dramatic diversification that is currently underway in the United States, gaining cultural competence may someday reach a status comparable to that of computer literacy. Twenty-five years ago, computer skills were an isolated novelty. Today, it is difficult to compete successfully in any job market without them. The same may eventually be true of cultural competence.

The Fear and Pain Associated With Moving Toward Cultural Competence

It is my experience that most people are rather apprehensive of learning about race and ethnicity, and they approach the topic with some reluctance and even dread. The same may be true for readers of this book. When I start a new class, the tension in the room is palpable. Students don't know what to expect. Race is a dangerous subject for everyone. People can come unglued in relation to it. White students wonder if they will be attacked, called racists, and made to feel guilty. Students of Color wonder if the class is "going to be for real" or just another "White liberal whitewash job." Everyone wonders whether they will really be able to speak their mind, whether things might not get out of control, and if so, whether I will be able to handle it. Their concerns are understandable. Few Whites have had the experience of talking openly about race and ethnicity, especially cross-racially. Society has evolved strong taboos against it. What is more familiar are accusations and attacks, name-calling, and long, endless diatribes. Consider the diatribes about Rodney King, O. J. Simpson, affirmative action, and anti-immigrant legislation.

What one doesn't hear about or talk about, and what must become a focus of attention if there is ever going to be any positive change in this arena, is the pain and suffering caused by racism and the ways in which everyone is touched by it. I cannot help but think of past students and their stories. Of the young White woman who was traumatized as a young child when her mother found her innocently touching the face of their black maid. Of the Latina girl who was never the same after being accused of stealing the new bike that her parents had scrimped and saved to buy for her. Of the Jewish man who discovered at the age of 25 that his parents had been hiding from him the fact that they were Jews. Of the Asian woman, adopted at birth by White parents, who could not talk to them about how difficult it was for her living in an all-White world. And of the White woman consumed by guilt because of what she felt to be an irrational fear of African American and Latino men. There is clearly as much fear and nervousness about letting out such feelings as there is about the unknowns of working with clients from other cultures.

I try to alleviate some of the anxiety by reviewing the ground rules and assumptions that define how we will interact:

1. There will be no name-calling, labeling, or blaming each other. There are no heroes or villains in this drama; no good people or bad. Each of us harbors our own negative reactions toward those who are different. It is impossible to grow up in a society and not take on its prejudices. So, it is not a matter of whether one is a racist or not. We all are. Rather, it is a question of what negative racial attitudes one has learned so far, and from this moment on, what one is willing to do about them.
2. Everything that is said and divulged in this classroom is confidential, and it is not to be talked about with anyone outside of here. Students often censure, measure their words, and are less than honest in what they say out of fear of either looking bad or of having their personal disclosures treated insensitively or as gossip.
3. As much as possible, everyone will personalize their discussion and talk about their own experiences. There is much denial around racism that serves as a mechanism for avoiding responsibility. Only by personalizing the subject and speaking in the first, rather than the third, person can this be avoided.
4. You can say whatever you believe. This may, in turn, lead to conflict with others. That is okay. But you must be willing to look at it, take responsibility for your words, and learn from what ensues. Anything that happens during class is a learning opportunity. It can and may be analyzed as part of the process. The class is a microcosm of the outer racial world with all of its problems, and as such, honest interaction in class can shed valuable light on the dynamics of intergroup conflict.
5. My intention is to create a safety zone where students can talk about race in ways that cannot be talked about in most parts of the real world. Most students have serious questions about race and ethnicity that need to be answered or experiences in relation to them that must be processed and better understood. Significant learning about race and ethnicity cannot proceed without this happening. Opportunities to do so are rare, but only through such occasions can growth and healing begin.

Once some safety has been established, the floodgates open and students become emboldened by the frank comments of each other to share what is really on their minds. These are the kind of concerns that emerge.

"Why do so many immigrants to America refuse to learn English? If they want to live here and reap the benefits, the least they should be willing to do is learn our language. My parents came over from Italy. They were dirt poor, but made successful lives for themselves. They didn't have all this help. I really don't understand why it should be any different for People of Color."

"This is all really new to me. I grew up in a small town in rural Oregon. There was one Black family, but they stayed to themselves mostly. It's confusing, and to be perfectly honest, it is also pretty scary. There's just so much anger. If I had a client of Color, I'm not sure I would know what to say or do."

"My biggest issues are with Black men. I try to be supportive of them and understand the difficulties they face. But when I see them always with White women, overlooking me and my sisters and all we have to offer, I get really angry."

"To be perfectly honest, I hate being White. I feel extremely guilty about what we have done to People of Color and don't know how to make up for it. I don't feel I have any culture of my own. We used to joke about being Heinz 57 variety Americans. And I envy People of Color for all of their culture and togetherness. We tried practicing some Native American ways, but that didn't seem exactly right, and besides, we were never made to feel very welcome."

"I've come to realize how much racial hatred there was in my family while I was growing up, and this disturbs me greatly. I find it very hard to see my parents in this negative light and don't know what to do with all of this."

"It's gotten pretty hard being a White male these days. You've always got to watch what you say, and as far as getting a job, forget it. There's a whole line of women and minorities and disabled in front of you. I guess I sort of understand the idea of affirmative action, but just because I'm White doesn't mean I have it made. I find it very difficult just getting by financially. I don't see where all of this privilege is."

"I just can't buy all this cultural stuff. People are just people, and I treat everyone the same. I grew up in an integrated neighborhood. I always had a lot of Black and Latino friends and never saw them as different. Frankly, I think all of this focus on differences is creating the problem."

"I'm Jewish, but am finding it hard to discover where I fit in all of this. I don't feel White, but everyone treats me and classifies Jews as White. I was very involved in the Civil Rights Movement a number of years ago; even worked down in the South for a summer registering voters. But that seems so far away, and now Blacks hate Jews. What did we do?"

"I'm in this class because I have to be. I don't need to take a class on racism. I've lived it all my life. White people don't get it. They just don't want to see, and no class is going to open their eyes. What I'm not willing to do is be a token Person of Color in here."

Moving toward cultural competence is hard emotional work. Personal issues such as those just described have to be given voice and worked through. Students need good answers to their questions and support in finding solutions to personal conflicts with the material. Each of five skill areas described by Cross et al. (1989) represents a new set of developmental challenges. It is as if a whole new dimension of reality—that of culture—has been introduced into a student's phenomenological world. Old beliefs about oneself, others, and what one does and does not have in common must be examined and adjusted, where necessary. There are, in addition, vast amounts of information to learn and new cultural worlds to explore. Perhaps most exciting, however, are the ways in which one's mind has to stretch and grow to incorporate all of this new material. Students who have progressed in their learning about cultural matters often speak of a transformation that occurs in the ways they think about themselves and the world.

Bennett (1993) has tried to describe these cognitive changes. Of particular interest is the qualitative shift that occurs in a person's frame of reference; what he describes as movement from "ethnocentrism" to "ethnorelativism." In typical ethnocentric thinking, culturally different behavior is assessed in relation to one's own culture's standards; it is good or bad in terms of its similarity to how things are done in one's own culture. In ethnorelative thinking, "cultures can only be understood relative to one another and . . . particular behavior can only be understood within a cultural context . . . cultural difference is neither good nor bad, it is just different . . ." (Bennett, 1993, p. 26). People who make this shift increase their empathic ability and experience greater ease in adopting a process orientation toward living. When the actions of others are not assessed or judged, but just allowed to exist, it is far easier to enter into their felt experience and thereby empathize with them. Similarly, realizing that behavior, values, and identity itself are not absolute, but rather constructed by culture, frees one to more fully appreciate the ongoing process of living life as opposed to focusing entirely on its content or where one is going or has been. These skills not only transform how people think, but also prepare them for working more effectively with culturally different clients.

A Word to the Reader

In closing this chapter, I wish to address the reader in a more direct way regarding the pursuit of cultural competence and this book. The old adage is still true: You get as much out of reading as you put in. There is much useful information in the following pages which cannot help but contribute to your growth as a provider of cross-cultural services. And that certainly is worth the price of "admission." But it can also be the beginning of a journey that may change you in deep and unpredictable ways. As suggested earlier, engaging in the serious pursuit of cultural competence can be transformational, not so much in a religious sense, but rather in a perceptual one. You may in time think very differently than you do now. I can also guarantee that at times, if you take this latter course, you will be disturbed or disoriented or find yourself feeling very lost and alone. I can remember the first time I had the experience of cultural relativity and realized that what I had for my entire life taken to be absolute reality, the underpinnings of my world, was merely relative. It came from reading the books of Alan Watts on Zen Buddhism, and what I found so disturbing and unsettling was the realization that there was more than one way to understand reality. I was never quite the same person again, as if the center of my consciousness had shifted slightly, and everything looked a little different. It was an unhinging experience, to say the least, which was often repeated in miniversions as I continued to delve into cultural material.

Two things will make a difference in how you relate to this book and ultimately in your pursuit of cultural competence. The first is self-honesty. There is an aspect of ethnocentrism that is delusional. It seeks to hide the fact that human experience can be relative; that there might be another show in town. As shall become evident in Chapter 3, there is also a strong tendency to deny and hide from consciousness many of the negative feelings about race, ethnicity, and cultural differences that one has learned over the years. Together, the two conspire to keep one in the dark. Only by pushing oneself to critically engage the concepts and material of this book and discover precisely how they have played themselves out in the confines of individual lives can one truly begin to understand what it is about. Second is a sustained commitment to gaining cultural competence. The kind of learning that has been the topic of this chapter is long-term. It is as much process as content, tends to be cumulative in nature, and as Cross et al. (1989), Sue et al. (1992), and Bennett (1993) point out, is highly developmental, meaning that the learner goes through various predictable stages of growth, emotion, and change. This book is only a beginning. What happens next—what additional cultural learning experiences you seek and the extent to which you seriously engage in providing services cross-culturally—is up to you.

Chapter Three

Understanding
Racism and Prejudice

Ron Takaki (1993) begins his book *A Different Mirror* by recounting a simple but powerful incident. While riding in a taxi from the airport to a hotel in a large Eastern city for a conference on multiculturalism, the cab driver engaged Takaki in casual conversation. After the usual discussion of weather and tourism, the driver asked, "How long have you been in this country?" Takaki winced and then answered, "All my life . . . I was born in the United States . . . My grandfather came here from Japan in the 1880's. My family has been here, in America, for over a hundred years." The cab driver, obviously feeling uncomfortable, explained, "I was wondering because your English is excellent!" (p. 1).

Encapsulated in this incident are the basic feelings that fuel racial tensions in the United States. The cab driver was giving voice to a belief shared by the majority of White Americans that this country is European in ancestry and White in identity and that only those who share these characteristics truly belong. All others, no matter how long they have resided here, are viewed and treated with suspicion and relegated to the status of outsider. Takaki's wince tells the other side of the story. People of Color, who also call the United States home, are deeply disturbed by their second-class citizenry. Being reminded of their unequal and unwanted status is a daily occurrence. This country, they argue, has grown rich on the labor of successive generations of immigrants and refugees, and our reward should be the same as Whites: full citizenship and equal access to resources as guaranteed in the Constitution. The situation is only further exacerbated by White America's seeming indifference to the enormous injustice that exists in the system.

Cross-cultural service delivery is most usefully viewed against this back-drop. The helping relationship is, after all, a microcosm of broader society, and as such, is susceptible to the same racial tensions and dynamics. It was suggested in Chapter 2 that cultural competence depends on self-awareness, and this includes, above all, an awareness of the attitudes and prejudices that providers bring with them to their work. Neither provider nor client exists in a vacuum. Rather, both carry with them into the helping situation prejudices and stereotypes about the ethnicity of the other, and these, if unaddressed, cannot help but interfere with communication. This chapter explores the dynamics of racism: its structure and meaning, the functions it serves for the individual and for society, how it operates psychologically, and why it is so resistant to change. The chapter ends with a self-assessment tool: a series of exercises intended to help readers explore personal prejudices, stereotypes, and attitudes toward specific ethnic groups, issues of race and ethnicity in familiar agencies and institutions, and their own cultural background.

Defining and Contexualizing Racism

According to Wijeyesinghe, Griffin, and Love (1997), *racism* is "the systematic subordination of members of targeted racial groups who have relatively little social power . . . by members of the agent racial group who have relatively more social power" (p. 88). It is supported simultaneously by individuals, the institutional practices of society, and dominant cultural values and norms. Racism is a universal phenomenon, exists across cultures, and tends to emerge wherever ethnic diversity and differences in perceived group characteristics become part of a struggle for social power. In the case of the United States, African Americans, Latinos/as, Native Americans, and Asian Americans—groups we have been referring to as People of Color—have been systematically subordinated by the White majority.

There are three important points to be made initially about racism. The first is the distinction between prejudice and racism. Allport (1954) defines *prejudice* as an "antipathy," that is, a negative feeling, either expressed or not expressed, "based upon a faulty and inflexible generalization which places [a group of people] at some disadvantage not merited by their actions" (p. 10). Thus, prejudice is a negative, inaccurate, rigid, and unfair way of thinking about members of another group. All human beings hold prejudices. This is true for People of Color as well as for majority group members. But there is a crucial difference between the prejudices held by Whites and those held by People of Color. Whites have more power to enact their prejudices, and therefore negatively impact the lives of People of Color, than vice versa. It is not that members of one group can garner more animosity than the other. Rather, it is the fact that one group (in this case, Americans of Northern European descent), because of its position of power, can more fully translate its negative feelings into real social, political, economic, and psychological consequences for the targeted group. Because of this difference, the term *racism* is used in relation to the racial attitudes and behavior of majority group members. Similar attitudes and behaviors on the part of People of Color are referred to as prejudice and discrimination (a term commonly used to mean actions taken on the basis of one's prejudices). Another way of describing this relationship is that prejudice plus power equal racism.

Second, racism is a broad and all pervasive social phenomenon that is mutually reinforced at all levels of society. In this regard, J. M. Jones (1972) distinguishes three levels of racism: individual, institutional, and cultural. *Individual racism* refers to "the beliefs, attitudes and actions of individuals that support or perpetuate racism" (Wijeyesinghe et al., 1997, p. 89). *Institutional racism* involves the manipulation of societal institutions to give preferences and advantages to Whites and at the same time restrict the choices, rights, mobility, and access of People of Color. While individual racism resides within the person, the institutional variety is wired into the very fabric of social institutions: into their rules, practices, and procedures. Some forms of institutional racism are subtle and hidden; others are overt and obvious. All, however, serve to deny and limit access to those who are culturally different. *Cultural racism* is the belief that the cultural ways of one group are superior to those of another. In the United States, it takes the form of practices that "attribute value and normality to White People and Whiteness, and devalue, stereotype, and label People of Color as 'other,' different, less than, or render them invisible (Wijeyesinghe et al., 1997, p. 93). Cultural racism can be found both in individuals and in institutions. In the former, it is often referred to as *ethnocentrism*. Each of these levels of racism supports and reinforces the others, and together they contribute to its general resistance to change. Later sections of this chapter explore the workings of each in depth as well as inquire into its relevance for providers working with culturally different clients.

The third point is that people tend to deny, rationalize, and avoid discussing their feelings and beliefs about race and ethnicity. Often, these feelings remain unconscious and are brought to awareness only with great difficulty. It is hard to look at and talk about race because there is so much pain and hurt involved. Children's natural curiosity about human differences are quickly tainted and turned into negative judgments and discomfort. They, often imperceptibly, pick up parental prejudices with little awareness (at least at first) that the racial slurs and remarks that come so easily cut to the very core of their victim's self-esteem.

In a society so riddled with racial tensions, everyone is eventually hurt by racism. Accompanying the pain, there is always enormous anger, and anger, whether held inside or directed toward someone else, is hard to deal with. When such emotions become overwhelming, people defensively either turn off or distance themselves from the source of the feelings. Such defensives become habitual, and by adulthood, they are usually firmly in place, effectively blocking emotion around the topic of race.

There is an interesting dynamic that exists around empathizing with those who have been the target of racism. When young children hear the stories of People of Color, they tend to deeply and sincerely feel with the storyteller. "We are really sorry that you had to go through that" is the most common reaction of children. By the time one reaches adulthood, however, the empathy is gone. Reactions instead tend to involve minimizing, justifying, rationalizing, or other forms of emotional blocking. Human service providers are no less susceptible to such defensive behavior, but must force themselves to look inward if they are sincere in their commitment to work effectively cross-culturally. For this reason, the present chapter concludes with a set of activities and exercises aimed at stimulating self-awareness.

Individual Racism and Prejudice

The burning question that arises when one tries to understand the dynamics of individual racism is: Why is it so easy for individuals to develop and then retain racial prejudices? As suggested earlier, racism seems to be a universal phenomenon that transcends geography and culture. Human groups have always exhibited it, and if human history is any lesson, always will. The answer, according to Allport (1954), lies in the fact that racial prejudice has its roots in the "normal and natural tendencies" of how human beings think, feel, and process information. For instance, people tend to feel most comfortable with those who are like them and be suspicious of those who are different. They tend to think categorically, to generalize, and to oversimplify their views of others. They tend to develop beliefs that support their values and basic feelings and avoid those that contradict or challenge them. And they tend to scapegoat those who are most vulnerable and subsequently rationalize their behavior. In short, it is out of these simple human traits and tendencies that racism grows.

Traits and Tendencies Supporting Racism and Prejudice

The idea of in-group and out-group behavior is a good place to begin. There seems to be a natural tendency among all human beings to stick to their own kind and to separate themselves from those who are different. One need not attribute this fact to any nefarious motives; it is just easier and more comfortable to do so. Ironically, inherent in this tendency to love and be most comfortable with one's own are the very seeds of racial hatred. As Allport (1954) suggests, "We prize our mode of existence and correspondingly underprize or actively attack what seems to us to threaten it" (p. 26). Thus, what is different can always be, and often is, perceived as a threat. The tendency to separate oneself from those who are different only intensifies the threat because separation limits communication and, thus, heightens the possibility of misunderstanding. With separation, knowledge of the other also grows vague, and this vagueness seems to invite distortion, the creation of myths about members of other groups, and the attribution of negative characteristics and intent to them.

Prejudice is also stimulated by the human proclivity for categorical thinking. It is a basic and necessary part of the way people think to organize perceptions into cognitive categories and to experience life through these categories. As one grows and matures, certain categories become very detailed and complex; others remain simplistic. Some become charged with emotions; others remain factual. Individuals and groups of people are also sorted into categories. These "people" categories can become charged with emotion and vary greatly in complexity and accuracy. On the basis of the content of these categories, human beings make decisions about how they will act toward others. For example, I have the category "Mexican." As a child, I remember seeing brown-skinned people in an old car at a stoplight and being curious about who and what they were. As we drove by, my father mumbled, "Dirty, lazy Mexicans," and my mother rolled up the window and locked her door. This and a variety of subsequent experiences, both direct and indirect (e.g., comments of others, the media, what I read, etc.), are filed away as part of my Mexican category and shape the way I think about, feel, and act toward Mexicans.

But it is even more complicated than this, for categorical thinking by its very nature leads to oversimplification and prejudgment. Once a person has been identified as a member of an ethnic group, he or she is experienced as possessing all of the categorical traits and emotions internally associated with that group. I may believe, for instance, that Asian Americans are very good at mathematics and that I hate them because of it. If I meet individuals I identify as Asian American, I will both assume that they are good at mathematics and find myself feeling negative toward them.

Related is the concept of stereotype. Weinstein and Mellen (1997) define stereotype as "an undifferentiated, simplistic attribution that involves a judgement of habits, traits, abilities, or expectations . . . assigned as a characteristic of all members of a group" (p. 175). For instance, Jews are short, smart, and money-hungry; Native Americans are stoic, violent, and abuse alcohol. What is implied in these stereotypes is that all Jews are the same and all Native Americans are the same (i.e., share the same characteristics). Ethnic stereotypes are learned as part of normal socialization and are amazingly consistent in their content. As a classroom exercise, I ask students to list the traits they associate with a given ethnic group. Consistently, the lists they generate contain the same characteristics down to minute details and are overwhelmingly negative. One cannot help but marvel at society's ability to transmit the subtlety and detail of these distorted ethnic caricatures. Not only does stereotyping lead to oversimplification in thinking about ethnic group members, but it also provides justification for the exploitation and ill treatment of those who are racially and culturally different. Because of their negative traits, they deserve what they get. Because they are seen as less than human, it is easy to rationalize ill treatment of them.

Categorical thinking and stereotyping also tend to be inflexible, self-perpetuating, and highly resistant to change. Human beings go to great lengths to avoid new evidence that is contrary to existing beliefs and prejudices. First, situations where old beliefs may be challenged or where contrary information might be found are avoided. In a similar manner, people holding like views are sought out as a means of reinforcing existing beliefs. That is why segregated housing and neighborhoods were such an effective means of perpetuating the racial status quo. Often, when contrary information is encountered, it is unconsciously manipulated so as to leave ethnic categories unaffected. Say for instance, I believe that African Americans are lazy. But one day, a new employee, an African American, is hired in my office, and I have never seen anyone work as hard or as diligently as this person. So how do I make sense of this fact, given my beliefs about African American laziness? What I do is treat him as an exception; that is, he is not like other African Americans. Allport (1954) calls this "re-fencing." Contrary information is, thus, briefly acknowledged. But by excluding this exception to my general stereotype ("He is really not like other African Americans"), I can retain my beliefs about African Americans in light of seemingly contradictory evidence.

A similar phenomenon involves the actual distortion of perceptions. Social psychologists have amply demonstrated that individuals perceive and remember material that is consonant with their attitudes and beliefs. They have even shown that perceptions can be distorted to avoid the introduction of contrary information. A classic example is the recall of ambiguous pictures. Pictures are shown to subjects at such high speeds that they can barely perceive the content. The more ambiguous the exposure, the easier it is for the subject to distort perception so as to support existing prejudices. Thus, an individual with extremely negative attitudes toward African Americans, when shown a drawing of an African American man being followed by a White man who is carrying a sticklike object in one hand, may report seeing an African American with a knife or club chasing a White man.

Psychological Theories of Prejudice

Psychologists, like Allport, suggest that the different factors just discussed—in- and out-group behavior, categorical thinking and stereotyping, avoidance, and selective perception—together set the stage for the emergence of racism. But without the existence of some form of internal motivation, an individual's potential for racism remains largely dormant. In a similar manner, Wijeyesinghe et al., (1997) distinguish between active and passive racism: the extent to which an individual actively engages in or advocates violence and oppression against People of Color as opposed to taking a more covert and passive stand. Various theories have been offered regarding the psychological motivation behind prejudice and racism. In reality, there does not seem to be a single theory that can adequately explain the impetus toward racism in all individuals. More likely, there is some truth in all of the theories that follow, and in the case of any given individual, one or more of these may be actively at work.

Probably the most widely held theory of prejudice is known as the *frustration-aggression-displacement hypothesis*. This theory holds that as people move through life they do not always get what they want or need and, as a result, experience varying amounts of frustration. Frustration, in turn, creates aggression and hostility, which can be alternately directed at the original cause of frustration, directed inward at the self, or displaced onto a more accessible target. Thus, if my boss reprimands me, I go home and take it out on my wife, who in turn yells at the kids, who then kick the dog. Such displacement, according to the theory, is the source of racism. How does one choose an appropriate target for displacement? There are a number of competing theories. Williams (1947) believes that the target must be "visible and vulnerable." Dollard (1938) sees any group with which one is in competition as a potential target. Still others believe that the target often symbolizes certain attributes that the individual detests. Another theory holds that societal norms dictate the acceptable targets for displacement. Finally, there is the belief that the choice of targets depends on the "analytic" mechanism of projection. Individuals displace their hostility on groups who possess "bad" attributes, which are in reality unconsciously similar to attributes they detest in themselves. The irrationality of displacement requires the person to find a justification for his or her hatred. This is often done by creating myths about why the group being discriminated against really deserves such treatment or by drawing on existing stereotypes, negative traits, and theories of inferiority. During the period of American slavery, for example, many slave owners asserted that African Americans were subhuman and incapable of caring for themselves, and because of this, slavery was actually a benign and kindly institution.

A second theory holds that prejudice is part of a broader, global personality type. The classical example is the work of Adorno, Frankel-Brunswik, Levinson, and Sanford (1950) on what has become known as the *authoritarian personality*. Growing out of the horrors of World War II and the willingness of so many to collaborate and "merely follow orders," Adorno and his colleagues postulated the existence of a global bigoted personality type manifesting a variety of traits revolving around personal insecurity and a basic fear of everything and everyone different. Such individuals are believed to be highly repressed, insecure, and experience low self-esteem and high alienation. In addition, they tend to be highly moralistic, nationalistic, and authoritarian, to think in terms of black and white, to have a high need for order and structure, to view problems as external rather than psychological, and to feel anger and resentment against members of all ethnic groups.

Other theories suggest the following about racial prejudice: that it is manipulated within a society to promote certain economic and political objectives; that it is a means of buoying up one's own self-esteem by viewing members of other groups as inferior; that it is socially sanctioned in certain geographical areas against specific ethnic groups and that many people who discriminate are adjusting to a social norm; and that it is based not on racial differences as much as on perceived dissimilarities in belief systems (i.e., people tend to dislike those who think differently than they do). What all of these theories share, however, is the idea that through racist beliefs and actions individuals meet important psychological and emotional needs. To the extent that this process is successful, their hatred remains energized and reinforced. Within such a model, the reduction of prejudice and racism can only occur when alternative ways of meeting emotional needs are found.

Implications for Providers

What does all of this information about individual racism have to do with human service providers? Put most directly, it is the source or at least a contributing factor to many of the problems for which culturally different clients seek help. Some clients present problems that revolve around dealing with racism directly. They live with it on a daily basis. Relating to the racism they encounter in a healthy and non-self-destructive manner is, therefore, a major life challenge. To be the continual object of someone else's hatred as well as that of an entire social system is a source of enormous stress, and such stress takes its psychological toll. It is no accident, for example, that African American men suffer from and are at particularly high risk for stress-related physical illnesses.

Other clients present with problems that are a more indirect consequence of racism. A disproportionate number of People of Color find themselves poor and with limited resources and skills for competing in a White-dominated marketplace. The stress caused by poverty places people at high psychological risk. More affluent People of Color are no less susceptible to the far-reaching consequences of racism. Life goals and aspirations are likely blocked or at least made more difficult because of the color of their skin. There is a saying among professionals of Color that one has to be twice as good as one's White counterpart to make it. This too is a source of inner tension, as are the doubts a professional of Color may have as to whether he or she earned a job or promotion because of ability or skin color.

It is equally important that providers become aware of the prejudices that they hold as individuals. There are a number of exercises at the end of this chapter. If undertaken with honesty and seriousness, they can provide valuable insight into the feelings and beliefs that one holds about other racial and ethnic groups. Without such awareness, it is all too easy for providers to confound their work with their own prejudicial material. For example, if I think stereotypically about clients of Color, it is very likely that I will too narrowly define their potential, miss important aspects of their individuality, and even unwittingly guide them in the direction of taking on the very stereotyped characteristics I hold about them. My own narrowness of thought will limit the success I can have working with culturally different clients. It is critical to remember that prejudice often works at an unconscious level and that professionals are susceptible to its dynamics. It is also critical to be aware that, after a lifetime of experience in a racist world, clients of Color are highly sensitized to the nuances of prejudice and racism and can identify it very quickly. Finally, it is important to reemphasize that professional codes of conduct consider it unethical to work with a client with whom one has a serious value conflict. Prejudice and racism are considered such a value conflict.

Institutional Racism

Consider the following statistics from Hacker (1992) about African Americans in the United States:

- 45.3% of the prisoners behind bars in the United States are African American.
- 44.8% of African American children live below the poverty level.
- Life expectancy of African Americans is 93% that of Whites.
- The infant mortality rate for African American babies is twice that of White babies.
- African Americans are 7 times as likely to contract tuberculosis, 2.5 times as likely to get diabetes, and 1.40 more likely to suffer from heart disease than Whites.
- The income of African American families is 58% that of White families.
- Unemployment rates among African Americans is 2.76 times that of Whites.
- African Americans are overrepresented in low-pay service occupations (e.g., nursing aides and orderlies, 30.7%) and underrepresented among professionals (e.g., architects, 0.9%).
- Whites are 1.92 times more likely to have attended 4 or more years of college than African Americans.
- In the state of Illinois, 83.2% of African American children attend segregated schools.

These are examples of the consequences of what was described earlier as institutional racism: the manipulation of societal institutions to give preferences and advantages to Whites and at the same time restrict the choices, rights, mobility, and access of People of Color. In each of these varied instances, African Americans are seen at a decided disadvantage or at greater risk compared to Whites. The term *institutions* refers to "established societal networks that covertly or overtly control the allocation of resources to individuals and social groups" (Wijeyesinghe et al., 1997, p. 93). Included are the media, the police, courts and jails, banks, schools, organizations that deal with employment and education, the health system, and religious, family, civil, and governmental organizations. Something within the fabric of these institutions causes discrepancies such as those just listed to occur on a regular and systematic basis. In many ways, institutional racism is far more insidious than individual racism because it exists beyond the attitudes and behaviors of the individual in the bylaws, rules, practices, procedures, and organizational culture. Thus, it appears to have a life of its own and seems easier for those involved in the daily running of such institutions to disavow any responsibility for it.

Determining Institutional Racism

How does one go about determining the existence of institutional racism? The most obvious manner is through the reports of victims themselves: those who regularly feel its effects, encounter differential treatment, and are given only limited access to resources. But such firsthand reports are often held suspect and are too easily countered by explanations of "sour grapes" or "they just need to pull themselves up by their own bootstraps" by those who may not, for a variety of reasons, want to look too closely at the workings of racism.

A more objective strategy is to compare the frequency or incidence of a phenomenon within a group to the frequency within the general population. One would expect, for example, that a group which comprises 10% of this country's population would provide 10% of its doctors or be responsible for 10% of its crimes. When there is a sizable disparity between these two numbers (i.e., when the expected percentages don't line up, especially when they are very discrepant), it is likely that some broader social force, such as institutional racism, is intervening.

One might alternatively argue that there is something about members of the group itself, rather than institutional racism, that is responsible for the statistical discrepancy. Such explanations, however, with the one exception of cultural differences (to be described), must be assessed very carefully, for they are frequently based on prejudicial and stereotypical thinking. For instance, members of Group X consistently score lower on intelligence tests than do dominant group members. One explanation may be that members of Group X are intellectually inferior. But there is a long history of debate over the scientific merit of taking such a position that has yet to prove anything more substantial than the fact that proponents who argue on the side of racial inferiority in intelligence tend to enjoy the publicity they inevitably receive. An alternative and more scientifically compelling explanation is that intelligence tests themselves are culturally biased and, in addition, favor individuals whose first language is English.

There are indeed aspects of a group's collective experience that do predispose members to behave or exhibit characteristics in a manner different from what would be expected statistically. For instance, because of ritualistic practices, Jews tend to experience relatively low rates of alcoholism. There-fore, it is not surprising to find that the percentage of Jews suffering from alco-hol abuse is disproportionately lower than their representation in the general population. Such differences, however, tend to be cultural rather than biological.

Consciousness, Intent, and Denial

Institutional racist practices can be conscious or unconscious and intended or unintended. Conscious or unconscious refers to the fact that those working within a system may or may not be aware of the practices' existence and impact. To be intended or unintended means that the practices may or may not have been purposely created, but they nevertheless exist and substantially affect the lives of People of Color. A similar distinction was made early in the Civil Rights Movement between de jure and de facto segregation. The former refers to segregation that was legally sanctioned and the existence of actual laws dictating racial separation. De jure segregation was, thus, both conscious and intended. De facto segregation, on the other hand, implies separation that exists in actuality or after the fact, but may not have been consciously created for racial purposes.

It is important to distinguish among consciousness, intent, and account-ability. I may have been unaware that telling an ethnic joke could be hurtful. Nor might I have intended such harm. But I am still responsible for the conse-quences of my actions and the hurt that may result. Similarly, someone I know works in an organization that unknowingly excludes People of Color from receiving services, and it was never his intention to do so. But again, intention does not justify consequences, and as an employee of that institution, he should be responsible for being aware of its actions. Thus, lack of intent or awareness should never be regarded as justification for the existence of institu-tional or individual racism.

Although denial is an essential part of all forms of racism, it seems espe-cially difficult for individuals to take personal responsibility for institutional racism. Acknowledging the existence of one's own prejudicial thoughts or stereotypes is far easier than feeling that one has played an active role in the creation of an institution, organization, or agency of which one is a part. First, institutional practices tend to have a history of their own that may precede the individual's own tenure in the organization. To challenge or question such practices may also be presumptuous and beyond one's power or status. Or one might feel that he or she is merely following the prescribed practices expected of an employee or the dictates of a superior, and thus, cannot fairly be held responsible for them. Similar logic is offered in discussions of slavery and White responsibility. "I never owned slaves; neither did my ancestors. That happened 150 years ago. Why should I be expected to make sacrifices in my life for injustices that happened long ago and were not of my making?" Sec-ond, people tend to feel powerless in relation to large organizations and institutions. Sentiments such as "You can't fight city hall" or "What can one person do?" seem to prevail. The distribution of tasks and power and the perception that decisions are made "above" contribute further to feelings of powerlessness and alienation. Third, institutions are by nature conservative and oriented toward keeping the status quo. Change requires far more energy and is generally considered only during times of serious crisis and challenge. Specific procedures for effecting change are seldom spelled out, and important practices tend to be subtly yet powerfully protected. Fourth, the practices of an institution that support institutional racism (i.e., that keep People of Color out) are multiple, complicated, mutually reinforcing, and therefore, all the more insidious. Even if one were to undertake such efforts sincerely, it is often difficult to know exactly where to begin.

A Case Study

To provide a better sense of the complexity with which institutional racism asserts itself, I would like to share an excerpt from a cultural evaluation of an agency in which I was involved. The purpose of the project was to assess the organization's ability to provide culturally sensitive services to its clients and to make recommendations as to how it might become more culturally competent. Since space is limited, I focus only on issues related to staffing patterns. Although the report does not directly point to instances of institutional racism, they become obvious as one reads through the text and its recommendations.

> Currently, People of Color are under-represented on the staff of _____.
> In the Units under study, only two workers are of Color: a Latino man and an African American man. Neither are supervisors. In the entire office only seven staff members are of Color: two Latino/as, one African American and three Asian Americans. Two Asian Americans are supervisors. There are no People of Color in higher levels of management. An often-cited problem is the fact that there are few minority candidates on the state list from which hiring is done. What is required to compensate is special and proactive recruitment efforts to get People of Color on the lists as well as the creation of special positions and other strategies for circumventing such lists. At a systems level attention must be given to screening practices that may inadvertently and unfairly reject qualified minority candidates. While at least parity in numbers of staff of Color to population demographics should be an important goal, holding to strict quotas misses the point of cultural competency. The idea is to strive for making the entire organization, all management and staff, more culturally competent, that is, able to effectively work with those clients who are culturally different. Nor is it reasonable to assume that all staff of Color will be culturally competent. While attempting to add more staff of Color, it is highly useful to fill the vacuum through the use of community resources and professionals hired specifically to provide cultural expertise.
>   In general, the staff interviewed were found to be in need of cultural competency training. This would include: awareness of broader issues of culture

and cross-cultural communication, history and cultural patterns of specific minority cultures and implications of cultural differences for the provision of client services. Especially relevant was knowledge of normal vs. dysfunctional family patterns within different cultural groups, so that culturally sensitive and accurate assessments might be carried out. In moving towards a family support model within the agency as was indicated by several staff members during our interviews, it is critical to understand family dynamics of a given family from the perspective of its culture of origin as opposed to a singular, monocultural Euro-American perspective. Also evident was a basic conflict within the organization between treatment and corrections models of providing services. Staff adhering to the latter tended to devalue the importance of cultural differences in working with clients of Color and in addition tended to see youth of Color as using racism and cultural differences as an excuse for not taking responsibility for their own behavior.

White staff members report the following needs and concerns in regard to working with children of Color: need help in identifying culturally appropriate resources and placements; discomfort in dealing with issues of race; don't know the right questions to ask; families often unwilling to discuss or acknowledge race as an issue; the need for more and better training; lack of knowledge about biracial children; and need for a better understanding of the role of culture in the service model they use.

Staff of Color did not report any experiences of overt discrimination and felt respected by their colleagues. They felt that _____ was in fact trying to deal with the problem of cultural diversity, but that this interest was of rather recent vintage and motivated primarily by political and legal concerns. They also felt that the liberal climate of the organization did much to justify a pervasive attitude that "we treat everyone the same" and "I know good service provision and can deal with anyone." Together, such attitudes often served as an excuse for not dealing directly with cultural differences in clients. They also believed that cultural diversity was experienced by some co-workers as an extra burden and merely more work to do. As in most work situations, the staff of Color did experience some distance from co-workers. The onus of keeping up good relations was often felt to be on the person of Color to put their White co-workers at ease. Staff of Color we interviewed were subject to especially high burnout potential and needed their own resources and support outside the organization. We found both staff of Color of the Units under investigation to be especially strong and competent individuals who were particularly stretched thin between their regular duties and their roles within the organization as cultural experts.

The recent hiring of a Latino/a professional by _____ as a means of dealing with a growing Spanish-speaking population deserves some comment. The need for providing services to this population has been well documented by the extent of the demand that has already arisen for his services. We are concerned, however, that the way in which the position has been created will be a set-up for eventual burnout and failure, and that much more support for the position must be consciously and systematically provided. We perceive an expectation from within and from without the organization that this individual will be able to "do it all": help organize an advisory board and provide services to it, do outreach to the Latino/a community, be an inhouse cultural expert, be an advocate with other agencies and referral source for all

Latino/a members of the community, and carry a full caseload of Latino/a and non-Latino/a families. The work demands are already cutting into personal time, and as he deals with other agencies and realizes the lack of culturally-relevant services available elsewhere, he becomes even further burdened. Providing culturally competent services to the Latino/a community, as _____ is now trying to do, will merely open the floodgates of additional demands for services. The current position holder suggested: "The agency doesn't realize that this is only the tip of the iceberg." It is likely that _____ will soon be faced with adding additional bicultural, bilingual staff to meet the growing need. In this regard two caveats should be offered. First, culturally sensitive workers and those assigned caseloads of individuals from non-Euro-American cultures tend to work most effectively and creatively when they are allowed maximum flexibility, leeway and discretion in how they carry out their duties. Rules and policies established within the context of serving Euro-American clients may be of little help and possibly obstructive to working with culturally-different groups. Second, the existence of a defined cultural expert within an organization should not be viewed in any way as a justification for not actively pursuing the cultural competence of the agency in general and its staff.

Implications for Providers

What, then, are the implications of institutional racism for human service providers? First and foremost, the vast majority of providers work in agencies and organizations that may suffer in varying degrees from institutional racism. To the extent that the general structure, practices, and climate of an agency make it impossible for clients of Color to receive culturally competent services, the efforts of individual providers, no matter how skilled, are drastically compromised. It is just not possible to divorce what happens between a provider and clients from the larger context of the agency. Culturally different clients may avoid seeking services from an agency once they are familiar with its practices. (Such information travels very quickly within a community.) If they must come, their willingness to trust and enter into a working relationship with the individual provider to whom they are assigned is seriously compromised. Again, their work with individual staff members is affected by how they perceive and experience the agency as a whole. In their eyes, the provider is always a part of the agency and perceived as responsible for what it does. Finally, the ability to do what is necessary to meet the needs of a culturally different client may be limited by the rules and atmosphere of the workplace. Is there support, resources, and knowledgeable supervision for working with culturally different clients? Is the provider afforded enough flexibility so as to be able to adapt services to the cultural demands of clients from various cultural groups? If the answer to either of these questions is no, then the provider must be willing to try to initiate changes in how the organization functions—its structure, practices, climate—so that it can be more supportive of efforts to provide more culturally competent services.

Cultural Racism

Closely intertwined with institutional racism is cultural racism: the belief that the cultural ways of one group are superior to those of another. Whenever I think of cultural racism, I remember a Latino student once telling a class about painful early experiences in predominantly White schools:

> "One day a teacher was giving us a lesson on nutrition. She asked us to tell the class what we had eaten for dinner the night before. When it was my turn, I proudly listed beans, rice, tortillas. Her response was that my dinner had not included all of the four major food groups and, therefore, was not sufficiently nutritious. The students giggled. How could she say that? Those foods were nutritious to me."

Institutions, like ethnic groups, have their own cultures: languages, ways of doing things, values, attitudes toward time, standards of appropriate behavior, and so on. As participants in institutions, people are expected to adopt, share, and exhibit these cultural patterns. If they don't or can't, they are likely to be censured and made to feel uncomfortable in a variety of ways. In the United States, the cultural form that has been adopted by and dominates all social institutions is White Northern European culture. The established norms of how things are done in this country are dictated by the various dimensions of this dominant culture. Behavior outside its parameters is judged as bad, inappropriate, different, or abnormal. Thus, the eating habits with which my student was raised in his Latino home, in that they differed from what White culture considers nutritious, were judged as unhealthy, and he was made to feel bad and ashamed because of it.

Herein lies the real insidiousness of cultural racism: Those who are culturally different must either give up their own ways, and thus a part of themselves, and take on the ways of majority culture or remain perpetual outsiders. (There are those who believe it is possible to be bicultural, that is, learn the ways and function comfortably in two very different cultures. This idea is discussed in Chapter 5.) Institutional and cultural racism are thus two sides of the same coin. Institutional racism keeps People of Color on the outside of society's institutions by structurally limiting their access. Cultural racism makes them uncomfortable if they do manage to gain entry. Its ways are foreign to them, and they know that their own cultural traits are judged harshly.

Wijeyesinghe et al. (1997) offer the following examples of cultural racism:

> Holidays and celebrations: Thanksgiving and Christmas are acknowledged officially on calendars. "Traditional" holiday meals, usually comprised of foods representing the dominant culture, have become the norm for everyone . . . Holidays associated with non-European cultures are given little attention in United States culture . . .

Personal traits: Characteristics such as independence, assertiveness, and modesty are valued differently in different cultures.

Language: "Standard English" usage is expected in most institutions in the United States. Other languages are sometimes expressly prohibited or tacitly disapproved of.

Standards of dress: If a student or faculty member dresses in clothing or hairstyles unique to their culture, they are described as "being ethnic," whereas the clothing or hairstyles of Europeans are viewed as "normal."

Standards of beauty: Eye color, hair color, hair texture, body size, and shape ideals exclude most People of Color. For instance, black women who have won the Miss America beauty pageant have closely approximated white European looks . . .

Cultural icons: Jesus, Mary, Santa Claus, for example, are portrayed as white. The devil and Judas Iscariot, however, are often portrayed as black. . . . (p. 94)

Implications for Providers

Cultural racism has relevance for human service providers in several ways. First, it is important that providers be aware of the cultural values that they, as professionals, bring to the counseling session and acknowledge that these values may be different from and even at odds with those of their clients. This is especially true for White providers working with clients of Color. It is not unusual for clients of Color to react to White professionals as symbols of the dominant culture and to initially act out their frustrations with a society that so systematically negates their cultural ways. Second, all helping across cultures must involve some degree of negotiation around the values that define the helping relationship. Most important, therapeutic goals and the general style of interaction must make sense to the client. Yet, at the same time, they must fall within the broad parameters of what the provider conceives as therapeutic. Most likely, the provider will have to make significant adaptations to standard methods of helping to fit the needs of the culturally different client. Third is the realization that traditional training as helping professionals and the models that inform this training are themselves culture-bound and have their roots in dominant Northern European culture. As such, what exactly are the values and cultural imperatives that providers bring to the helping relationship? And what relevance do these have for clients whose cultural worldview might be very different?

Cultures differ greatly in how they view healing and how they conceive of the helping process. The notion of seeking professional help from strangers makes little sense in many cultures. Similarly, questions of what is healthy behavior and how one treats dysfunction vary greatly across cultures. Given all of this cultural variation and the ethnocentricity of traditional helping models and methods, helping professionals must answer for themselves a number of very knotty questions. Is it possible, for example, to expand present culture-bound models so they can become universally applicable (i.e., appropriately applied multiculturally)? And if so, what would such a model look like? Or is there, perhaps, some truth to the contention of many minority professionals that something in the Northern European dominant paradigm is inherently destructive to traditional culture, and radically different approaches to helping must be forged for each ethnic population? These questions are addressed in Chapter 4.

A Self-Assessment

A theme that has reverberated throughout this chapter is the critical nature of self-awareness. Again, it is not just a question of whether one holds racist attitudes and stereotypes or if one is involved with practices of institutional or cultural racism. We all do and are. Rather, the issue is discovering in what ways a provider's thinking is slanted racially, how this will affect his or her role as a helper, and what can be done to change it. The exercises that follow are meant to stimulate increased self-awareness. They are necessary in counteracting natural tendencies toward denial, avoidance, and rationalization in matters of race and ethnicity. They are useful to the extent that the reader takes them seriously, gives sufficient time to adequately process and complete them, and approaches them with candor.

Exercise I

This exercise involves a series of questions about your experiences with ethnicity and cultural differences. Several ask you to identify a time or event in the past. Allow yourself to relax and visualize the time or event you have identified. Try to reexperience it as much as possible. When you are finished, describe the experience in writing. Include how you felt at the time, how you now feel about it, how it has affected you today, and any other associations, images, or strong feelings that may come up. Use as much time and detail as you need.

1. When did you first become aware that people were different racially or ethnically?
2. When did you first become aware of yourself as a member of a racial or ethnic group?
3. When were you first made aware of people being treated differently because of their race or ethnicity?
4. When did you first become aware of being treated differently yourself because of your own race or ethnicity?
5. Are there things about you as a person that make you feel that you are different from other people? Describe them and how having these qualities makes you feel and how it has affected you over time.

6. When were you proudest being a member of the group to which you belong?
7. When were you least proud of being a member of the group to which you belong?
8. How do you identify yourself racially/ethnically? Culturally? How has your sense of race/ethnicity or culture changed over time?
9. How would you describe the extent of your contact with people who are racially/ethnically different from you? How has this changed over time?

You can increase the intensity and learning value of this exercise by sharing your answers with someone else. After you have shared each answer, use it as a springboard for further soul-searching and personal discussions of each topic.

Exercise 2

This exercise involves writing a detailed autobiography focusing on issues of race and ethnicity. You might find it helpful to do this chronologically. With the experiences of Exercise 1 as stimuli, write a personal history of your experiences with prejudice and racism, how your own ethnic background has impacted these, contact with those who are culturally different from you, and the general experience of being different.

You can increase the power of this exercise by taking turns reading your autobiography with another person or in a small group. In relation to either, have the other person or people respond to various aspects of your writing and then follow this up with a discussion of their various reactions.

Exercise 3

This exercise gives you an opportunity to verbalize and identify your experiences with, attitudes toward, and beliefs about members of different racial and ethnic groups. Answer the following questions or carry out the requested activity in relation to each of the following groups toward which you feel an affinity or dislike: (a) African Americans, (b) Latinos/as, (c) Asian Americans, (d) Native Americans, (e) White Northern Europeans, (f) White ethnic groups (Jews, Irish, Italians, etc.).

1. Describe in detail experiences you have had with members of this group.
2. At present, how do you feel about members of this group (describe your reactions in detail and, if possible, relate them to specific experiences) and how has that changed over time?
3. Are there any characteristics, traits, or other things about members of this group that make it difficult for you to approach them?

4. Without censoring yourself, generate a list of characteristics—one-word adjectives—that describes your beliefs and perceptions about members of this group.

5. What reactions, feelings, thoughts, or concerns come to mind when you think about working professionally with members of this group?

6. What kinds of answers, information, learning experiences, contact, and so forth do you need to become more comfortable with members of this group?

Exercise 4

This exercise is intended to help you identify dynamics and aspects of institutional and cultural racism in organizations and agencies. Choose a particular agency or organization with which you are familiar. It may be one in which you are currently working or volunteering or one you are familiar with from the past. Answer the following questions about it. Some of the questions may require you to do research or seek additional information. As part of your organizational assessment, answer the following in detail.

1. How many People of Color or other ethnic group members work in this organization and what kind of jobs do they hold?

2. How are people hired or brought into the organization? Is there anything about this process or what might be required that you feel may differentially affect People of Color or other ethnic group members?

3. Does the organization take any position on promoting cultural diversity within its ranks? Do any mission statements, plans, or projections in this direction exist? Can you discern any unwritten feelings or attitudes that prevail around race and ethnicity within the organization? Has it done anything specific to promote greater diversity?

4. How would you describe the organizational culture? Do you feel that members of various communities of Color would be comfortable entering and being a part of it? Specify your answers by group and explain in detail. How do you feel your co-workers or fellow volunteers would react to the entry of a Person of Color?

5. How is the organization run? Who has the power? Who makes decisions? Is there anything about the organization's structure that makes it accessible or inaccessible to People of Color?

6. What does it feel like working or volunteering in this organization? Are there extensive rules, policies, and styles of working that are unique or unusual? Would you say that the organization's culture is predominately Euro-American? Explain.

7. If it is a service organization or agency, who are its clients? Are there any efforts being made (or have there ever been any efforts) to broaden the racial and ethnic composition of the clientele?

You may find it particularly informative to have other co-workers or fellow volunteers answer these same questions and then compare answers or use the questions as stimuli for discussing the cultural competence of the organization.

Exercise 5

This last exercise is intended to help you become more aware of your own cultural roots and identity as well as prepare you for better understanding the material in Chapter 4, Understanding Culture and Cultural Differences. The following is a detailed list of questions to be answered in relation to each ethnic group constituting your culture of origin. The questions were developed by Hardy and Laszloffy (1995). In answering them, you are encouraged to seek additional information from parents or other relatives.

1. What were the migration patterns of the group?
2. If other than Native American, under what conditions did your family (or their descendants) enter the United States (immigrants, political refugee, slave, etc.)?
3. What were/are the group's experiences with oppression? What were/are the markers of oppression?
4. What issues divide members within the same group?
5. Describe the relationship between the group's identity and your national ancestry (if the group is defined in terms of nationality, please skip this question).
6. What significance does race, skin color, and hair play within the group?
7. What is/are the dominant religion(s) of the group? What role does religion and spirituality play in the everyday lives of members of the group?
8. What role does regionality and geography play in the group?
9. How are gender roles defined within the group? How is sexual orientation regarded?
10. (a) What prejudices or stereotypes does this group have about itself?
    (b) What prejudices or stereotypes do other groups have about this group?
    (c) What prejudices or stereotypes does this group have about other groups?
11. What role (if any) do names play in the group? Are there rules, mores, or rituals governing the assignment of names?
12. How is social class defined in the group?
13. What occupational roles are valued and devalued by the group?
14. What is the relationship between age and values of the group?
15. How is family defined in the group?

16. How does this group view outsiders in general and mental health professionals specifically?
17. How have the organizing principles of this group shaped your family and its members? What effect have they had on you? (Organizing principles are "fundamental constructs which shape the perceptions, beliefs, and behaviors of members of the group." For example, for Jews an organizing principle is "fear of persecution.")
18. What are the ways in which pride/shame issues of the group are manifested in your family system? (Pride/shame issues are "aspects of a culture that are sanctioned as distinctively negative or positive." For example, for Jews a pride/shame issue is "educational achievement.")
19. What impact will these pride/shame issues have on your work with clients from both similar and dissimilar cultural backgrounds?
20. If more than one group comprises your culture of origin, how are the differences negotiated in your family? What are the intergenerational consequences? How has this impacted you personally and as a therapist? (p. 232)

As a second part of this exercise, and as a way of focusing more specifically on cultural content, the reader is asked to carry on an inner dialogue while reading the next chapter. As different dimensions of culture are introduced and discussed (e.g., experiencing time), ask yourself where you fit on each dimension and from where in your cultural past this characteristic is likely to have derived.

Chapter Four

Understanding Culture and Cultural Differences

There is a Zen story about a millipede that is stopped by an earthworm and asked how it can possibly manage to walk with so many legs to coordinate. The next moment the millipede is lying on its back in a ditch, trying to figure out which leg to put in front of the next. Many Americans have become like that millipede vis-à-vis culture. My White students often complain that they have no culture: They know nothing and feel nothing about where they came from. What they mean, I believe, is that they lack the kind of connection to a cultural heritage and community that they see among People of Color and White ethnics. And they are jealous. When culture is alive and vibrant, it provides the kind of inner programming that keeps the millipede walking along. It's always there, much of the time beyond awareness. It gives life structure and meaning. When it becomes fragmented, however, a central part of what it is, and what it can offer, gets lost.

This chapter discusses a number of issues related to culture. What exactly is it and how does it function in the life of a person? Why are social scientists finding it more preferable to describe group difference in terms of culture rather than race? Along what cultural dimensions do groups differ and in what ways do the cultures of Euro-Americans and People of Color clash? What happened to White culture? Are the theories that inform professional helping culture-bound as some practitioners have suggested? And finally, is there such a thing as multicultural counseling (i.e., a single approach that can adjust itself to the needs of all cultural groups)? Answers to these questions provide a better understanding of the ways in which culture affects service delivery.

What Is Culture?

Culture is a difficult concept to grasp. The problem lies in the fact that it is so basic to human societies and so intertwined with our very natures that its workings are seldom acknowledged or thought about by those who have internalized it. It is so all-encompassing, like water to a fish, that it remains largely preconscious and is obvious only when it is gone or has been seriously disturbed. Anthropological definitions point to certain aspects of it. *Culture* is comprised of traditional ideas, related values, and is the product of actions (Kroeber & Kluckhohn, 1952); it is learned, shared, and transmitted from one generation to the next (Linton, 1945); and it organizes life and helps interpret existence (Gordon, 1964). I also like the notion of culture as the ways a people have learned to respond to life's problems. For instance, all human groups must deal with death. But there is great variation from culture to culture in the rituals and practices that have developed around it. What these definitions lack, however, and what would be particularly helpful for the present purposes, is a more felt sense of how culture functions within the individual. To get at this, the concept of paradigm is most useful.

Kuhn (1970) introduced the term *paradigm* in his book *The Structure of Scientific Revolutions* to describe the totality of how a science conceives of the phenomena it studies. He argues that sciences change over time, not through the slow accumulation of knowledge (as was always taught in high school physics), but rather through paradigm shifts. A paradigm is a set of shared assumptions and beliefs about how the world works, and it structures the perception and understanding of the scientists in a discipline. For example, in physics, when Newton's theory of how physical matter operated no longer fit the accumulating evidence, it was eventually replaced by Einstein's theory of relativity, which was a qualitative shift in thinking. The new paradigm was a radical departure from its predecessor and gave physicists a totally different way of thinking about their work. What is so engaging about Kuhn's idea is that it suggests that our beliefs (paradigms) define what we perceive and experience as real.

The notion of paradigm was quickly appropriated by psychologists to describe the cognitive worldview through which human beings relate to their world. Their paradigms, without being very aware of them, tell people how human existence works: What is possible and impossible, what the rules are, how things are done. In short, they shape an individual's experience of reality. People think through their paradigms, not about them. "I'll see it when I believe it" is a more accurate description of how beliefs can give form to what is experienced as "real." People also grow emotionally attached to their paradigms and give up or change them only with great difficulty and discomfort. Having one's paradigm challenged is experienced as a personal threat, for ego gets invested in the portrayal of how things should be. Having one's paradigm shattered is somewhat akin to the chaos of psychosis. When the world no longer operates as it "should," one feels cut adrift from familiar moorings, no longer sure where one stands or who one is.

Culture is the stuff that human paradigms are made of. It provides their content: the identity, beliefs, values, and behavior. It is learned as part of the natural process of growing up in a family and community and from participating in societal institutions. These are the purveyors of culture. In short, one's culture becomes one's paradigm, defining what is real and right. Different cultures, in turn, generate different paradigms of reality, and each is protected and defended as if a threat to it was a threat to a group member's very existence. From this perspective, it is easy to understand why the imposition of a Northern European cultural paradigm onto the lives of People of Color, who possess and live by very different cultural paradigms, is experienced so negatively.

Culture Versus Race in the Definition of Group Differences

Before describing the dimensions along which cultures differ, it is useful to take a short digression to discuss difficulties with the concept of race. Increasingly of late, social scientists have chosen to distinguish between human groups on the basis of culture rather than race. For example, when they refer to tribal subgroupings within the broader racial category of Native Americans as separate ethnic groups, they are emphasizing cultural differences in defining group identity as opposed to biological or physical ones. I have followed a similar practice here by using terms such as ethnic group and culturally different clients to describe human diversity. Ethnic group was defined in Chapter 1 as any distinguishable people whose members share a common culture and see themselves as separate and different from the cultural majority. The emphasis is on shared cultural material as a basis for identification. It is not likely that the concept of race and its usual breakdown into five distinct human groupings will ever disappear from use. It is just too deeply ingrained in the fabric of American society. Rather, its importance as a social as opposed to a biological concept will increasingly be emphasized.

There are many serious problems with the concept of race. First, physical anthropologists have shown quite conclusively that what has always been assumed to be clear and distinct differences between the races are not very clear or distinct at all. In fact, it appears that there is as much variability in physical characteristics within racial groups as there is between groups. It is not uncommon, for example, to see a wide array of skin colors and physical features among individuals who are all considered members of the same racial group. It is believed that there has been so much racial mixing throughout history that, today, groups that may have once been genetically distinct are no longer distinguishable.

Second, the term has become so emotionally charged and politicized that it can no longer serve a useful role in any scientific discussion.

Third, racial categories have been consistently used throughout U.S. history to simultaneously oppress People of Color and justify White privilege. For example, U.S. census classifications of race and color have changed each year from 1989 to the present. In 1890, they included "White, Black, Mulatto, Quadroon, Octoroon, Chinese, Japanese, and Indian." In 1998, they include "White, Black, Indian, Eskimo, Aleut, Asian or Pacific Islander, Chinese, Filipino, Hawaiian, Korean, Vietnamese, Japanese, Asian Indian, Samoan, Guamanian, Other." What is particularly interesting about the redefinition of racial groups every 10 years is that the list closely parallels increased immigration restrictions. Thus, an increased demand for entry into the United States from groups who are perceived as threats by the White establishment results in reduced immigration quotas.

Fourth, defining race biologically and genetically opens the door for pseudoscientific arguments about intellectual and other types of inferiority among People of Color.

Fifth, the social reality of race in the United States does not conform to the existence of five distinct groups. Rather, there are only two that bear any real social meaning: White and Color. The notion of the great melting pot, for instance, was in actuality only about melting White ethnics. The myth was never intended to apply to People of Color. For White ethnics, upper mobility involved discovering and asserting their group's whiteness as a means of setting themselves apart from and above the groups of Color who perpetually resided at the bottom of America's social hierarchy. When they first arrived in America, various White ethnic groups were met with prejudice and scorn and were merely tolerated because they represented a source of much needed cheap labor. In time, however, as they acculturated into the system, they discovered that they could progress most quickly by identifying themselves as White and by taking on the prejudices against People of Color, which were an intrinsic part of White culture.

For all of these reasons, it has become increasingly compelling to set aside the term race as a distinguishing feature between groups and to turn to cultural differences as a more useful and less controversial yardstick.

The Dimensions of Culture

Cultural paradigms define and dictate how human beings live and experience life. Brown and Lundrum-Brown (1995) describe the dimensions along which cultures can differ. The content and specifics of each vary from culture to culture. It is because of these differences, and the natural tendency to ethnocentrically assume that everyone else views the world in the same way as we do, that cross-cultural misunderstanding occurs.

Psychobehavioral modality refers to the mode of activity most preferred within a culture. Do individuals actively engage their world (doing), more passively experience it as a process (being), or experience it with the intention of evolving (becoming)?

Axiology involves the interpersonal values that a culture teaches. Do they compete or cooperate (competition vs. cooperation)? Are emotions freely expressed or held back and controlled (emotional restraint vs. emotional expressiveness)? Is verbal expression direct or indirect (direct verbal expression vs. indirect verbal expression)? Do group members seek help from others or do they keep problems hidden so as not to shame their families (help seeking vs. "saving face")?

Ethos refers to beliefs that are widely held within a cultural group and guide social interactions. Are people viewed as independent beings or as interdependent (independence vs. interdependence)? Is one's first allegiance to oneself or to one's family (individual rights vs. honor and protect family)? Are all individual group members seen as equal or is there an acknowledged hierarchy of status or power (egalitarianism vs. authoritarianism)? Is harmony, respect, and deference toward others valued over controlling and dominating them (control and dominance vs. harmony and deference)?

Epistemology summarizes the preferred ways of gaining knowledge and learning about the world. Do people rely more on their intellectual abilities (cognitive processes), their emotions and intuition (affective processes, "vibes," intuition), or a combination of both (cognitive & affective)?

Logic involves the kind of reasoning process that group members adopt. Are issues seen as being either one way or the other (either/or thinking)? Can multiple possibilities be considered at the same time (both/and thinking)? Or is thinking organized around inner consistency (circular)?

Ontology refers to how a culture views the nature of reality. Is what's real only what can be seen and touched (objective material)? Is there a level of reality that exists beyond the material senses (subjective spiritual)? Or are both levels of reality experienced (spiritual and material)?

Concept of time involves how time is experienced within a culture. Is it clock-determined and linear (clock-based)? Is it defined in relation to specific events (event-based)? Or is it experienced as repetitive (cyclical)? *Concept of self*, finally, refers to whether individual group members experience themselves as separate beings (individual self) or as part of a greater collective (extended self).

In relation to these dimensions, each culture evolves a set of cultural forms—ritual practices, behavioral prescriptions, and symbols—to support them. For example, a given culture stresses the doing mode on the first dimension. Certain kinds of child-rearing techniques tend to encourage directed activity. Parents differentially reinforce activity over passivity. They also model such behavior. Cultural myths portray figures high on this trait, and moral teachings stress its importance. The group's language likely favors active over passive voice. What makes a culture unique, then, is the particular profile of where it stands on each of these dimensions combined with the specific cultural forms it has evolved.

As will become apparent shortly, the dimensions of culture are not totally independent. Rather, some tend to cluster with each other. In relation to Ethos, for instance, beliefs concerning independence, individual rights, egalitarianism, and control and dominance tend to occur together in the belief system of a culture as do interdependence, honor and family protection, authoritarianism, and harmony and deference. This is because such clusters tend to be mutually reinforcing. It will become clear that certain cultures share a number of dimensions. The cultures of Color in the United States, for example, have many dimensional similarities, and as a group, differ considerably from Northern European culture.

Finally, it is important to note that each culture generates a unique felt experience of living. The quality of life differs in tone, mood, and intensity. So do the kind of mental health issues that members must face as well as the emotional strengths they develop. A most dramatic example of this occurred many years ago. I was a graduate student running a personal growth group for students at a multicultural weekend retreat. The students who showed up for my group were all White with the exception of one young Latino man, who it turned out was there to spend more time with one of the young women in the group. Such groups seldom attracted non-White participants, for it was the belief of most students of Color that it was a "White thing" and something that "Whites really needed." "As for us, we don't have any trouble relating to other people." The group was quite successful, and it did not take long until people were sharing deeply: talking about feelings of disconnection from parents, isolation, and loneliness. At a certain point, the young Latino man could contain himself no longer and said, "I don't understand what you are all talking about. I am part of a big extended family; there is always someone around. I can't imagine feeling alone or isolated." Only after that did I realize that what I had thought to be the "universal malaise" of loneliness and isolation was, in fact, a cultural experience and artifact of the Northern European lifestyle.

Comparing Cultural Paradigms in America

M. Ho (1987) compared the cultural paradigm of White, European Americans to those of the four cultures of People of Color on three of Brown and Landrum-Brown's dimensions listed earlier as well as two of his own. It is worth reviewing these in some detail to better appreciate the breadth of difference that can exist. It should be remembered, however, that these comparisons speak in generalities and may not necessarily fit or apply to individual group members, especially those who have acculturated. In addition, each of the five "racial" groups described are in actuality made up of numerous subgroups whose cultural content may differ widely. In the United States, for example, Manson and Trimble (1982) identified 512 federally recognized Native "entities" and an additional 365 state-recognized Indian tribes, each with its own cultural uniquenesses.

Nature and the Environment

Ho classifies the four cultures of Color—Asian Americans, Native Americans, African Americans, and Latino/a Americans—as living in "harmony with" nature and the environment, whereas European Americans prefer "mastery over" them. For the former, the relationship is one of respecting and coexisting with nature. Human beings are seen as part of a natural order and, as such, must live respectfully and nonintrusively with other aspects of nature. To destroy a fellow creature is to destroy a part of oneself. European American culture, on the other hand, views human beings as superior to the physical environment and entitled to manipulate it for their own benefit. The world is a resource to be used and plundered. The cultures of Color see the component parts of nature as alive and invested with spirit, to be related to respectfully and responsibly. Great value is placed on being ever attentive to what nature has to offer and teach. Out of such a perspective comes notions such as the Native American idea of Turtle Island, a mythology that views the nonhuman inhabitants of the continent as an interconnected system of animal spirits and archetypal characters. A "mastery" mentality results in environmental practices such as runaway logging, strip mining, and oil drilling as well as the impetus for institutions such as human slavery, which exploit "inferior" human beings for material gain.

TIme Orientation

There is great diversity among the five cultural groups in regard to how they perceive and experience time. European Americans are dominated by an orientation toward the future. Planning, producing, and controlling what will happen are all artifacts of a future time orientation. What was and what is are always a bit vague and subordinated to what is anticipated. At the same time, European Americans view time as compartmentalized and incremental, and as such, being on time and being efficient with one's time are positive values. Asian and Latino/a cultures are described as past–present oriented. For both, history is a living entity. Ancestors and past events are felt to be alive and impacting present reality. The past flows imperceptibly into and defines the present. In turn, both Native Americans and African Americans are characterized as present oriented. Focus is directed toward current experience of the here and now, with less attention to what led up to this moment or what will become of it. As a group, and as distinct from European American culture, the cultures of Color share a view of time as an infinite continuum and, as a result, find it difficult to relate to the White "obsession" with being on time. Interestingly, each of these groups has evolved a term to describe their "looser" sense of time: "Colored people's time," "Indian time," "Asian time," and "Latin time." Invariably, time becomes an issue when non-Whites enter institutions where European American cultural values predominate. Lateness is often mistakenly interpreted as indifference, provocative, or symptomatic of a lack of basic work skills.

People Relations

Ho distinguishes European Americans as having an "individual" social focus compared to a "collateral" one for the four cultures of Color. Individual behavior refers to actions undertaken to actualize the self, while collateral behavior involves doing things not for oneself but in light of what they may contribute to the survival and betterment of family and community. These differences, in turn, become a basis for attributing value to different, and opposing, styles of interaction. European Americans, for example, are taught and encouraged to compete, to seek individual success, and to feel pride in and make public their accomplishments. Native Americans and Latino/a Americans, in particular, place high value on cooperation and strive to suppress individual accomplishment as well as boasting and self-aggrandizement.

Having pointed out this shared collateral focus, it is equally important to understand that the four communities of Color differ significantly in their communication styles and the meaning of related symbols. Native Americans place high value on brevity in speech, while for African Americans, the ability to rap is treated like an art form. It is considered impolite in certain Asian American subgroups to say "no" or refuse to comply with a request from a superior. Among Latino/a Americans, differential behavior and the communication of proper respect depends on perceived authority, age, gender, and class. And the same handshake can be given in one culture to communicate respect and deference and in another to show authority and power.

Work and Activity

On the dimension of work and activity (similar to Brown and Landrum-Brown's Psychobehavioral Modality), European Americans, Asian Americans, and African Americans are described as "doing" oriented compared to Native Americans and Latino/a Americans who are characterized as "being-in-becoming." Doing is an active mode. It involves initiating activity in pursuit of a given goal. It tends to be associated with societies where rewards and status are given on the basis of productivity and accomplishment. But even here, there are differences in motivation. European Americans' work and activity are premised on the idea of meritocracy—that hard work and serious effort ultimately bring the person financial and social success. Asian Americans, on the other hand, pursue activity in terms of its ability to confer honor on one's family and concurrently to avoid shaming them or losing face. African Americans fall somewhere between these two extremes. Being-in-becoming, in turn, is more passive, process oriented, and focused on the here and now. It involves allowing the world to present opportunities for activity and work rather than seeking them out or creating them. It is a mode of activity that can easily be misinterpreted from a doing perspective as "lazy" or "lacking motivation.

On a recent trip to the Sinai in Egypt, one of my traveling companions was a hardworking lawyer from New York City, clearly high on the doing dimension. After spending several hours visiting a Bedouin village, he could barely contain his shock at how the men just sat around all day. Our guide, himself a Bedouin, suggested that they were not merely sitting, but thinking and planning. "There is a lot to think about: where to find water, missing goats, perhaps a new wife, maybe a little smuggling." This didn't satisfy the lawyer, however. "I don't understand how they can get anything done without meetings. Give me 6 months and I'd have this whole desert covered with condos."

One last point. Activity and work, whether of the doing or becoming variety, must occur in the context of other cultural values. For example, in many cultures, work does not begin until there has been sufficient time to greet and properly inquire about the welfare of one's family. To do otherwise is considered rude and insensitive. In White European American business culture, such activity would be seen as lazy, wasteful, and the shirking of one's responsibilities.

Human Nature

This dimension of culture deals with how groups view the essence of human nature. Are people inherently good, bad, both, or somewhere in between? According to Ho, African Americans and European Americans see human nature as being both good and bad and as possessing both potentials. But for each, the meaning is quite different. In African American culture, where all behavior involves a collateral focus, or what Nobles (1972) calls "experiential communality," good and bad are defined in relation to the community. It is laudable if it benefits the community and bad if it does not. Thus, human nature is seen as existing in the interaction between the person and the group. European American culture, on the other hand, sees good and bad as residing in the individual. Freud's view of human nature is an excellent example. The instinctive urges of the id are seen as a negative force that must be controlled. The ego and the superego are assigned this task and, as such, play a positive role in containing baser drives. In addition, Freud hypothesized a life instinct that is balanced by a death instinct. Thus, the two sides of human nature, the good and bad, are seen in constant opposition and conflict.

Ho describes Asian Americans, Native Americans, and Latino/a Americans as sharing a view of human nature as good. This tendency to attribute positive motives to others has, however, at times proven less than helpful in interaction with members of the dominant culture. Early treaty negotiations between Native American tribes and the U.S. government are a case in point. Tribal representatives entered these negotiations under the assumption that they were dealing with honest and honorable men and that whatever agreements were struck would be honored. By the time sufficient experience forced them to reevaluate their original assumptions, it was too late and their lands had been stolen. Similarly, in the workplace, when members of such groups exhibit helpfulness, generosity, and caring for their fellow workers (behavior that follows from an assumption that others are basically good), they are frequently viewed as naive, gullible, and in need of "smartening up."

A Case of Cross-Cultural Miscommunication

Sue and Sue (1990) offer the following example of cross-cultural miscommunication:

> Several years ago, a female school counselor sought the senior author's advice about a Hispanic family she had recently seen. She seemed quite concerned about the identified client, Elena Martinez, a 13-year-old student who was referred for alleged peddling of drugs on the school premises. The counselor had thought that the parents "did not care for their daughter," "were uncooperative," and "were attempting to avoid responsibility for dealing with Elena's delinquency." When pressed for how she arrived at these impressions, the counselor provided the following information.
>
> Elena Martinez is the second oldest of four other siblings, ages 15, 12, 10, and 7. The father is an immigrant from Mexico and the mother a natural citizen. The family resides in a blue-collar neighborhood in San Jose, California.
>
> Elena had been reported as having minor problems in school prior to the "drug-selling incident." For example, she had "talked back to teachers," refused to do homework assignments, and had "fought" with other students. Her involvement with a group of Hispanic students (suspected of being responsible for disruptive school-yard pranks) had gotten her into trouble. Elena was well-known to the counseling staff at the school. Her teacher last year reported that she was unable to "get through" to Elena. Because of the seriousness of the drug accusation, the counselor felt that something had to be done, and that the parents needed to be informed immediately.
>
> The counselor reported calling the parents in order to set up an interview with them. When Mrs. Martinez answered the telephone, the counselor had explained how Elena had been caught on school grounds selling marijuana by a police officer. Rather than arrest her, the officer turned the student over to the vice-principal, who luckily was present at the time of the incident. After the explanation, the counselor had asked that the parents make arrangements for an appointment as soon as possible. The meeting would be aimed at informing the parents about Elena's difficulties in school and coming to some decision about what could be done.
>
> During the phone conversation, Mrs. Martinez seemed hesitant about choosing a time to come in and, when pressed by the counselor, excused her-

self from the telephone. The counselor reported overhearing some whispering on the other end, and then the voice of Mr. Martinez. He immediately asked the counselor how his daughter was and expressed his consternation over the entire situation. At that point, the counselor stated that she understood his feelings, but it would be best to set up an appointment for tomorrow and talk about it then. Several times the counselor asked Mr. Martinez about a convenient time for the meeting, but each time he seemed to avoid the answer and to give excuses. He had to work the rest of the day and could not make the appointment. The counselor stressed strongly how important the meeting was for the daughter's welfare, and that the several hours of missed work [were] not important in light of the situation. The father stated that he would be able to make an evening session, but the counselor informed him that school policy prohibited evening meetings. When the counselor suggested that the mother could initially come alone, further hesitations seemed present. Finally, the father agreed to attend.

The very next day, Mr. and Mrs. Martinez and a brother-in-law (Elena's godfather) showed up together in her office. The counselor reported being upset at the presence of the brother-in-law when it became obvious he planned to sit in on the session. At that point, she explained that a third party present would only make the session more complex and the outcome counterproductive. She wanted to see only the family.

The counselor reported that the session went poorly with minimal cooperation from the parents. She reported, "It was like pulling teeth," trying to get the Martinezes to say anything at all.

(From *Counseling the Culturally Different*, 2e by S. W. Sue & D. Sue, pp. 118–119. Copyright © 1990 John Wiley & Sons, Inc. Reprinted with permission.)

This is a clear case of misunderstanding cultural differences. The counselor proceeds with her normal modus operandi, irrespective of the very obvious cultural differences that exist between her and the Martinez family. She misreads their reactions and intentions and draws erroneous and insulting conclusions about them as parents. She communicates these to the Martinezes, who immediately withdraw and become nonreactive. What are some of the assumptions she made and cultural artifacts that she missed?

First, it is very possible that because of her ethnicity and her involvement with a group of other Hispanic students, Elena was being carefully watched as a potential troublemaker. Second, the counselor appears unaware that in a traditional Mexican family, the wife would not make a decision without first consulting her husband, which she did by "whispering on the other end." Similarly, it is the husband who represents and talks for the family in any formal situation such as this. Third, the counselor assumes that Mr. Martinez is indifferent about his daughter because he seemed reluctant to miss work on her behalf. She had no idea of what his work situation was or what the consequences of missing work might be for him and his family. But like any middle-class professional, she assumes he can make himself available during the day and even presumes to moralize at him, something he is probably not used to from a woman, about several hours of missed work being more important than his daughter. But at the same time, she is unwilling to accommodate herself to the family's need for an evening session and hides behind bureaucratic rules to avoid doing so. Finally, she thinks too narrowly about what constitutes a family, is used to dealing with nuclear as opposed to extended families, and has no idea of the appropriateness of the brother-in-law's presence. Godfathers in Latino/a culture are responsible for the spiritual life of their godchildren, and Elena was possibly in the midst of serious spiritual difficulties.

Are Theories of Helping Culture-Bound?

In Chapter 3, cultural racism was defined as the belief that the cultural ways of one group are superior to those of another. It can exist within the mind of an individual, as in the case of Elena's counselor, who seems largely unaware that she is imposing her cultural values on the Martinez family. Cultural racism can also assert itself through the workings of institutions such as the agencies in which most providers work and through the theories and practices they hold and subscribe to as professionals. It is the strong belief of many researchers that the assumptions and practices of mainstream service delivery are based on Northern European cultural values (Draguns, 1981; Kim & Berry, 1993; Sue & Sue, 1990). Because of this, serious questions exist as to whether practitioners can adequately serve culturally different clients.

Anthropologists draw a distinction between emic and etic approaches to working cross-culturally. *Emic* refers to looking at a culture through concepts and theories that are indigenous to it. For example, making traditional healers available to Native American clients is an emic approach to service delivery. *Etic* means viewing a culture through "glasses" that are external to it. This is the strategy that the helping professions have adopted. It has been assumed that their approach has relevance for all people irrespective of their cultural backgrounds, but this may not be true. Some critics argue that since the helping profession has its origins and roots in Northern European ideas, values, and sensibilities, it cannot appropriately be applied to individuals who hold different cultural values and assumptions (Duran & Duran, 1995). They further contend that such models are at best "pseudoetic" (Draguns, 1981), which means that they naively misjudge the universality of their approach and that what in reality has been created are "emic approaches to counseling that are designed by and for middle-class European Americans" (Atkinson, Morten, & Sue, 1993, p. 54).

Key Aspects of the Helping Process

If one looks carefully at the assumptions and practices that are central to the helping professions as they currently exist, it becomes immediately clear that much is in conflict with the general cultural worldview of non-White clients.

Four key aspects of the helping process can be identified as especially problematic. These include the importance of verbal expressiveness and self-disclosure, the setting of long-term goals, the relative importance placed on changing the client versus changing the environment, and the definition of what is mentally healthy.

Verbal Expressiveness and Self-Disclosure

Most practitioners believe that verbal expressiveness and self-disclosure by clients are critical parts of the helping process. The cultures of Color do not, however, share this value or feel comfortable talking about themselves or disclosing personal material to relative strangers. Asian Americans, for example, learn emotional restraint at an early age and are expected to exhibit modesty in the face of authority as well as subtleness in dealing with personal problems (Atkinson, Whitely, & Gin, 1990; D. R. Ho, 1994). To reveal intimate details of one's life to strangers is seen as bringing shame on the family and is experienced as "losing face." Similarly, it has been shown that Native Americans and Latino/a Americans also feel threatened with the demand for such disclosure (Fleming, 1992; Vontress, 1981). For both, intimate sharing is done only with friends of long standing. Only European Americans seem comfortable revealing intimate details of their life to relative strangers. Foreign travelers to the United States are often shocked by the amount of personal information revealed to them by fellow passengers.

African Americans, in turn, tend to be suspicious of requests by White providers for intimate life details (Gordon, 1964; Sue & Sue, 1990). It is seen by the African American community as dangerous and potentially self-destructive to not hide one's feelings from Whites until their trustworthiness can be assured. I am reminded of a very bizarre but sad incident when minority youth leaders, mostly African American, from a major urban area were taken to an isolated part of the Grand Canyon for a sensitivity training experience by a group of White professionals. Communications between the two groups broke down very quickly, and only when it was learned that the African American youth had come to believe that they had been taken there to be assassinated was it possible to defuse the situation. Helping professionals obviously need to be aware of how culturally different clients view their efforts at helping as well as careful in drawing conclusions about a client's reluctance to self-disclose. Such behavior is normative in many cultural groups and should not be interpreted as defensiveness or as reflecting depression, shyness, or passivity.

Long-Term Goals

Psychodynamic approaches to counseling and other forms of helping place importance on long-term treatment planning. Helping is envisioned as a long-term, ongoing process where therapist and client interact in a rather unstructured situation with the aim of making significant changes in the interpsychology of the client. Clients of Color, on the other hand, tend to be more action-oriented and desirous of concrete advice and immediate solutions to the problems for which they seek help (Sue & Sue, 1990). They seem to find directive as opposed to nondirective approaches most helpful and often express confusion or frustration around the idea of abstract, long-term goal setting. The differences may result from differing time orientations, a belief that the individual's purpose is to serve the collective (rather than the self), or just the fact that "sitting around and talking" is a luxury they just can't afford or can't see as potentially helpful. Again, the helper must avoid the temptation to interpret their "reluctance" to go along with long-term goal planning as resistance.

Changing the Client Versus Changing the Environment

Practitioner and client can differ greatly in how they conceive and think about the change process: Is it important to change the client to fit their circumstances, or vice versa. These are referred to technically as *autoplastic* versus *alloplastic* solutions. Helping clients cope with a difficult life situation by accommodating or adapting to it (i.e., changing themselves in that direction) is autoplastic; encouraging or teaching clients to impose changes on the external environment so that it better fits their needs is alloplastic.

Cultures of Color differ widely on this question. Asian American culture tends to stress a passive acceptance of reality and a transcendence of conflict by adjusting one's perceptions so that harmony can be achieved with the environment (D. R. Ho, 1994). African Americans, on the other hand, tend to point to a racist environment as the cause of many of their distresses and advocate changing it as opposed to themselves (Kunjufu, 1984). To this end, in the late 1960s, African American psychologists in the state of California called for and got a moratorium on testing minority children in the public schools (Bay Area Association of Black Psychologists, 1972). They argued that culturally biased psychological assessment was being used to funnel culturally different children into special education classes by White teachers and administrators who were not comfortable with their non-White ways. In a similar vein, Braginsky and Braginsky (1974) and others have called the helping profession to task for serving as a "handmaiden to the status quo" by encouraging culturally different clients to adapt their behavior to the demands of White institutions as opposed to encouraging their clients to pursue societal change. Northern European culture, for its part, tends to encourage the confrontation of obstacles in the environment that restrict one's freedom (Holtzman, Diaz-Guerrero, & Swartz, 1975).

Among helpers, what seems most critical is the particular theory they follow. Psychodynamic approaches, by their nature, locate problems and conflicts within the individual and dictate inner changes as the exclusive solution. More behaviorally and cognitively oriented theories do the opposite. They advocate changing the environment to change behavior.

Sue and Sue (1990) offer an interesting perspective on this question. They suggest that much client behavior can be understood as resulting from their beliefs about locus of control and locus of responsibility. *Locus of control* refers to whether individuals feel that they are in control of their own fate (internal control) or that they are being controlled externally (external control) and with their actions having little impact on changing the external world. *Locus of responsibility* refers to whether individuals believe that they are responsible for their own fate (internal responsibility) or that they cannot be held responsible because there are more powerful forces at work (external responsibility). Sue and Sue propose four different "worldviews" based on combining these two dimensions and argue that People of Color may exhibit any of the four. Generally, Northern European American helpers believe in internal control and internal responsibility—that clients are in control of their own fate, their actions do affect their outcomes, and success or failure in life is related to their personal characteristics and abilities. If this does not match with a client's perception of how the world works, there are likely to be serious differences regarding treatment goals and just what constitutes helping.

Definitions of Mental Health

The human service professions have tended to adopt Northern European cultural definitions of what constitutes healthy and normal functioning. Self-reliance, autonomy, self-actualization, self-assertion, insight, and resistance to stress are seen as hallmarks of healthy adjustment and functioning (Saeki & Borow, 1985; Sue & Sue, 1990). These are the characteristics toward which clients are encouraged to strive. They are not, however, the same personal qualities that are valued in all cultures. For example, Asian American cultures value interdependence, inner enlightenment, negation of self, transcendence of conflict, and passive acceptance of reality (D. R. Ho, 1994). This view is largely antithetical to that of mainstream Western thought. What Asian American culture shares with the other three cultures of Color, and what sets them apart from Northern European culture, is the diminished importance of individual autonomy and self-assertion. A similar idea is expressed in the way Native American culture views health and illness (Duran & Duran, 1995). Illnesses, both mental and physical, are thought to result from disharmony of the individual, family, or tribe from the ways of nature and the natural order. Healing can only occur when harmony is restored. This is the goal of traditional healing practices.

Another way of describing this important difference is the distinction between the individual and the extended self (Brown & Landrum-Brown, 1995). The individual self is characteristic of Northern European culture. It exists autonomously, is fragmented from its social context, and has as its goal personal survival and betterment. The self develops very differently in cultures that limit its narcissism and free expression. The term *extended self* is used to describe ego development in group members who conceive of themselves not as individuals, but as part of a broader collective. All behavior occurs with an awareness of what its impact will be not on the self, but more important, on the larger social group of which the person is a part. Referring back to the Axiology and Ethos dimensions suggested by Brown and Lundrum-Brown, the subvalues of competition, emotional restraint, direct verbal expression, and help seeking and the subbeliefs of independence, individual rights, egalitarianism, and control and dominance (all typical of the Northern European cultural paradigm) represent ideas that support the existence of an individual self. Similarly, their opposites (the subvalues of cooperation, emotional expressiveness, indirect verbal expression, and "saving face" and the subbeliefs of interdependence, honor and family protection, authoritarianism, and harmony and deference), most typical of the worldview of the communities of Color, are related to an extended self. Independence, for example, allows for greater self-assertion; interdependence allows for greater intergroup harmony. In speaking of the extended self, I am reminded of a former graduate student of Color who, when introduced to a model of identity development in People of Color which described the final stage of growth as "transcending specific group identities," reacted: "This can't be right. How can they see this as optimal growth. The person is no longer a part of the community."

Thus, practitioners must be aware of when there is incongruence between their notion of what is healthy and where treatment should be leading and that of the client. Where differences exist, they must be respected, and great care must be taken both to not project one's own values onto the helping process or unintentionally judge a client's behavior that varies from one's own standards as inferior and deficient.

Conflicting Strategies Over Cross-Cultural Service Models

In turning to the question of what a practitioner can do about these potential areas of conflict, the easiest and most immediate answer is fairly simple: Alter and adjust the helping model to accommodate them. Recall from Chapter 2 that one of the central skills associated with cultural competence is being able to adapt mainstream practices to the needs of culturally different groups. For example, it does not seem unreasonable or impossible to expect providers to alter their expectations, especially in the early stages of working together, regarding self-disclosure or verbal openness and fluency. The provider should also be able to learn to adjust the type of interaction that occurs and, when helpful, move into a less ambiguous and more directive problem-solving mode. Similarly, it should be possible to adapt the provider's view of where change should take place (changing the individual vs. changing the environment) to align with the client's cultural tendencies and to rethink treatment goals and outcomes in light of the client's cultural beliefs.

Sue and Zane (1987) suggest two additional strategies for improving provider credibility. First is to ensure that clients feel that their problems or reasons for seeking help are understood by the provider in terms of their own cultural viewpoint. This involves both appreciating their worldview in terms of the intricacies of their cultural background and being able to communicate that awareness to them. Second is to ensure that the client gets some immediate benefit or reinforcement from the helping process. This may involve advocating for them with another agency, teaching them some skill or practice that might help them better navigate the system, or even directly intervening in a situation on their behalf. Although such interventions push the boundaries of what is considered appropriate among mainstream providers, it should be remembered that such helping practices were developed primarily for working with dominant culture clients. Such limitations may just not make cultural sense for working with clients of Color.

Some critics, however, believe that merely making adjustments to a predominantly Northern European model of helping is not sufficient. Their belief is that approaching the problem of cross-cultural service delivery in this manner is something akin to "rearranging the deck chairs on the *Titanic.*" They argue that merely making cosmetic changes in a process that is by its very nature highly destructive to traditional people and their culture does not get to the real heart of the problem. Duran and Duran (1995), for example, believe that Northern European culture and its application through Western psychology have been instrumental in fragmenting Native American culture and lifestyle. They contend further that inherent in Western thought is an inability to tolerate the existence of alternative ways of knowing and experiencing the world:

> The critical factor in cross-cultural psychology is a fundamentally different way of being in the world. In no way does Western thinking address any system of cognition other than its own. Given that Judeo-Christian belief systems include notions of the Creator putting human beings in charge of all creations, it is easy to understand why this group of people assumes that it also possesses the ultimate way of describing psychological phenomena for all of humanity. In reality, the thought that what is right comes from one worldview produces a narcissistic worldview that desecrates and destroys much of what is known as culture and cosmological perspective. (p. 17)

Diamond's (1987) work on "primitive" versus "civilized" offers a useful metaphor through which to compare the nature of traditional cultures (which include the cultures of Color in the United States) with that of postmodern Northern Europe. Like Duran and Duran, Diamond believes there is something inherently wrong with civilized culture, and something essential has been lost. Only through a careful analysis of the dimensions of traditional culture can one discern what that is. Diamond summarizes eight characteristics of primitive culture that he believes have been lost to the civilizing process. These include good psychological nurturance; many-sided, engaging relationships throughout life; various forms of institutionalized deviance; celebration and fusion of the sacred–natural and individual–society in ritual; direct engagement with nature and natural processes; active participation in culture; goodness, beauty, and the natural environment are equated; and socioeconomic support is a natural inheritance. One consequence of the breakdown of traditional culture due to the civilizing process, according to Diamond (1987), was a radical increase in mental disorders and mental ill health:

> These prominent features of primitive society should lead us to anticipate an exceedingly low incidence of the chronic characterological or psychoneurotic phenomena that seem to be growing with civilization . . . This reflects my own experience; I would add only that the disciplined expressiveness of primitive societies, together with traditional social and economic supports, also results in a greater tolerance of psychotic manifestations, or better, converts the latter into a normal, bounded human experience. (p. 171)

Elsewhere, like Duran and Duran and Diamond, I (Diller, 1991) document a similar destructive tendency in contemporary Western culture. Specifically, I look at Jewish emancipation in 19th-century Europe and describe ways it radically altered traditional Jewish culture. The result was widespread fragmentation and the destruction of traditional Jewish ways, community, and identity:

> As chaos reigned supreme within the ghetto, it simultaneously intruded itself into the inner psyche of the assimilating Jew, rupturing previous bases for self-understanding and identity. The internal consequences were staggering. One major symptom was a fragmentation in the way people thought. Mind increasingly came to function independent of emotion and intuition, and the integrity of the Jewish self fell prey to self-consciousness and compartmentalization. With the Enlightenment, Jews became self-conscious about their own Jewishness and in time they grew alienated from it. In the ghetto, being a Jew was a given, a fact of life that required no further exploration. Jews uncritically followed customs and habits thousands of years old and participated in a lifestyle that defined all aspects of their existence. They questioned the fairness of God, the reasons for their sad plight and exile, but never the fact of who they were.
>
> A given becomes a matter of debate, an absolute becomes relative, only when there is an alternative available. Emancipation provided Jews with that alternative in the form of potential escape and assimilation, the possibility of no longer being Jews. In so doing, it forced them to inquire into the nature of their Jewishness, thereby objectifying it and setting them apart from it. By asking the questions: "Why am I a Jew and what does that mean?" by tasting of the tree of Knowledge as Adam had, postemancipation Jews set into motion a process which would eventually and permanently alienate them from the past. (p. 32).

These concerns have led researchers in different directions in seeking alternatives to merely adapting and adjusting the dominant helping service model. The first has been to call for the creation of individual ethnic-specific (emic) models or "psychologies," each developed by providers and researchers from a given ethnic community, aimed at defining a unique and unbiased understanding of the mental health and treatment issues of that community. In arguing for the wisdom of a "Black psychology," White (1972) contends that "principles and theories developed by white psychologists to explain the behavior of white people simply do not have sufficient explanatory power to account for the behavior of blacks" (p. 2). C. Clark (1972), in a similar vein, suggests the need for "creating an alternative framework within which black behavior may be differently described, explained, and interpreted" (p. 1). According to Jones (1972), Mosby "makes the case for qualitative differences in the life experiences of blacks which lead to differences in developmental, social, personal, intellectual, educational, and family functioning. Black Psychology would account for the differences" (p. 2). Each of the evolving models would dictate a unique and culturally sensitive approach specific to providing helping services to members of that community.

A second approach is suggested by Duran and Duran (1995), who advocate a return to the use of traditional healing practices from the client's own culture. Each community of Color has over time developed its own conceptions of health and illness as well as unique indigenous healing practices. Availing oneself of such services, first of all, guarantees that the help being received has not been compromised by dominant cultural ways. Second, it provides an avenue for strengthening ethnic identity and cultural ties. Finally, offering such services is especially useful to clients who remain steeped in traditional cultural ways and values and for whom dominant American culture has little relevance or feels unsafe.

A logical compromise, at least for the present, to the general question of the most appropriate model for delivering cross-cultural services is to include traditional healers and healing practices as part of a broad range of helping services available within a community. Such a strategy above all provides a strong statement about the value of cultural diversity to the human services. Most culturally different clients, however, have experienced some level of acculturation, or to put it differently, are in varying degrees bicultural. For these individuals, a full return to traditional, cultural ways is probably neither possible nor desirable. More relevant to their situation is the use of models of helping that have been sensitively and extensively adapted to the cultural needs of their group by practitioners, either indigenous or culturally different, who are truly culturally competent. As the demand for cross-cultural helping continues to grow and increasingly complex and effective strategies for serving culturally diverse clients are developed, it is just a matter of time before dominant forms of helping begin to lose their decidedly Northern European perspective and become increasingly infused and informed by the wisdom of a variety of other cultures.

Chapter Five

Ethnic Children, Parenting, and Families

Ethnic parents face a most difficult and thankless task of preparing their children for entry into a society that does not value them. Their children, in turn, may encounter difficulties navigating some of the normal developmental tasks of childhood because of the preponderance of negative messages they receive about themselves from the White world. Particularly problematic are internalizing a positive self-concept and developing an unconflicted sense of ethnic identity. Ethnic families, which are culturally very different from their mainstream counterparts, must serve as a buffer zone between family members and White society. Within the family system, individuals struggle with differential rates of language acquisition and acculturation as well as differences in traditional identification. These differences may be especially acute in families that have recently immigrated.

Previous chapters focused on cultural competence, racism, and culture. With this chapter and the two that follow, attention is redirected toward exploring the psychological experience of clients of Color. This chapter focuses first on issues related to child development: ethnic differences in temperament at birth, the development of racial identity and its impact on self-concept, personal identity formation in adolescents, and differences in cognitive and learning styles. Next, it takes up the question of parenting. What unique tasks face ethnic parents vis-à-vis society and their children? Finally, it explores issues related to ethnic families, ending with a consideration of a special subset of these families: those that are biracial or bicultural.

Three Scenarios

The following three scenarios drawn from real-life situations highlight the kinds of differences, demands, and dilemmas that characterize ethnic families. Most striking is the complexity of the dynamics that impact these children, parents, and families and to which they must respond and adapt. More often than not, forces in the broader environment impact them in negative ways, requiring some form of creative intervention or accommodation if the child or the family system is allowed to follow its normal developmental course. Frequently, this involves drawing on the strengths and unique attributes of the family's cultural ways. Readers are encouraged to return to these situations after completing the chapter and see how their thinking has expanded or changed.

Scenario 1.   K. B. Clark (1963) describes the following situation of a Black child referred to therapy because of severe racial identity confusion. "'I got a sun-tan at the beach this summer,' a seven-year-old Negro boy repeated over and over again to a psychologist. His mother, he said, was white and his father was white and therefore he was a 'white boy.' His brown skin was the result of a summer at the beach. He became almost plaintive in his pleading, begging the adult to believe him" (p. 37). Clark goes on to comment more broadly on this phenomenon. "General studies of a thousand Negro psychiatric patients in a mental hospital and detailed case histories of eight of them revealed that Negro patients frequently had delusions involving the denial of their skin color and ancestry. Some of these patients insisted that they were white in spite of clear evidence to the contrary" (p. 49).

Scenario 2.   I was once awakened early in the morning to attend an emergency meeting of a Jewish religious school's board of directors. During the previous night, someone had broken into the school, made a mess of the place, sprawled anti-Semitic graffiti all over the walls, and destroyed various religious articles and artwork. A night janitor had discovered the break-in, and board members were meeting to decide how best to handle the situation. In the very heated and emotional discussion, some argued that the school should not be reopened the next morning and remain closed until all signs of the vandalism were removed. They felt that it would be too traumatic for the children, ages 5–12, to witness because they were not old enough to understand what had happened. One parent summarized this position as follows: "There will be plenty of time in their future for the children to learn about this kind of hatred." Others felt that it was "never too early." Their suggestion was that students be shown the school now and be given ample opportunity to talk about what had happened. Yet others favored only exposing the older children to the reality of what had happened or letting the choice be up to individual parents.

Scenario 3.   As part of my private practice, I once saw an interracial couple for marital problems. The husband, of Chinese American descent, and the wife, Irish American, disagreed bitterly about the role his mother should play in their lives. He said that it was normal in his culture for the mother of the family to give advice and guidance to the daughter-in-law and that, even though it might at times be a little "heavy-handed," it was done out of love and caring. He further believed his wife should be more tolerant out of respect for his culture. She, in turn, responded that she had spent the last 10 years trying to recover from an abusive home situation and refused to subject herself to any further abuse from the mother-in-law no matter how pure her intentions or how normal such behavior might be in Chinese culture. "I married you, not your family, and don't feel it is fair or very loving to ask me to continue to subject myself to your mother's intrusive and abusive ways." The husband just lowered his eyes, as if embarrassed by what his wife was saying.

Ethnic Children
Temperament at Birth

The characteristics and development of children from different ethnic groups vary greatly from birth (Trawick-Smith, 1997). It is easy to discern dramatic differences, for instance, in temperament and activity levels of newborns and infants. Freedman (1979) offers the following examples. White babies (of Northern European background), cry more easily and are harder to console than Chinese babies, who tend to adapt to any position in which they are placed. Navajo babies show even more calmness and adaptability than the Chinese. They calmly accept being placed on a cradleboard, while White babies cry and struggle to get out of the strapped confinement. Japanese children, in turn, are far more irritable than either the Chinese or Navajo. Australian aboriginal babies react strongly, like Whites, to being disturbed, but are more easily calmed.

Differences are also found in the ways mothers and infants interact (Seifer, Sameroff, Barrett, & Krafchuk, 1994). There is far less verbal interaction between a Navajo mother and baby than between a White mother and baby. The Navajo mother is actually rather silent and gets her baby's attention via eye contact. White mothers talk to their children constantly and their children respond with great activity. The mothers are equally adept, however, at gaining their children's attention. According to Freedman, the differences result from the continual interplay of inherited genetic predispositions and patterns of cultural conditioning through child–parent interaction. Thus, children's genetic temperamental tendencies are reinforced by cultural learning about the proper way to respond emotionally, and the result is children who increasingly take on the temperamental style of their culture (Garcia Coll, 1990; Scarr, 1993).

Development of Racial Identity

Ethnic children are aware of racial differences (i.e., differences in skin color and facial and body features) as early as 3 or 4, and by age 7, one can begin to discern the rudiments of a racial identity (Aboud, 1988; Grant & Haynes, 1995). Majority group children, in comparison, are generally slower to develop a consciousness of the fact that they are White because race is not as central to their families' lives as it is to People of Color (York, 1991). Racial identity evolves in relation to the sequential acquisition of three learning processes. The first is *racial classification ability* (Aboud, 1987; Williams & Morland, 1976) and involves the child learning to apply ethnic labels accurately to members of different groups. For example, in the classic doll studies designed by Clark and Clark (1947) to measure racial identity in African American children, the child is asked: "Show me the Black doll" or "Show me the White doll" when presented with dolls of varying skin tones. The child who can accurately perform such labeling on a regular basis is ready to move on to the next stage of forming a *racial identification* (Aboud & Doyle, 1993). Put simply, racial identification involves children learning to apply the newly gained concept of race to themselves. According to Proshansky and Newton (1968), this process requires a kind of inner dialogue through which children learn that because of their own skin color, they are members of a certain group (i.e., that the child is black or yellow or brown) and, as such, visibly different from others. Thus, racial identification results from an interaction between children's comparisons of their own skin color with those of parents, siblings, and others and what they are told about who they are racially. The final stage, called *racial evaluation* by Proshansky and Newton, involves the creation of an internal evaluation of one's own ethnicity. It is how children come to feel about being black or yellow or brown. Racial evaluation develops as children internalize the various messages regarding their own ethnicity received from significant others and society in general. By age 7, most ethnic children are aware of the negative evaluation that society places on members of their group (Thornton, Chatters, Taylor, & Allen, 1990).

Racial Identity and Self-Esteem

Early studies of racial identity formation by Clark and Clark (1947), Kardiner and Ovesey (1951), and Goodman (1952) found that African American children had difficulty successfully completing the last two stages just described. These children would either deny the fact that their skin was black (as in Scenario 1), devalue people with black skin and black culture in general, or do both. In addition, it was found that these same African American children often exhibited negative self-concepts. The authors concluded that such outcomes were inevitable for children of Color: By living in White-dominated society, they could not help but internalize the negative attitudes and messages that bombarded them daily, and the resulting negative self-judgments would inevitably translate into a diminished self-image.

As the ethnic pride movements of the 1960s gained momentum, however, the inevitability of such conclusions was vehemently challenged. Some referred to this early work as the "myth of self-hatred" (Trawick-Smith & Lisi, 1994). Earlier studies were criticized as being methodologically weak or as reflecting an earlier psychological reality that was no longer accurate. New studies showed no differences in self-esteem between African American and White children (Powell, 1973; Rosenberg, 1979). In racially homogeneous settings, in fact, African American children scored higher than their White counterparts (Spenser & Markstrom-Adams, 1990). The more extensive their interaction with Whites and the White world, however, the lower were their self-concept scores. The accuracy of these findings was, in turn, challenged as too conveniently fitting the researchers' political agenda.

The Usefulness of a Dual Perspective

Critics of the earlier studies argue for the usefulness of a dual perspective in resolving this question. They believe that the messages sent by the child's immediate environment (made up of home, community, and significant others), not those of broader society, are internalized and, thus, become the basis for self-esteem. Earlier researchers had assumed that society's negative views and stereotypes were directly reflected onto the child and internalized into the sense of self. Norton (1983) argues for differentiating the child's immediate environment from that of general society. For majority group members, there is little difference between the two kinds of messages. However, the situation is very different for People of Color, where the two systems offer very different and conflicting messages. Norton asserts that the more immediate interpersonal world of the child is critical to the development of healthy self-esteem and that the family can act as a buffer between the child and the broader society and, thus, become the primary sculptor of feelings about self. Norton concludes her argument by raising a number of questions that still need answers: "What happens in the interaction between black parents and their children in those stable nurturing families from any educational or socioeconomic level who manage to rear children with a strong sense of self? How and with what patterns do these families defy the 'mark of oppression'? How can we determine the strengths and healthy coping mechanisms in the interaction between black parents and their children?" (p. 188).

Clarifying the Question

To bring further clarity to these questions, Williams and Morland (1976) carried out an extensive longitudinal study of racial identity formation in African American and White preschoolers that followed them into their teenage years. Part of the value of their study was that it controlled for the various methodological criticisms that had been leveled at the earlier "doll" studies. What they found can be summarized as follows.

First, by the age of 3, preschoolers were responding differently to the colors black and white. Both "Euro" and "Afro" children (I use their terms) tended to favor the color white over the color black. This trend continued for both groups throughout elementary school. By junior high school, however, the Afro children had done a complete turn around in attitude and were generally favoring the color black over white. The authors suggest that the initial preference for white over black in all children probably derives from a biological tendency to prefer light over darkness and that this generalizes to the differential favoring of white over black. They further suggest that this early preference creates a general context in which specific learning about race can occur. But this is all merely conjecture.

Second, racial identification was measured by asking children which of the various colored dolls (light- or dark-skinned) looked like them or looked like a parent. Preschool Euro children chose the light-skinned figure 80% of the time and the dark-skinned figure 20%, whereas Afro preschoolers evenly distributed their choices between the dark- and light-skinned dolls 50%–50%. By the third grade, however, the Afro children were also choosing the dark-skinned figures 80% of the time, paralleling the differential responses of the same aged Euro children. By junior high school, both groups were almost 100% in their respective choices.

Third, racial evaluation was assessed by asking the young subjects to choose a figure (light- or dark-skinned) in response to a description that included a positive or negative adjective (e.g., choose the good parent). Both Euro and Afro preschoolers overwhelmingly assigned the positive features to the light-skinned figures (pro-Euro response) at a rate of 90% and 80%, respectively. These same patterns repeated for both groups through late elementary school. In junior high school, however, the Afro students' responses changed dramatically to pro-Afro (i.e., positive adjectives assigned to dark-skinned figures), ending with a rate equal to that of Euro junior high students.

Fourth, racial acceptance was measured by showing the subjects photos of dark- and light-skinned individuals and asking if they would like to play with this person. Euro preschoolers were significantly less accepting of Afro photos than Afro preschoolers were of Euro photos. In fact, Afro preschoolers accepted Euro pictures slightly more frequently than they did Afro photos. By elementary school and beyond, both Afro and Euro students grew increasingly less accepting of photos of the other group, with Afros always a bit more accepting than Euros.

By way of summary, Williams and Morland found that by third grade African American children were appropriately aware of their racial identity, accepted it, and preferred playmates from their own group. They did find African American preschoolers regularly making pro-Euro responses on all measures, which could be interpreted as indicating some early identity confusion (as suggested in the pre-1960s studies discussed earlier). The authors, however, attribute this to early response bias rather than any underlying pathology, and their interpretation seems to be borne out by the fact that with further socialization and by the third grade all except one of the measures showed group-appropriate responses. Regarding racial evaluation, however, there does seem to be lingering pro-White attitudes among Black youth until junior high school, when there is a dramatic reversal to predominantly pro-Afro responses. From these data, it seems likely that African American children do internalize to some extent the attitudes of society at large. But it is not clear from this study whether their pro-Euro preferences can be interpreted as indicative of negative feelings toward themselves or their own group. In any case, the effects are not lasting, and there doesn't seem to be any concurrent difficulty in racial identification itself. It is probably fair to say, however, that this is a critical period in the developmental life of the ethnic child and may be potentially problematic for the development of self-esteem as long as pro-Euro attitudes linger. Of course, all of these data are based on statistical analyses and do not imply that individual children can't potentially develop serious problems with racial identity and self-esteem, especially if their "home" environment does not counteract the negative effects of broader society.

What can be concluded about where ethnic children stand today vis-à-vis identity development and self-esteem? Recent studies by Spenser and Markstrom-Adams (1990) and Williams and Morland (1976), clearly show that children of Color often exhibit positive self-esteem and unconflicted ethnic identities. It is clearly time to set aside the "myth of self-hatred." But this does not mean that racism poses any less risk for children of Color. It simply means that active measures can be taken to protect them. Norton's (1983) notion of the value of a dual perspective points to the importance of creating a buffer zone around the child. McAdoo (1985) points to ethnic pride as a critical factor that insulates the child psychologically from the experience of racism. Critics do not disagree with the usefulness of a dual perspective or the value of ethnic pride, but rather warn against underestimating the insidiousness of racism on personality development in children of Color.

An additional perspective on the question of the impact of racism on self-esteem can be gleaned from interviews with ethnic group members who came to the United States as adults after growing up in countries where they were in the racial majority (Diller, 1997). It was only after they arrived in this country that they had their first personal experiences with prejudice and racism. How did they respond? Their first reported reaction was shock and disbelief. Once, however, they had sufficient time to process what had happened and to label it as a "racial attack," they were able to put up sufficient ego defenses to protect themselves emotionally as well as physically. They quickly learned to identify such situations before or as they happened and to deal with them quickly and effectively. They uniformly believed that it was only because of their own strong sense of self and well-developed ego defenses as adults that they were able to come out of these experiences relatively unharmed. When asked how they might have felt as children facing such experiences, they all indicated that they would have been clearly overwhelmed and likely scarred in some essential way.

Formation of Adolescent Identity

Another area of potential difficulty for ethnic children involves the formation of personal identity in adolescents. In a study comparing lower class urban African American and White adolescent boys, Hauser and Kasendorf (1983) found very different patterns of identity formation in the two groups. Building on the work of Erikson (1968), they looked at the manner in which adolescent boys come to integrate various images of themselves into a coherent sense of self. Erikson sees adolescence as a time of self-exploration during which the young person tries to find a comfortable synthesis of past experiences, sense of family, present questions and concerns, and hopes and plans for the future. The authors found that the African American adolescents formed a stable integration of self-images much earlier than did their White counterparts, who seemed to experience a lot more confusion, disequilibrium, and personal exploration. In fact, it took the White youth all 4 years of high school to reach the same level of identity stability as the African American youth after 1 or 2 years.

At the same time, African American adolescents showed a striking sameness in how they saw themselves compared to Whites, who showed much greater variability and flexibility in content. According to Erikson's model of adolescent identity development, the Whites were experiencing "identity progression and moratorium," (i.e., slow but steady movement toward a coherent definition of self with extensive confusion and time-out for exploration). The African American adolescents, on the other hand, were seen as exhibiting "identity foreclosure," stabilizing their identities very early with a premature closing off of possibilities in terms of content.

Hauser and Kasendorf (1968) found additional difficulties for the African American youth. Images of themselves as future parents were equally fixed and rigid, especially if the father had been absent from the home. In such cases, fathers were disparaged figures who foreshadowed what they themselves would look like as fathers, and on the basis of this, there was little hope for it being any different. Thus, early foreclosure seemed a natural consequence. Similarly, their image of the future was rigid and established early, connoting little hope for what was to be. Images of the past self showed great discontinuity, reflecting some discomfort and shame over the historical past (slavery and exploitation), instability in families (not knowing one parent's background), and even a kind of racial self-hatred (although there was no desire to be White). Finally, similar negative patterns were evident in relation to the kinds of fantasies they reported: lacking hope for their futures, especially in relation to what they can accomplish and become, work available to them, and the kinds of role models they could emulate.

Although times have changed since this study (with many People of Color having significantly improved their financial and social situations), it still clearly points to the kinds of difficulties that can exist for ethnic children growing up in a racist environment which dramatically limits the possibility of what they can do and become. The data also show the great capacity for coping that exists within these young African American men, for on a daily basis of living there was little evidence of the negativity and hopelessness that one might have predicted. Their current self-images, in fact, differed little from those of their White counterparts. Finally, it should be acknowledged that there may be cultural differences related to these findings. Erikson's model is clearly Northern European in origin and reflects a view of adolescence (and what should be happening during this period) that may not be accurate or appropriate for a different cultural group. Some anthropologists have even suggested that the prolonged period of confusion and moratorium that typifies Western adolescence is in reality a symptom of the loss of much needed rites of passage, which in many other cultures create a clear sense of direction and identity for the young person.

Academic Performance and Learning Styles

There is clear evidence that frequently children of Color perform academically at a lower level than their White counterparts in the public school system. Obgu (1978) distinguishes between three types of ethnic minorities and their relative success in academic performance: autonomous, immigrant, and caste-like. The first group, which includes relatively small populations such as Jews, Amish, and Mormons tends to experience prejudice but not widespread oppression. They tend to possess distinctive cultural traits related to academic success as well as cultural models of success and do not suffer from disproportionate amounts of school failure. The second group includes recent immigrants to the United States, such as Koreans and Chinese. They came here voluntarily to improve their life conditions, and although mainstream individuals may view them negatively, they do not hold similar views of themselves. Their living conditions in this country are a marked improvement over what they experienced in their countries of origin, and if they were to grow dissatisfied here, there is always recourse to returning. In spite of cultural differences, their children perform well in school and on academic tests. The third group, what Obgu calls "castelike minorities," includes African Americans, Latinos/as, and Native Americans and tends to experience disproportionate amounts of school failure. They are the objects of systematic racism and disadvantage both within and outside of the schools and, according to Ogbu, often view school success not as a path to advancement but rather as "acting White" or "Uncle Tom" behavior.

Closely related to poor school performance among these populations is the issue of cultural differences in learning styles. Each culture has its own preferred manner of learning, and as children grow, they internalize it and become progressively more comfortable and proficient with its use. There is much evidence to show that poor school performance among ethnic group children is related to conflicts in learning style; that is, the United States school system as an institution is based on and rewards a mode of learning that is characteristic of Northern European culture (Anderson & Adams, 1992; Wolkind & Rutter, 1985). Those who are not adept or comfortable interacting educationally in this mode are clearly at a disadvantage and likely over time to fail. When efforts have been made to adjust classroom interaction to the cultural needs of different groups, the results have shown dramatic increases in performance and school success (Wolkind & Rutter, 1985).

By way of example, as in all cultures, the learning style of Native Americans developed out of necessity and in relation to the environment that was their home. Their survival depended on "learning the signs of nature" and thus observation became a central mode of learning: "watching and listening, trial and error" (Fleming, 1992). In addition, oral tradition was the primary mode of teaching values and traditional attitudes, and such storytelling was often stylized through the use of symbols, anthropomorphizing, and metaphor, a particularly powerful way of teaching extremely complex concepts. Today, according to Fleming (1992), "modern Indian children still demonstrate strengths in their ability to memorize visual patterns, visualize spatial concepts, and produce descriptions that are rich in visual detail and the use of graphic metaphor" (pp. 161–162).

Contrast this with the very different learning paradigm that is emphasized in White schools: auditory learning, conceptualization of the abstract, and a heavy emphasis on language skills. Similarly, African Americans (Hale-Benson, 1986), Hawaiians (Gallimore, Boggs, & Jordan, 1974), and Mexican Americans (Kagan & Madsen, 1972) exhibit learning styles that have a heavy relational component as opposed to the Northern European style, which emphasizes individualism and competition. Mexican American children, for example, are less willing than White students to enter into rivalries or competition with each other or to internalize a drive to perform well to meet the expectations of teachers. Nor do Hawaiian children feel any need to forsake their strong need to affiliate with peers for a more individualistic modality that reinforces goal-orientated behavior. Although children from these cultures can potentially learn to process information in this manner, it is counter to their preferred mode of interacting. Put simply, it just feels foreign and unnatural, and for most students of Color, rather than adapting, they choose to shut down in a variety of ways and thereby exit the formal U.S. education system. The real task of education in a multicultural society is to broaden the dimensions of the classroom to make room for the learning styles of all students (Collett & Serrano, 1992). Similarly, human service providers should be aware of optimal learning styles for clients to maximize their learning potential during the helping process.

Ethnic Parenting

Margaret Burroughs captures the dilemma that faces all ethnic parents:*

> What shall I tell my children who are black
> Of what it means to be a captive in this dark skin?
> Of how beautiful they are when everywhere they turn
> They are faced with abhorrence of everything that is black . . .

There are three tasks that an ethnic parent must face and carry out that go beyond what might be called "normal parenting." Normal parenting involves creating a safe environment in which the child can move without harm through the various developmental tasks and stages that present themselves as part of growing up. Threats to the child's health or safety, when they exist, are random and unpredictable. Ethnic children, on the other hand, are born into an environment in which they are systematically subjected to the harmful effects of racism. Ethnic parents, having grown up under similar conditions, are aware of what awaits their children and of the fact that there is only so much they can do to protect them from what is to come. First, as suggested earlier, parents can help create a buffer zone in which children are protected from negative attitudes and stereotypes that abound in the broader society. Part of this process is to instill in them a sense of ethnic pride. In such a safe environment, they are more likely to develop a healthy sense of self-esteem. Second, children can be prepared cognitively for what they will encounter in the world outside the buffer zone. Third, they can be taught and guided in how to deal emotionally with the negative experiences around race that are sure to come.

Creating a Buffer Zone

The idea of creating a buffer zone in which the child can develop without harmful intrusions from the outside is actually the essence of all good parenting. All young children must be protected and nurtured until they are able to venture forth into the outside world with sufficient skills and abilities to protect themselves. But ethnic children are always at risk, and it is especially critical for their parents to create within them a good psychological base grounded in a strong and positive sense of self with which to go out into the world. Research, for example, has repeatedly shown that positive self-concept is correlated with effective social functioning, higher levels of cognitive development, and greater emotional health and stability (Curry & Johnson, 1990). The buffer zone (against racism and negative racial messages) can provide a place and time for optimal personal growth. Children's concept of self results

---

*Excerpt from poem "What shall I tell my children who are black?" by Margaret Burroughs. Reprinted by permission of the author.

directly from the messages they receive about themselves from the world. Theories of the development of the self speak of mirroring and reflection and imply that children take in and make a part of themselves the reflected views of others (Wylie, 1961). If they are loved, they will love themselves; if they are demeaned or devalued, that is how they will feel about themselves. In this regard, K. B. Clark (1963) has written: "Children who are consistently rejected understandably begin to question and doubt whether they, their family, and their group really deserve no more respect from the larger society that they receive" (pp. 63–64). This is why the idea of a buffer zone is so critical to ethnic parents. By substituting the reflection of loving parents and significant others for that of a hostile environment that routinely negates the value of children because of their ethnicity, a more positive sense of self is literally guaranteed. Norton (1983) describes the optimal ingredients for parent–child interaction most likely to foster heightened self-esteem as follows: "Early consistent, loving, nurturing interaction is the ideal process of interaction leading to a good sense of self. The child who is loved, accepted and supported in appropriate reality-oriented functioning in relationship to others comes to love himself and to respect himself as someone worthy of love" (p. 185).

The idea of a buffer zone should not, however, be limited merely to parents and family. The entire ethnic community with its own various institutions can function in a similar way to protect its children. The African adage that "it takes an entire village to raise a child" is relevant here. The idea of ethnic separatism, as currently practiced by Black Muslims, is predicated on such a notion of creating a safe, supportive, and economically viable system that does not depend on Whites and, in fact, limits interaction with them and their institutions.

Preparing the Child Cognitively for Racism

Equally important to providing children with a strong emotional base is preparing them for what will be encountered in the broader world. This is the issue that members of the Jewish religious school board were arguing about in Scenario 2 presented earlier. Although many researchers have written about this process, the early work of Lewin (1948) is most compelling in offering a number of good suggestions for how parents should go about preparing children for the eventual experience of prejudice and discrimination. First, never deny children's ethnicity or underestimate the impact it may have on their lives. Some parents feel that it is best to put off such discussions as long as possible, thereby protecting children from the "horror of racism" until it can no longer be avoided. There are real problems with this approach. It models, first of all, a kind of denial of reality that not only confuses children, but also sets them on a life course of not actively dealing with their ethnicity. Parents who choose to avoid discussions of race also tend to underestimate the level of children's knowledge and may be avoiding issues that have already become real and problematic for children. (Remember, as cited earlier, some ethnic children are aware of racial differences as early as 3 years of age, and by 7, all are aware of the negative judgments that society holds about their group.) Ethnic children might very much like and need to discuss experiences related to race that they have already encountered, but may feel that they cannot do so and must remain silent because of the family rule: "We do not talk about these things." By such tactics, parents unintentionally remove themselves as important resources to their children.

Lewin also points out, using the analogy of adoption, that "learning the truth" can be much more damaging and hurtful the older the child is. In other words, the longer one lives with a given picture of reality, the more devastating it can be to have that reality shattered. Although Lewin's work focused initially on assimilating Jews who could more easily hide their identities than most people of Color, his points are still well taken about avoiding the topic of ethnicity. It is clearly best to allow children to bring up the subject and deal with it in the context of their ongoing reality. Parents should answer questions in as simple a manner as possible and not overwhelm children with more knowledge than they currently need. More often than not, a small amount of information will suffice. Parents should answer questions in a manner that fits with the child's level of cognitive development. Similarly, the child should not be overwhelmed emotionally with difficult information or stories. Preparing children for dealing with racism is not a single-time event. It is an ongoing developmental process. As they encounter it in the real world, it should be discussed and processed, and as they mature, information and explanations should also grow in depth and comprehensiveness.

Second, it is critical to help children develop a strong and positive ethnic identity based on values inherent in group membership so as to internally counteract the negative experiences of being an object of prejudice. "I am an African American and I come from a rich cultural tradition of which I am very proud. Sure, I experience a lot of racism, but that is just the way it is, although at times I get very angry. But I would never trade it for being White or anything else, even if it meant life would be a lot easier." An ethnic identity based solely on negative experiences of racial hatred is a very fragile thing that disappears as soon as the adversity is gone. If children are made to feel bad because of how they are different, it is psychologically crucial that they possess positive feelings about who they are ethnically to draw upon. If they do not, it is likely that they may in time come to hate their group membership, seeing it as the source of all of their problems. Jewish parents, for example, are now beginning to realize that identities based exclusively on the experience of the Holocaust or a long history of oppression eventually drive their children from the fold.

Third, racism should always be presented as a social, and not as an individual or personal, problem. For example, "Why did Joey call me that bad name? I didn't do anything to him." "Of course, you didn't. Sometimes when people get angry or unhappy, they take it out on others who are different from them. There is something wrong with people when they do that." It is vital that children not come to believe, consciously or unconsciously, that something they did brought on the racist behavior. Parents should never just assume that a child has not personalized a negative racial experience. They must check it out. Young children, in their egocentric mode of experiencing the world, tend to take responsibility for most things that happen to them. Parents must actively make sure this is not the case. I have seen too many instances where an ethnic child is transformed (e.g., from a very happy and carefree young person to one who is negative and sullen) by a single experience with racism. I believe quite strongly that much of the damage could have been alleviated if the incident had been carefully worked through with the child. Parents must also be careful to not expect "special things or behaviors" from their children because of who they are ethnically. Such expectations also communicate to children that they are in some way responsible for their own plight and that better behavior on their part may have averted the incident. This is an enormous burden to unintentionally place on a child.

Fourth, it is important that children learn two lessons about ethnic group membership. The first is that group membership is based not only on obvious physical or cultural features but also on an interdependence of fate. In other words, members of an ethnic group share the experience of being treated similarly by the world, and this should serve to heighten awareness of being part of a single whole. It is very easy for children to learn to vent their frustration on subgroups within their community, blaming them for the bad treatment that all group members experience. Such internalized racism can become a tyranny of its own and lead to destructive intergroup wrangling and bickering. I am thinking, for example, of the caste systems based on lightness and darkness of skin color that exist in all communities of Color.

The second lesson is that it is acceptable to have multiple allegiances and belong to different social groupings at the same time. If children are made to unnecessarily choose between alternatives, they grow resentful and eventually find a way of getting even with parents, usually through the rejection of group membership at some level. Some parents, for instance, are very critical of their children's attempts at being bicultural (i.e., of trying to become competent in the ways of the dominant culture as well as their own). Fearing that their children may lose touch with traditional ways and values, they force them to choose, and the result is great unhappiness for all concerned.

Fifth, parents must realize that their child's feelings about ethnicity, ethnic identity, and group belonging cannot be any more positive or less conflicted than their own. Put in a slightly different manner, parents cannot help but pass on inner conflicts and issues about their own ethnicity to their children. The lesson to be learned here is that parents, in preparing their children for a hostile world, must not focus only on their children, but also on themselves as role models.

Preparing the Child Emotionally for Racism

Poussaint (1972) offers some good insights into how to help children deal emotionally with the negative racial experiences they encounter. He first emphasizes the fact that children should not be allowed to feel alone in their struggle. They must not only feel the support of their parents and peers, but also understand that they are part of a long history of African Americans, for example, who have similarly struggled against racism. Parents should model active intervention and mastery over the environment as well as help their children develop competence and the ability to achieve personal goals. If children can experience their parents as powerful, they gain a certain sense of power vicariously. Children should generally be allowed to try to deal with racial situations on their own, with the parent prepared to intervene if necessary. It is the parent's job to be sure that the situation is resolved quickly and satisfactorily and, above all, that the child's self-esteem is protected.

Poussaint describes a number of "compensatory mechanisms" that African American parents adopt in the process of trying to support and prepare their children for life. What they are compensating for is, in reality, their own insecurities. More often than not, these efforts tend to become highly counterproductive. Some parents, for example, subject their children to a verbal regimen of "Black is beautiful," hoping to reinforce a strong sense of positive identity and self. Children, however, may begin to wonder why they are being asked to repeat the same phrases over and over again and that perhaps the compulsive need to do so in actuality points to the possibility that maybe "Black is not so beautiful after all." Other parents adopt a permissive stance, being overly generous and accommodating with their children, as if to assuage their own guilt or make up for the harshness that the child will eventually encounter. The problem with this strategy is that it does not allow children to test themselves and their abilities in the real world and, in so doing, develop feelings of competence and self-worth. Still other parents are overly authoritarian and feel that the best they can do for their children is to toughen them up so they will be familiar with functioning in a hostile environment. But this strategy leads to abuse, which in turn teaches children to be abusive in their own right. It also gives them a green light to act out in the world. A final compensatory mechanism involves encouraging the child to remain passive and to avoid aggressive behavior of any kind, as if such a strategy would somehow mollify racial hatred.

Poussaint also points out the importance of helping children learn to manage the righteous anger that they will feel as objects of racial hatred. Suppressing anger eventually leads to feelings of self-loathing and low self-esteem. Overgeneralized anger is counterproductive, leading nowhere and consuming a vast amount of undirected energy. Rather, a more balanced approach seems optimal: teaching children to assert themselves sufficiently, to display their anger appropriately, and to sublimate and channel much of it into constructive energy for actively dealing with the world. "Our job," Poussaint writes, "is to help our children develop that delicate balance between appropriate control and appropriate display of anger and aggression, love and hate" (p. 110). He continues as follows, offering an excellent summary for this section on ethnic parenting. "As parents we must try to raise men and women who are emotionally healthy in a society that is basically racist. If our history is a lesson, we will continue to survive. Many black children will grow up to be strong, productive adults. But too many others will succumb under the pressures of a racist environment. Salvaging these youngsters is our responsibility as parents" (p. 111).

Ethnic Families

The key to understanding and working with ethnic families is an appreciation for their extreme diversity. Their form, first of all, varies from culture to culture. As Gushue and Sciarra (1995) suggest, each culture has "differing ways of understanding 'appropriate' family organization, values, communication and behavior" (p. 588). For example, Mexican American families share certain general cultural forms. They tend to be hierarchical and male-dominated, religious, traditionally sex typed, and often bilingual with deep extended family roots. But to push such generalizations too far is to enter into the realm of stereotyping. McGoldrick (1982), who almost single-handedly has crafted the recent interest in the importance of culture in working with families, argues that no two families are ever culturally the same. Each internalizes in its own way aspects of the cultural norms of the group. Some become very important; others are disregarded. McGoldrick sees the latter as "starting points" for understanding a given family. She goes on to enumerate a variety of other factors that impact "the way ethnic patterns surface in families." Included here are acculturation, class, education, ethnic identity, reason for migration to the United States, language status, geographic location, and stage in the family life cycle when they migrated.

It is vitally important that cultural differences in family structure not be interpreted as cultural "deficits." The Moynihan Report (Moynihan, 1965) on the status of the Black family, also referred to as "the myth of the Black matriarchy" and named for its sociologist turned U.S. senator author, is an excellent case in point. The report, which had great impact on public welfare policy in the 1960s and 1970s, implied that the strong influence of the mother in African American families was an aberration caused by racism. It further implied that with the coming of more equitable times, African American family structure would return to a more patriarchal form. Critics of the report argue that the existence of strong women in the African American family is instead a cultural artifact which belies greater role equality and flexibility for men and women than is true for White families. They further point to it as an example of the kind of creative and adaptive strategies and strengths that have emerged out of the African American family as a necessity for dealing with a hostile social environment. The critical conceptual difference here is seeing this phenomenon as a creative adaptation of a traditional African American cultural form and as a strength as opposed to a deficit in African American lifestyle.

Family Therapy With African Americans

Much of the work on adapting family therapy to cultural needs of ethnic families has focused on African Americans, and by way of example, I would like to review some of this literature. All of it emphasizes: (a) understanding the cultural context of the African American family; (b) viewing differences in family dynamics as adaptive strategies and strengths; and (c) developing practices that take into account the needs, cultural dynamics, and style of the African American family. Further, the researchers referred to favor interventions that mobilize existing Black family structures and strengths as opposed to creating new forms similar to those in White families. Hill (1972) identifies three such factors: strong kinship bonds, flexibility of family roles, and the emphasis on religion. Each will be explored in some depth.

Kinship Bonds.   Most African American families are embedded in complex kinship networks of blood and nonrelated individuals. Stack (1975) found patterns of "co-residence, kinship-based exchange networks linking multiple domestic units, elastic household boundaries, and a lifelong bond to three generation households" as typical (p. 124). White (1980) points to a series of "uncles, aunts, big mamas, boyfriends, older brothers and sisters, deacons, preachers, and others who operate in and out of the Black home" (p. 45). Such extended patterns and the multiple resources they provide must be acknowledged and worked with by family therapists as a legitimate locus of intervention. Key family members must be identified and included in the treatment planning, even if they do not fit traditional definitions of the family. It is critical that they play significant roles in the family system. One is reminded of Elena's godfather in the case study of the Martinez family in Chapter 4.

Hines and Boyd-Franklin (1982) and Boyd (1982) suggest the use of genograms or family trees to map out the role of family actors and their relationships and conflicts. Caution, however, should be exercised in the collection of such data because African American families are often suspicious of "prying" professionals. These authors suggest delaying data collection until adequate trust has been developed and that information be sought in a natural as opposed to a forced manner. Extended kinship bonds also suggest the usefulness of working with subgroups of the extended family and including only those who are directly relevant to a particular issue. It may also be necessary to schedule family sessions in the home to include key figures who cannot or will not visit clinics. Again, entering the home, like seeking information, should be done with sensitivity in light of past abuses of the welfare system against poor families.

Role Flexibility.   Role flexibility within the African American family, like extended kinship bonds, is highly adaptive for coping with the stresses of oppression and socioeconomic ills. It is most evident in the greater role diversity found among African American men and women as well as in the existence of unique familial roles such as the *parental child*. African American males have been traditionally seen by social scientists as "peripheral" to family functioning (Moynihan, 1965). Hill (1972), among others, has challenged this notion. He argues that the father's frequent absence from the home reflects neither a lack of parenting skill or interest, but rather the time and energy required to provide basic necessities for the family. The father's precarious economic position coupled with the need for African American females to work outside the home often lead to extensive role reversals and flexibility in child-rearing and household responsibilities. These circumstances have led White (1972) to suggest that, as a result, African American children may not learn as rigid distinctions between male and female roles as their White counterparts. In approaching therapy, Hines and Boyd-Franklin (1982) caution against routinely excluding the father, as has frequently been the case with those who subscribe to the myth of peripheralness. Instead, they suggest doing everything possible to include him, even if for only a single session. They encourage the therapist to regularly keep him abreast of events and developments in therapy when he is unable to attend. They also caution against assuming the absence of a male role model when the father has abandoned the family. Given the variety of extended family figures, someone often emerges to fill this role.

While the African American male has been viewed as peripheral, the African American female, often forced to assume responsibilities well beyond those typically taken on by White women, has frequently been mislabeled as overly dominant. African American couples are, in fact, often more egalitarian than their White counterparts. Scanzoni (1971), for example, found that, more often than Whites, Black males and females grow up with the expectation that both will work. Minuchin, Montalvo, Guerney, Rosman, and Schumer (1967) offer some interesting insights into the dynamics between African American males and females. Discord tends to be dealt with indirectly and not through direct confrontation. Solutions to long-term disharmony are typically informal, and long periods of separation may occur without the thought of divorce. African American couples tend to remain together for life, often for the sake of the children, and typically seek therapy for child-focused issues rather than for marital dissatisfaction. In spite of ill-treatment by a husband, African American women tend to resist the dissolution of a relationship. Hines and Boyd-Franklin (1982) suggest that this may result from three factors: (a) greater empathy for the husband's frustration in a racist society, (b) an awareness of the extent to which they outnumber Black males, and (c) a strong religious orientation that teaches tolerance for suffering.

Economic demands and oppressive forces have, in addition, created unique roles in the African American family. Included are the parental child, which involves parental responsibilities allocated to an older child when there are many younger children to attend to or when both parents are absent from the home for considerable amounts of time, and the extended generational system of parenting, in which the parent role is shared and distributed across several generations within the home. It is important to emphasize that such adaptive strategies within the African American family, while clearly a potential positive force, can in themselves become sources of problems that require intervention. This occurs when their intended function becomes distorted, overutilized, or rigidified. According to Pinderhughes (1982), "if the mother's role is overemphasized . . . it can become the pathway for all interactions within the family. This requires children to relate primarily to her moods and wishes rather than to their own needs. The result is emotional fusion of the children with the mother . . . " (p. 113). Or parental children can be forced to take on responsibilities well beyond those of which they are capable and at the expense of necessary peer group interactions (Minuchin, 1974). Or shared parenting in the multigenerational family can become highly chaotic or a source of open conflict and dispute. In each of these cases, the goal of therapy should not be to eliminate or "repair" the adaptive pattern (i.e., to move the family closer to White middle-class norms). Such patterns may, in fact, be necessary for family survival. Rather, the goal should be to set it back on its purposeful course so that it can once again function as intended.

Religion.   Religion is an extremely important factor in the life of the African American community and provides a valuable source of social connection as well as self-esteem and succor in times of stress. According to Boyd (1977), however, it is frequently overlooked by clinicians in therapy. Specifically, religious issues are seldom discussed; African American families seeking help from mental health agencies may be those unconnected to church networks; and clients may dichotomize problems as appropriate either for discussion with ministers or with mental health professionals. For clients with elaborate church connections, such networks can represent valuable resources. This might include seeking necessary information from religious leaders, calling on the network for help and resources during times of crisis, or including ministers as "significant others" in therapy or as cotherapists. In addition, religiosity is not infrequently related to a family's presenting problem. For example, Larsen (1976) reports the case of a highly religious family dealing with the rejection of religion and traditional values by a rebellious preadolescent. An understanding of its impact on behavior (e.g., strict adherence to harsh physical punishment and discipline of children based on religious maxims such as "spare the rod and spoil the child") is critical to any potentially successful therapeutic intervention.

Although I have focused only on therapy issues related to African Americans, this section should serve to highlight the kinds of differences that exist for ethnic families in general.

Bicultural Families

There are two kinds of bicultural families: ones in which the parents come from two different cultures and ones in which the parents come from the same culture with a child adopted from another culture. This section focuses primarily on the first, but I comment briefly about the second at the end.

Bicultural families and children are definitely on the increase. Perkins (1994) estimates that there are around a million interracially married couples in the United States, an increase of 250% from 1967 to 1987. According to government statistics, approximately 1 million children, or 3% of the population born between 1970 and 1990, were of mixed races, and this number is probably a substantial underestimate because there is no formal category for counting such individuals in the U.S. census. Smolowe (1993) estimates that the increase in birthrate of multiracial children is 26 times that of any other group. In spite of these increasing numbers, however, there still exists a number of myths and distorted beliefs about bicultural children. (This is perhaps not so surprising, given the fact that only 30 years ago there were laws against interracial marriages in 16 states.) Kerwin and Ponterotto (1995) describe three of the most prevalent myths: (a) bicultural children turn out to be very tragic and marginal individuals, (b) each must choose an identity with only one of their parent's groups, and (c) they are very uncomfortable discussing their ethnic identity.

Each of these is far from the truth. First, biracial children are quite capable of developing healthy ethnic identities and finding a stable social place for themselves. Second, contrary to having to choose membership in one group over the other, healthy identity development involves integrating both cultural backgrounds into a single sense of self that is an amalgam of both and yet uniquely different from either. Third, biracial children welcome the opportunity to discuss and explore who they are ethnically. Such myths are more than likely created and sustained by individuals who are uncomfortable with the idea of interracial relationships and who project their own discomfort onto the children.

Bicultural Couples

My clinical work with bicultural spouses (as in Scenario 3) yields a very interesting psychological profile. First, I have found that bicultural couples tend to approximate extremes in healthy functioning. They are either very high functioning, and bring to the relationship advanced communication skills, good cultural understanding of each other, and a strong motivation toward openness and working through difficulties. Or they enter the relationship with a culturally different partner for unconscious reasons of which they were largely unaware and bring to the relationship very poor interpersonal skills and little insight.

Jacobs (1977) carried out extensive interviews with African American and White bicultural couples and their children and because of his sampling methods found his adult subjects to be primarily high functioning. All emphasized personal attraction rather than race as their reason for getting involved with their spouse. Jacobs found that several of the spouses acknowledged a drive toward asserting autonomy as a secondary motive. For the White spouses this tended to be autonomy from rigid and overcontrolling families, while for the African American spouses it tended to represent "overcoming limits placed on them by racism." None of the 14 spouses reported feeling any guilt over their relationship. Couples in Jacobs's sample also seemed rather well differentiated from each other and, because of this, were able to allow their children to separate and become their own selves. The parents did report that it seemed easier to give their children more autonomy because the child was experienced as "being different" and not exactly like either of them.

Only two of the seven White spouses reported that both parents accepted their intention to marry. In contrast, all seven of the Black spouses reported their families of origin as generally accepting of their partner choice. This parallels previous research findings that ethnic community members seem more accepting of bicultural relationships and marriages than Whites. But there are some notable exceptions to this rule, especially among Asian American subgroups. White spouses reported an interesting sequence of reactions to parental rejection, which again attests to the basic maturity and emotional health of the partners in Jacobs's sample. After a period of initial anger, lasting anywhere from several months to a number of years, they were able to develop empathy and understanding for the rejecting parent and continued attempting to reestablish contact and attachment. Members of couples who I would describe at the other end of the continuum (i.e., as rather unhealthy) would find it impossible to make such movement and efforts at reconciliation. They tend to be flooded with guilt over their marriage, heavily preoccupied with race (the healthier couples were not so preoccupied), harbored serious prejudices of their own, and continued to act out behaviorally the same conflict that had drawn them into the interracial relationship in the first place.

Second, I have found bicultural couples to be particularly evolved in regard to issues of race and ethnicity. Being in close and intimate interaction with someone who is culturally different cannot help but elicit racial material from both partners. Such issues must be discussed honestly and worked through if the marriage is going to continue to function. What exists in effect is a microcosm of race relations in the home with numerous opportunities to explore resolving cross-cultural problems. Memmi (1966) suggests that during arguments between bicultural couples racial prejudices and stereotypes often surface in the heat of battle. Because of the hurtful nature of such attacks, resolution must be pursued and found. Jacobs (1977) also found that his interracial couples were much freer to discuss topics of race and ethnicity than were either African American or White monocultural couples.

Third, bicultural couples tend to be rather isolated as a unit, often experiencing social rejection and preferring social contact with other bicultural couples who can more easily understand what they face in the world. In reaction, they often evolve patterns of strong interdependence, which on the negative side seems to lead to an unwillingness to acknowledge problems or seek help. The isolation and mutual dependence may make the airing of problems a particular threat.

Fourth, bicultural couples face an added challenge that monocultural couples do not. Not only must they deal with their own individual differences and conflicts, but they must also navigate through the often complex and difficult terrain of cultural differences. Thus, interfaith couples (e.g., Jewish and Christian) must agree on shared practices in the home and their children's religious education. Or bicultural couples may find that they have very different styles, values, priorities, or expectations that are cultural in origin For example, Northern Europeans become quiet and distant during interpersonal conflicts and tend to move away from the partner, while individuals from more traditional cultures tend to become more verbal and emotional and move toward their partner in an effort to resolve things. If problems are ever to be resolved by such a bicultural couple, they must learn to accommodate these differences in style.

Patterns of Bicultural Marital Discord

Falicov (1986) believes that cross-cultural marriages demand from both partners a certain kind of cultural transition. According to her, the couple must "arrive at an adaptive and flexible view of cultural differences that make it possible to maintain some individuated values, to negotiate conflictual areas, and even to develop a new cultural code that integrates part of both cultural streams" (p. 431).

Falicov identifies three patterns of cultural problems that are most often presented clinically. First is what she refers to as "conflicts in cultural code." This involves cultural differences in how marriages are conceived and structured. Particularly important are differences in rules related to the inclusion and exclusion of others (especially extended family members) and the relative power and authority between spouses. In the hope of mutually adapting to each other's style, partners often minimize or maximize cultural differences. In either case, they tend to have only limited knowledge of the other's culture and are generally unable to carry out what Falicov sees as a necessary developmental task for the marriage: that of negotiating together a new cultural code that implies the melding of their different ways. She also points out that errors in this arena often stem from "ethnocentric or stereotyped views of the other." As a result of this limited knowledge, cultural differences may be "mistaken for negative personality traits" of the other.

The second type of problem deals with "cultural differences and permission to marry." Here, Falicov includes problems related to parental disapproval of the relationship and cultural artifacts such as trends toward enmeshment which make separating from family of origin a difficult and conflictual task. She goes on to identify two patterns of adaptation in couples who have not received emotional permission to marry. In the first, partners "maximize their differences and do not blend, integrate, or negotiate their values and life styles. They lead parallel lives, each holding on to their culture and/or family of origin. Often, the counterpoint of the marital distance is an excessive involvement of one or both parties with the family of origin. There may also be unresolved longings for the past ethnic or religious affiliations, even if these were of little importance previously" (p. 440). The second pattern is one of minimizing and even denying the differences, including the possibility of joining a third and alternative culture or cutting ties with culture and family. Such couples often develop an attitude of "us against them" (meaning the world) or "we only have each other." Structurally, they tend to construct rigid boundaries with the outside (especially with families of origin) and diffuse boundaries with each other.

Falicov's third problem area in cross-cultural marriages is "cultural stereotyping and severe stress." In such problems, some impending stress (e.g., the death of a parent) initiates the maximizing of cultural differences as well as increased cultural stereotyping of each other. Falicov suggests that cultural material, which has in the past been dealt with constructively, is being used as a defense against looking at other noncultural problems and that the stress currently affecting the couple has worn down their ability to cope.

Bicultural Children

While monoethnic children must eventually face the actions of a hostile social environment, bicultural children must additionally come to grips with their parents' racial drama and the perpetually repeated question: "What are you?" Kich (1992) suggests that the interracial child represents not only the parents' racial differences but also a unique individual who must work through very personal identity issues. Kerwin and Ponterotto (1995) summarize the development of racial identity in biracial children. In many ways, it parallels that of monoethnic children, but with the added task of simultaneously exploring two (or more) rather than one ethnic heritage and then integrating these into a single unique identity. Perhaps, the most salient point to remember in working with biracial and multiracial children is that psychologically they are unique entities. They are not merely reflections of their two or more sides but rather unique integrations of them.

Biracial children on the average develop an awareness of race and racial differences even earlier than monoethnic children, usually by 3 or 4. This is because they are exposed to such differences from birth in the confines of their own family. It is also likely that their parents are more attuned to these differences because of their own interracial relationship. Upon entry into school, biracial children are immediately confronted with questions of "What are you?" which serve as major stimuli for their internal processing of this question. At about the same time, they begin to experiment with labels for themselves. Children may create their descriptions based on perceptions of their skin color (e.g., coffee and cream), or adopt parental terms (e.g., interracial). Generally, biracial children are more successful moving through the identity formation process when race is openly discussed at home and parents are available to help them sort out the various issues of self-definition. Rate of development also depends on the amount of integration in their school and the availability in school of role models from their two cultural sides. During preadolescence, children begin to use racial or cultural as opposed to physical descriptions of themselves regularly. They are becoming increasingly aware of group differences other than skin color (physical appearance, language, etc.) and of the fact that their parents belong to distinct ethnic groups. Exposure to "racial incidents" and first-time entry into either integrated or segregated settings also accelerate learning.

Adolescence is particularly problematic for bicultural children. It is a time of marked intolerance for differences both for children and their peers. There are likely to be strong pressures on bicultural adolescents to identify with one parent's ethnicity over the other: usually with the parent of Color if one of the parents is White. Peers of Color push the adolescent to identify with them, and increasingly, Whites perceive and treat the bicultural adolescent as a Person of Color. Jacobs (1992) believes that vacillation between identification with one ethnic side and the simultaneous rejection of the other, and then vice versa, is a natural part of identity formation in bicultural youth. Perhaps only by internalizing one aspect of the self at a time, and even vacillating between the two over the duration of adolescence and young adulthood, can there be any real integration of both identities. Adolescence is also when dating begins, and this seems to accentuate race as a central life issue. It is not unusual for biracial youth to experience rejection because of their color or ethnicity, and these experiences are likely to have a great impact on their emerging sense of identity. The heightened sexuality of adolescence also stimulates interesting questions: "If I become pregnant or make someone pregnant, what will the baby look like?"

Interactions between bicultural children and their parents are at times complex and conflictual. As children grow more mature and aware, they are increasingly confronted with and confused by the experience of being different. The experience has been described by some as akin to "going crazy" or having no way of making sense out of how the world is reacting to them. Monoethnic parents often have a difficult time understanding exactly what the child is going through, for they tend to see the child as an extension of them rather than as an amalgam of them and their spouse. The growing realization from the child's point of view that he or she is really not like either parent, but something beyond both, can be quite anxiety provoking.

In family situations where one of the parents has detached from his or her group of origin, bicultural children may feel the need to protect this parent. Similarly, they may feel particularly close to the parent of Color when he or she is feeling bad or rejected because of racism. Divorce can be especially traumatic for biracial children because it represents a severing of the two sides of their identity. They may feel a real need to keep their warring parents together at any cost. It may become especially difficult for the child if the parents begin to use race against each other. Nor is it uncommon for the child to take on the prejudices of the individual parents during divorce. In single-parent families, difficulties can arise when the lone parent, usually the mother, feels great hostility toward the father for abandoning them and unconsciously turns her resentment toward the child as a very visible reminder of the union.

Adopted Children

Intercultural adoption is the second form of bicultural families. Communities of Color, especially African American and Native American, have taken very strong stances against adoption and foster care across racial lines. Their feeling is that White parents are not capable of providing ethnic children with adequate exposure and connection with their cultures of birth or training in how to deal with the racism they will inevitably experience. Serious efforts have been made to sensitize and train adoptive parents in cultural competence as well as to encourage them to keep their child connected to his or her ethnic community of origin. There are, however, real questions as to whether such efforts can overcome the enormous cultural gaps, let alone a racially hostile social environment. White adoptive parents seldom understand the enormity of difficulties that their children face as People of Color. In addition, they often unconsciously deny differences that exist between themselves and their children. This puts children in a most difficult psychological situation. They feel isolated in dealing with the very complex issues of race and ethnicity. Often, there is the aforementioned sense of "going crazy" caused by the enormous gulf between how they are being reacted to in the world and at home. Finally, it can become very confusing for adopted children of Color when their adopted parents simultaneously represent nurturance and emotional support on one side and the oppressor on the other. A process somewhat akin to the identity vacillation suggested by Jacobs may occur for these bicultural children as well.

Readers are reminded to return to the scenarios presented at the beginning of the chapter and to see in what ways their understanding of ethnic children, parents, and families has expanded.

Chapter Six

Mental Health
Issues

In a most extraordinary book entitled *Black Rage*, psychiatrists William Grier and Price Cobbs (1968) explore the enormous anger they see lurking below the surface of the African American patients who seek their help. They begin by describing the life circumstances of three patients. Roy was an overachieving painter who had become impotent and unable to work after a fall from scaffolding. He sought help because there was no physical basis for his malaise or reason for the way his life had fallen apart after the accident. Bertha entered treatment because of a severe depression. She was very dark-skinned, had grown up in the South, and had experienced a series of abusive relationships with working-class men who were far below her socially and intellectually. In treatment, she revealed deep feelings of self-hatred, self-deprecation, and a self-image as Black, ugly, ignorant, and dirty. Her depression had become clinical after a marriage to a fellow professional and the birth of a child. John was a highly trained professional with a severe anger problem that had lost him a series of good jobs. He sought treatment after entering a very promising executive training program in which he was doing poorly because of his discomfort in supervising and competing with White co-workers.

The patterns that these patients presented with were very typical of Grier and Cobbs's general African American clientele. All had been living reasonably functional lives until an emotional crisis knocked them down, and each had a difficult time recovering. Psychotherapy had revealed very negative perceptions of self which were deeply intertwined with their experiences as African Americans in the United States. According to the authors, African

Americans, because of their circumstances of having to live in, adapt to, and survive in a hostile and racist world, are at perpetual risk for developing serious physical and emotional disorders. Most, in fact, survive. Many even grow strong from it. But all pay an emotional price that may, with sufficient stress and personal difficulty, end up in some type of psychological breakdown. For many, the ultimate consequence is depression and grief, which are understood by Grier and Cobbs to be nothing less than "hatred turned toward the self." But when these patients are helped to feel the depth of their sorrow, their grief begins to lift, and enormous anger is set free. According to the authors, African Americans stand at a precarious juncture, "delicately poised, not yet risen to the flash point, but rising rapidly nonetheless" (p. 213). As if looking into a crystal ball, they anticipated a growing violence that has increasingly become a part of race relations in America since the 1970s.

This chapter and the one that follows turn our attention to mental health issues that plague ethnic group members. This chapter explores a number of factors, like the racism described by Grier and Cobbs, that put populations of Color at risk for mental and emotional difficulties. Chapter 7, in turn, focuses on the related question of bias in the delivery of mental health services. Why is it that, in spite of a clearly documented need, ethnic clients consistently under-utilize available mental health services? Together, these chapters should give the reader a good picture of the kinds of psychological issues with which culturally different clients struggle and ultimately bring with them into the helping situation. In this chapter, I offer a more detailed look at problems with ethnic identity and group belonging, discuss the effects of acculturation on traditional culture, introduce the concept of stress as a mediator between negative environmental forces (e.g., poverty and racism) and physical and mental symptoms, explore the idea of unresolved historic grief and trauma as a source of communal difficulties, and look at drug and alcohol use and their relationship to ethnicity.

Ethnic Identity and Group Belonging

The development of racial identity in children and the controversy over whether children of Color regularly experience problems in group identification and low self-concepts were discussed in Chapter 5. The conclusion, based on several sources of evidence, was that they did not, but without sufficient family and community support, ethnic children were certainly at risk for such problems. There was also some hesitancy to underestimate the deleterious effects of racism and the negative views that society in general holds of ethnic group members. In this section, I expand this picture to include identity difficulties in ethnic adults.

The Inner Dynamics of Ethnic Identity

The general term *identity* refers to the existence of a stable inner sense of who a person is and is formed by the successful integration of various experiences of the self into a coherent self-image. *Ethnic identity*, in turn, refers to that part of personal identity that contributes to one's self-image as a ethnic group member. Thus, when one speaks of African American identity or Native American identity or Jewish identity, what is being referred to is the individual's subjective experience of ethnicity. What does the person feel, consciously and unconsciously, about being a member of his or her ethnic group? What meaning do individuals attach to their ethnicity? What does their behavior reflect about the nature of their attachment to the group? Answers to these questions are subsumed under the notion of ethnic identity. Ethnic identity formation, like personal identity formation, results from the integration of various personal experiences one has had as an African American or, Native American or Jew combined with the messages that have been communicated and internalized about ethnicity by various family members and significant others. In general, ethnic identity can be defined as positive, negative, or ambivalent, and individuals as positive identifiers, negative identifiers, and ambivalent identifiers (Klein, 1980). The latter two situations have also been referred to in the literature as "internalized racism" and "internalized oppression."

As emphasized in the previous chapter, ethnic children, by the fact of being raised in a hostile and racist environment, are likely to have unpleasant experiences associated with their ethnicity. As these negative group-related experiences accumulate, it becomes increasingly difficult for the child, and later the adult, to integrate them into a coherent and positive sense of ethnic self. Instead, they are either actively rejected and disowned, and thus relegated to the unconscious and experienced as "not me" (negative identification) or allowed to remain conscious, but unintegrated. In time, they are likely to become a source of ambivalent feelings about the self as an ethnic group member (ambivalent identification). In this regard, Klein (1980) found that Jews with positive ethnic identities tend to be healthier psychologically and better adjusted than those with more conflicted feelings about their Jewishness. Similar logic would seem to hold for People of Color.

Inner conflicts in ethnic identity, such as those just described, ultimately find expression in some form of overt behavior. In the case of negative identification (i.e., where aspects of the ethnic self are actively rejected or disowned), there is, first of all, a tendency in the individual to deny, avoid, or escape group membership in whatever ways possible. In communities of Color, this is often referred to as "passing." It may include trying to change one's appearance so as not to look so typically ethnic, name changing, moving to nonethnic neighborhoods, dating and marrying outside of the group, and taking on majority group habits, language, and affectations. Such behaviors are usually experienced as offensive within ethnic communities. Specific derogatory terms have, in fact, been created in each of the communities of Color to described such individuals: "oreos" among African Americans, "coconuts" among Latinos/as, "apples" among Native Americans, and "bananas" among Asian Americans. All refer to such individuals as of Color on the outside, but White on the inside. As part of this rejection of ethnicity, one also finds the taking on of majority attitudes and habits, including the dominant culture's prejudices and stereotypes toward one's own group. For those who are unfamiliar with such patterns of "identity rejection and self-hatred," it is usually shocking to learn that some of the most virulent anti-Semites and racists can be Jews and Blacks, respectively.

In relation to ambivalent identification, where rejecting tendencies exist concurrently with positive feelings about group membership, there is either vacillation between love and hate (where individuals move back and forth, pulling away from feeling too identified if they get too close and moving back toward the group if they grow too distant) or the simultaneous expression of contradictory positive and negative attitudes and behaviors. One form of accommodation is to compartmentalize ethnic identity (i.e., retain certain aspects and reject others). For instance, a Latino/a might refuse to speak Spanish or identify as a Catholic or marry within the group, but at the same time have strong preferences for native foods, prefer living in a barrio, and become involved in civil rights activities.

However, psychological accommodations such as these tend to be precarious at best and often fall apart, or at least grow fragile, in relation to all forms of emotional upheaval and change. It is not uncommon, for example, for individuals to "rethink" their connection to ethnicity after the birth of a child, death of a parent or close relative, or after a personal near-death experience. It is perhaps most accurate to conceive of ethnic identity formation as an ongoing and lifelong process. As such, it involves a series of internal psychological adaptations (that may eventually translate into changes in behavior) to an ever-changing complex of unfolding ethnic experiences. Generally, core conflicts around ethnicity that occur early in life continue to feed basic feelings of negativity or ambivalence and are difficult to resolve completely. But even here, there are instances when dramatic and significant changes toward positive identification do occur (Diller, 1991).

Models of Ethnic Identity Development

Since the 1970s, there has been extensive theorizing about models of ethnic identity development. The writings of Helms (1990), W.E. Cross (1995), Hardiman and Jackson (1992), and Atkinson, Morten, and Sue (1993) offer good summaries of this work. These models, which were first developed in relation to the experience of African Americans, assume that there are strong similarities in the ways all ethnic individuals respond to the experience of oppression and racism. It is believed, further, that there is a series of predictable stages that People of Color (and also Whites) go through as they struggle to make sense out of their relationship to their own cultural group as well as to the oppression of mainstream culture.

Cross, for example, hypothesizes five stages. In Stage 1, *preencounter,* people are socialized into a strong preference for dominant cultural values. In Stage 2, *encounter,* some event or experience shatters the individual's denial and sends them deep into confusion about their own ethnicity. In Stage 3, *immersion–emersion,* they uncritically internalize a prominority view and completely reject dominant culture, immersing themselves in a separatist ethnic world. In Stage 4, *internalization,* their new positive identity becomes more comfortable and the need to rigidly hold on to group allegiances at the expense of personal autonomy lessens. In Stage 5, *internalization–commitment,* the movement initiated in Stage 4 continues with the person increasingly able to retain a strong but simultaneous commitment to intragroup, intergroup, and individual issues.

The value of these models for providers is that they suggest that individuals at different stages of development have very different needs and values and may have different perspectives on what might be helpful or therapeutic. Atkinson et al. (1993), for instance, differentiate the attitudes of clients at various stages in relation to counseling needs. Those at Stage 1 tend to seek help for issues unrelated to ethnic identity and generally prefer working with White providers. Those at Stage 2, on the other hand, tend to be preoccupied with issues of ethnicity, race, and identity. They seek counselors knowledgeable about their own cultural group and tend to do best with counseling modes that allow maximum self-exploration. Clients in Stage 3 are not as likely to seek counseling. They tend to be absorbed in reexploring and engaging in ethnic ways, and they see their problems almost exclusively as the result of oppression. Those in Stage 4 are struggling to balance group and personal perspectives and may seek counseling to help them sort out these issues. They may still tend to prefer a counselor from their own group, but can begin to conceive of receiving help from a culturally sensitive outsider. Those who have reached Stage 5 are again less in need of access to counseling. They have developed good skills at balancing personal needs and group obligations, have an openness to all cultures, and are able to deal well with racism when it is encountered. Their preference for a counselor, if needed, is most likely to be dictated by the personal qualities and attitudes of the counselor rather than by group membership. Of late, there has been a trend toward the development of culturally specific identity development models growing out of a sense that the experience of identity formation is sufficiently different in each cultural group to warrant its own separate treatment.

Assimilation and Acculturation

Ethnic group members can differ widely in the extent of their assimilation and acculturation. Conceptually, assimilation means the coming together of two distinct cultures to create a new and unique third cultural form. This is the "myth" of the "great melting pot," taken from a play by the same name, written by Jewish playwright Israel Zangwill at the beginning of the 20th century. It is referred to as a myth because it just never happened that way.

Gordon (1964) distinguishes several forms of assimilation including acculturation, structural assimilation, marital assimilation, and identificational assimilation. Acculturation involves taking on the cultural ways of another group, usually those of the mainstream culture. Structural assimilation means gaining entry into the institutions of a society. This is also called "integration" by Gordon. Marital assimilation implies large-scale intermarriage, and identificational assimilation involves developing a sense of belonging and peoplehood with the host society. It is probably most accurate to say that White ethnics—Irish, Italian, Jews, Armenians, and so forth—have assimilated into American society on all of these dimensions, but only to the extent that they have been willing to give up their traditional ways and values. People of Color, on the other hand, were never really considered part of the great melting pot image and have remained structurally separate. They have, however, acculturated in varying degrees to the dominant Northern European culture. Thus, in America, assimilation has always been a one-way process, perhaps, according to Healey (1995), better referred to as "Americanization" or "Anglo-conformity." Healey continues:

> This kind of assimilation was designed to maintain the predominance of the British-type institutional patterns created during the early years of American society. Under Anglo-conformity there is relatively little sharing of cultural traits, and immigrants and minority groups are expected to adapt to Anglo-American culture as fast as possible. Historically, Americanization has been a precondition for access to better jobs, higher education, and other opportunities. (p. 40)

Acculturation, again, is the taking on of cultural patterns of another group, in this case, dominant White culture. In relation to working with culturally different populations, acculturation has importance in two different ways. First, it is critical to be able to assess the amount of acculturation that has taken place within any individual or family and, simultaneously, to discover to what extent and in what specific areas traditional attitudes, values, and behavior still remain. Without such a "reading," it is impossible to know what form of helping process is most appropriate and most effective with culturally different clients. Just knowing that a client is Latino/a in origin tells us very little about who the person is or how he or she lives. To know where the individual falls on a continuum from traditional identification to complete acculturation offers more information. It is important, however, to not confuse group membership with the degree of acculturation that has occurred, or as Sue and Zane (1987) suggest, to "avoid confounding the cultural values of the client's ethnic group with those of the client" (p. 8).

Second, acculturation can create serious emotional strain and difficulties for ethnic clients. A special term, *acculturative stress*, has been coined to refer to such situations. Take, for example, a newly arrived Vietnamese family. The children have learned English relatively quickly in comparison to their parents. As a result, they may end up translating for and becoming the spokespeople for the family. This is not a traditional role for Vietnamese children, who are trained to be very deferential to their elders. Nor is it natural within their tradition for children to be in a position to wield so much power. As the children Americanize, they feel increasingly less bound by traditional ways. The result is enormous stress on the family unit, as is usually the case when traditional cultural ways are compromised or lost as a result of immigration and acculturation.

Views of Acculturation

Researchers have long argued over how best to conceptualize the process of acculturation. Is it unidimensional or multidimensional? That is, does acculturation exist on a single continuum ranging from identification with the indigenous culture at one end to identification with the dominant culture at the other? Or does it make more sense to conceive of an individual's attachment to the two groups as independent of each other, with the possibility of simultaneously retaining an allegiance to one's traditional culture as well as to dominant American culture? The unidimensional view implies that as one moves toward dominant cultural patterns, there must be a simultaneous giving up of traditional ways. This approach has generated the notion of the "marginal" person, an ethnic group member who tries to acculturate into the majority but ends up in a perpetual limbo, caught between the two cultures (Lewin, 1948; Stonequist, 1961). Such individuals have transformed themselves too much to return to traditional ways, but at the same time, cannot gain any real acceptance in majority culture because of their skin color. A variety of symptoms has been attributed to such marginality: feelings of inferiority, depression, hyperself-consciousness, restlessness and anomie, and a heightened sense of race consciousness.

Other writers see acculturation as bi- or multidimensional. Proponents of biculturalism believe that it is possible to live and function effectively in two or more different cultures (T.L. Cross, 1987; Oetting & Beauvais, 1990; Valentine, 1971). Unlike the marginal person who is suspended between cultures with little real connection to either, the bicultural individual feels connected to both and picks and chooses aspects of each to internalize. Thus, in this view, it is possible for an Asian American to remain deeply steeped in a traditional lifestyle, while at the same time interacting comfortably in the White world, perhaps in relation to work, some socializing, and political activity outside of the Asian American community. Problems with this notion arise when aspects of the two cultures are in clear conflict. For example, an immigrant Latina woman is forced to give up her traditional role and work outside of the home and yet tries to remain true to traditional sex roles. Even if she is able to integrate the two, it will be very difficult for her children, not having been fully enculturated in traditional ways, to do the same (Casas & Pytluk, 1995). It should also be pointed out that biculturalism is not seen as a virtue in all ethnic communities. Some view those who have become proficient in majority ways with contempt, as turn-coats who have rejected and turned away from their own kind.

A third perspective, typified by the work of Marin (1992), suggests that the impact of acculturation can best be assessed by discovering the kinds of material that have been gained or lost through acculturation. Marin distinguishes three levels of acculturation. The superficial level involves learning and forgetting facts that are part of a culture's history or tradition. The intermediate level has to do with gaining or losing more central aspects and behaviors of a person's social world (e.g., language preference and use, ethnicity of spouse, friends, neighbors, names given to children, and choice of media). The significant level of cultural material involves core values, beliefs, and norms that are essential to the very cultural paradigm or worldview of the person. For example, Marin (1992) points to Latino/a culture's values of "encouraging positive interpersonal relationships and discouraging negative, competitive and assertive interactions," "familialism," and "collectivism" (p. 239). When cultural values of this magnitude are lost or become less central, acculturation has reached a significant point, and one might wonder what remains of an individual's cultural attachment. For many Whites, traditional cultural ties progressively slipped away, generation by generation in America, according to Marin's model. The immigrant generation tended to trade more superficial cultural material. Their children, in turn, exchanged more immediate cultural material as they increasingly acculturated and so forth.

Immigration and Acculturation

Acculturative stress is most pronounced during periods of transition, especially during and after significant migrations (e.g., to the United States) and the exposure and necessary adjustment to a new culture. Landau (1982) points to a number of factors that either ease or make the transition more difficult. Included are: (a) reasons for the migration and whether or not the original expectations and hopes were met, (b) the availability of community and extended family support systems, (c) structure of the family and whether it was forced to assume a different form after migration (e.g., moving from extended family to exclusively nuclear), (d) the degree to which the new culture is similar to the old (the greater the difference, the more substantial is the stress), and (e) the family's general ability to be flexible and adaptive. According to Landau, when the stresses are severe, the support insufficient, and the family basically unhealthy, it is likely to try to compensate in one of three ways, each leading to even further stresses and a compounding of existing problems. The family may isolate itself and remain separate from its new environment. It may become enmeshed and close its boundaries to the outside world, rigidify its traditional ways, and become overly dependent on its members. Or it may become disengaged, wherein individual family members become isolated from each other as they reject previous family values and lifestyle. Especially problematic is the situation in which family members acculturate at very different rates.

Perhaps the most common and problematic consequence of acculturation is the breakdown of traditional cultural and family norms. Among Latino/a immigrants, for instance, this may take the form of challenges to traditional beliefs about male authority and supremacy, role expectations for men, and standards of conduct for females. But such changes may not be limited only to newer immigrants. Carrillo (1982) suggests that these same changing patterns are evident within the Latino/a community as a whole: "Clearly, Hispanics appear to be moving away from such strict concepts of role and authority within the family, and with this movement approaching new normative behavior for males and females" (p. 260). She goes on to warn helping professionals to exhibit caution in assessing pathology, appropriateness, and inappropriateness in relation to Latino/a sex-role behavior:

> An Hispanic man who prefers the company of other men and who behaves in an authoritative manner with his wife may be manifesting his "machismo" rather than indicating personal pathology. Such behavior among other cultural groups may imply "latent homosexuality," or an "inferiority complex," or that the woman is masochistic and prefers to be a "martyr." Such is not necessarily the case among Hispanic groups. (p. 261)

What is critical is knowledge of the norms of the group and subgroup of which the client is a member. This is not to say, however, that emotional problems do not develop as a result of cultural change. Quite the contrary. Carrillo (1982), in fact, points out a number of problems that can emerge in relation to the individual's "inability to accept, conform to or adhere to sex-role defined standards of conduct" (p. 258). For males, symptoms can include difficulties in relation to authority, preoccupation and anxiety over sexual potency, conflict over the need for role consistency, and depression and isolation over having to feel invincible. For females, it tends to include feelings of failure and depression over not being able to live up to the strict sex-role requirements that are placed on them as well as the somatization (development of bodily symptoms) of their frustration and rage.

Acculturation and Community Breakdown

A final dynamic worth exploring is the psychological consequences of the breakdown of the broader community as a result of assimilation. As acculturation proceeds and individual group members feel less attached to traditional ways, they often choose to leave the community (or ghetto) in the hope of avoiding some of the hatred and animosity that are routinely directed toward the group. Lewin (1948), drawing on observations of highly assimilated German Jews prior to World War II, suggests a very different outcome than one would predict. Specifically, he found that by leaving the ghetto, acculturated individuals put themselves at greater risk of being the objects of prejudice and racial hatred than was true when they resided within the traditional community: "If we compare the position of the individual Jew in the Ghetto period . . . with his situation in modern times . . . we find that he now stands much more for and by himself. With the wider spread and scattering of the Jewish group, the family or the single individual becomes functionally much more separated" (p. 153). In the ghetto, "he felt the pressure to be essentially applied to the Jewish group as a whole . . . Now as a result of the disintegration of the group, he is much more exposed to pressure as an individual . . . Even when the pressure on the whole group from without was weakened, that on the individual Jew was relatively increased" (pp. 153-155). In other words, with acculturation and assimilation, the ability of the community to protect the individual is weakened, and efforts to avoid racial hatred by distancing oneself from group membership are likely in the end to prove counterproductive.

Stress

A critical question that needs to be answered to understand the complex relationship between ethnicity and health is: How exactly does the negative impact of broad social factors, such as racism, acculturation, poverty, and so forth, get translated into the everyday physical and emotional distresses that disproportionately affect People of Color? According to Myers (1982), the mechanism is stress. Put most simply, being without resources and the perpetual object of discrimination make life more stressful and, in turn, increase the risks of disease, instability, and breakdown. Myers begins his argument by suggesting that "for many blacks, particularly those who are poor, the critical antecedents appear to be the higher basal stress level and the state of high stress vigilance at which normative functioning often occurs" (p. 128). In other words, poor African Americans tend to live a "stress-primed" state of existence.

Myers goes on to show how certain internal and external factors either increase or decrease (mediate) the subjective experience of stress and, as a result, the risk of stress-related diseases. Externally, current economic conditions set the stage for whether race- and social-class–related experiences will be sources of greater or lesser stress. Internally, individual temperament, problem-solving skills, a sense of internal control, and self-esteem reduce the likelihood that an event or situation is experienced as stressful. With these factors as a baseline, Myers describes two additional conditions that seem to mediate the individual's response when a stressful situation is actually presented: the actual episodic stressful event that occurs and the coping and adaptation of which the individual is capable. In relation to the former, Myers contends (a) for poor African Americans, episodic crises are more frequent and (b) because of their higher basal stress levels, such crises are more likely to be damaging and disruptive. "Thus, for example, the death of a spouse or relative, the loss of a job due to economic downturns is likely to be more psychologically and economically devastating to the person who is struggling to find enough money to eat, to pay the rent, and to support three or four children than it would to someone without those basic day to day concerns" (pp. 133-134). Myers has identified substantial differences among group members in their ability to cope and in the type of coping strategies used. Street youth, for example, resort to "cappin, rappin, conning, and fighting" as coping mechanisms for survival in the streets. For others, the "ability to remain calm, cool, and collected in the face of a crisis" is primary. Still others may turn to alcohol and drugs or religion as a means of gaining some distance.

Myers believes that for African Americans as a group, stress-related illness risks are higher than the general population. But he does point out that there are very real ways to reduce the risk:

> To the extent that ethnic cultural identity can be developed and stably integrated into the personality structure, to the extent that skills and competencies necessary to meet the varied demands can be obtained, to the extent that flexible, contingent response strategies can be developed, and to the extent that support systems can be maintained and strengthened, then resistances can be developed that will enhance stress tolerance and reduce individual and collective risk for disorders and disabilities." (Myers, 1982, p. 138)

Daly, Jennings, Beckett, and Leashore (1995) amplify on Myers's findings by describing specific coping mechanisms within the family, at the community level, and within organizations.

Unresolved Trauma and Historic Grief

The Lakota Sioux, like many other Native American groups, are beset by serious and widespread social problems. Their rate of death by alcoholism is 7 times the national average and 2.5 times that of other Native American People. Suicide rates are 3.2 times that of Whites. Historically, they have been plagued by high rates of coronary heart disease and hypertension. Unemployment rates on the Lakota reservation average from 50%–90% and about 50% of the group live below the poverty level. Yellow Horse Brave Heart (1995) contends that these depressing statistics are the result of generations of chronic, unresolved historic grief, "a repercussion from the loss of lives, land, and aspects of culture rendered by the European conquest of the Americas" (p. 2). This unre-solved grief has dual sources: (a) massive trauma that has endured from gener-ation to generation and (b) the systematic destruction of traditional Lakota ways of grieving at both the individual and communal levels. In other words, not only have the Lakota been devastated by an ongoing series of traumatic events, but also robbed of the traditional rituals that would allow them to ade-quately mourn and thereby resolve their grief. The result, according to Yellow Horse Brave Heart, has been frozen, unresolved grief, passed on across genera-tions, which is the real source of the community's out-of-control alcohol and mental and physical health problems.

Legters (1988) believes that the treatment of Native Americans in the United States meets the United Nations definition of genocide. Nowhere is this fact more evident than in the traumatic history of the Lakota Sioux. The mid-1800s saw the loss of traditional hunting grounds, the spread of smallpox and cholera, the killing, imprisonment, and relocation of hundreds of innocent tribal members, a bounty on Lakota scalps, and the death of hundreds by star-vation and exposure. In 1871, President Grant asserted that the government would no longer consider Indians to be nations with whom treaties would be negotiated. Instead, they were wards of the state. This declaration set the stage for increased persecution and widespread invasion of Lakota territories. An army attack in 1868 on a peaceful encampment led ultimately to the Lakota victory at Little Big Horn. This, however, only intensified government efforts to steal land and break the spirit of the People. In 1877, Lakota spiritual leader Crazy Horse was arrested and killed. The rise of Sitting Bull temporarily reunited and gave some encouragement to the People. By then, he alone remained a symbol of resistance to the White man and ensured the practice of traditional Native ways. His eventual assassination, the suppression of the spiritual Ghost Dance cult, and the massacre at Wounded Knee left the surviv-ing Lakota totally traumatized. The accumulated trauma of these events has been passed down through subsequent generations.

A series of more recent experiences has only intensified the cumulative effect of the historic past. The experience of Indian boarding schools (which represented generations of forced separations of children from parents, physi-cal and sexual abuses, and the destruction of traditional cultural knowledge among the children), death by tuberculosis, continued land loss, and relocation and government termination policies exacerbated the sense of loss. According to Yellow Horse Brave Heart, "with the rapidity and severity of these trau-matic losses over time, now extended by high death rates from accidents and health problems, Lakota grief has become complicated. There isn't sufficient time to mourn one loss before another loss occurs" (p. 33). Paralleling this mas-sive trauma and contributing to the difficulty in grieving was the systematic destruction of traditional beliefs, ceremonies, and rituals of grief. Boarding schools made many strangers to their own cultural heritage. Traditional ways were disenfranchised by government control of reservations, the prohibition of ceremonies, and the intrusion of White attitudes toward grieving. In other words, the massive trauma was accentuated by a lack of functional cultural methods of mourning the losses. The grief could not go away; it could only accumulate and be passed on from generation to generation.

To intervene in this process and see if it was possible to reintroduce traditional means of grieving to her people, Yellow Horse Brave Heart designed an experimental healing intervention to be used with a group of Lakota human service providers, healers, and community leaders. They, in turn, were to take the experience back to their respective communities and facilitate similar healing. Yellow Horse Brave Heart drew many of her ideas for treating trauma from research on Jewish Holocaust survivors and their children. There seemed to be strong parallels in intergenerational transmission of grief and difficulties in accessing cultural and communal forms of grieving between the Lakota People and Jewish survivors who remained in Europe. Survivors who found their way to Israel, for instance, had significantly more opportunities for collective mourning. The same is true of America. Ironically, only in Europe, where the trauma actually occurred, has there been a reluctance to acknowledge its existence. It was also only among European Jews, like the Lakota, that postwar survivors "lived among the perpetrators and murderers of their families" (Fogelman, 1991, p. 67). Fogelman points out other similarities between these survivors and the Lakota, including the difficulty in mourning a mass grave, the importance of community rituals and memorials, and the dynamics of collective grieving.

The Lakota intervention, which lasted 4 days, entailed a series of experiential exercises and presentations focusing on Lakota history, the nature and dynamics of trauma and grief, and traditional spiritual practices and ceremonies. It was designed with the purpose of "stimulating mourning resolution of historical grief" among the provider participants, all of whom were Lakota. Participants were tested before and after the intervention on a number of assessment instruments. Yellow Horse Brave Heart tested three specific hypotheses in the study. First was that "education about historical trauma would lead to an increased awareness of the trauma and its impact upon grief and related affects (emotions)" (p. 126). Second was that "sharing grief and related affects with others of similar background within a traditional Lakota context would lead to a cathartic sense of relief" (p. 126). Third, "a grief resolution process would be initiated, with a reduction in grief related affects, accompanied by a more positive group identity and commitment to community healing" (p. 126). All three hypotheses were strongly supported. Since this research, Yellow Horse Brave Heart has expanded her work by creating a network of "survivors" to do training and therapy in their respective Lakota communities and by helping communities carry out their own memorial ceremonies and grieving rituals.

In a similar manner, Duran and Duran (1995) argue that the psychological consequence of communal trauma and colonization for Native American males has been posttraumatic stress disorder (PTSD): "Once the warrior is defeated and his ability to protect the community destroyed, a deep psychological trauma of identity loss occurs" (p. 36). He will unconsciously turn against his loved ones and become abusive as his ego splits, one aspect in touch with the enormous pain and the other identifying with the aggressor. The rage that he feels and would like to turn on the destroyer of his culture is ultimately turned inward. The only way he can contain the rage and self-medicate the PTSD is through the use of alcohol. In discussing treatment, Duran and Duran (1995) warn against unintentionally perpetuating the trauma:

> Without the awareness of some of these dynamics . . . most practitioners continue to invalidate the experience of trauma in Native American people, which in its own right becomes an ongoing infliction of trauma on the patient. The Native American patient already feels decades of horrendous unresolved grief and rage, and the practitioner adds to this through the insensitivity of blaming the victim by pathologizing clients, as is so common in Western psychotherapy. Such iatrogenics perpetuates the suffering. (p. 42)

Yellow Horse Brave Heart's and Duran and Duran's work on resolving historical grief and trauma have relevance not only for Native Americans, but also for any ethnic group with a collective history of trauma and oppression. Such wholesale loss and disenfranchisement have certainly been the experience of People of Color in the United States. African Americans with the lingering effects of slavery and the ongoing trauma of racism; Latinos/as with the trauma of migration north, expatriation of lands in the Southwest and, for some, escape from political genocide in South and Central America; and Asian Americans with their oppression as an immigrant labor force, internment during World War II, and the traumatic experiences of refugees from the war in Southeast Asia. Similarly, there are Jews, Irish, Armenians, and the Gypsies (Rom) in the United States with long histories as victims of political and social oppression in their native lands. It is likely that individuals from these various groups, like the Lakota Sioux, currently suffer posttraumatic stress disorder and unresolved historical grief which have never been diagnosed or dealt with either individually or on a communal basis.

Drug and Alcohol Use

There are three important points to be made about substance use and ethnicity. First, there are numerous myths about substance abuse among People of Color. Rather than reflecting anything akin to empirical reality, they are based on distorted stereotypes of excessive use and abuse by People of Color, especially in comparison to beliefs about the consumption patterns of Whites. "All Mexicans use and sell drugs" is typical. Recently, for example, a report was issued regarding profiles of suspected drug traffickers to be routinely stopped and searched by the Oregon State Highway Patrol. Included among the characteristics that were sufficient to initiate a search was "being Hispanic." In reality, research shows that, with a few notable excepts (to be discussed shortly), People of Color tend to use drugs and alcohol much less frequently than do dominant culture Americans.

Second, there are real cultural differences in consumption patterns, in the meaning of drinking and substance use, and in what is socially acceptable across cultures. Like the interpretation of any cultural differences, it is dangerous to make clinical judgments about patterns of substance use by culturally different clients without knowledge of the norms that exist around drinking or drug use within their culture. The same consumption pattern in an Asian American male, for instance, may have very different meaning vis-à-vis possible excesses and pathology than it would for a similarly aged Native American male.

Third, the meaning of recovery and abstinence is very different for People of Color compared to dominant group members. While substance abuse among Whites tends to be best understood as a personal issue, for People of Color, it is as much a social-cultural issue as a personal one.

A good place to begin is by citing research findings on substance use and abuse in youth of Color. Drug research on youth is more plentiful than similar data on adults, and in general, it tends to reflect similar patterns to those of adults within the same culture. The following data are drawn from and summarized in Bernard (1991). With the exception of Native American youth, other ethnic populations exhibit use patterns that are significantly less than young Whites. This fact challenges commonly held beliefs and stereotypes about runaway abuse and addiction among minority youth. As ethnic groups members acculturate, however (and this is true for youth as well as adults), research shows that use levels increase and begin to approximate those of White counterparts. The lower use rates found among less acculturated African Americans, Latinos/as, and Asian Americans may reflect protective factors that exist in traditional ethnic cultures, including emphases on cooperation, sharing, communality, group support, interdependence, and social responsibility. These values are believed to mitigate against social alienation, which has regularly been shown to be associated with high substance abuse. It is interesting to note that complementary values (i.e., competition, individualism, self first, and non-sharing) are more closely aligned with Northern European dominant culture and are seen as risk factors implicated in the development of substance abuse problems. It has also been found that bicultural youth (i.e., those who can move effectively between the dominant culture and their culture of origin) tend to exhibit rather low levels of drug and alcohol use. Although youth of Color generally show lower rates of substance use, their use tends to lead to more behavioral and health problems. This is because there is a cumulative effect of substance abuse with other risk factors such as poverty, unemployment, discrimination, poor health care, and general depression, which correlate highly with ethnicity. It is believed that prevention is of little use unless these other risk factors are addressed. More specific information on use and abuse patterns for youth of Color by community is summarized in Tables 6.1–6.4.

Table 6.1

Key Research Findings From *Prevention Research Update Number Three: Substance Abuse Among Latino/a Youth*
- Hispanics are one of the largest, youngest, and fastest-growing of the nation's subgroups (half of the Hispanic population is now under age 18).
- While Hispanics in general have no higher levels of use prevalence than Whites or other ethnic groups, some research has found that Hispanics have more drug-related problems and that drug abuse is a serious, chronic, and multigenerational problem in many Hispanic families and communities.
- Hispanic youth who consume heavier quantities and experience more drinking problems than do other adolescents.
- Heavier use patterns beginning in late adolescence appear to result from a blending of the drinking patterns of the donor cultures with those common among U.S. youth and reflect the value that the right to drink is a rite-of-passage.
- Differential acculturation can produce stress in family relationships and behavioral problems in immigrant children who may acculturate to the U.S. culture at a faster rate than their parents.
- Prevention efforts must (1) encourage biculturalism and bilingualism, building on cultural strengths and pride while facilitating the development of skills necessary to succeed in U.S. society; (2) involve the community in community development efforts, especially the development of cultural arts centers; (3) involve the community in public awareness campaigns to counter the efforts of the alcohol/tobacco industry in Hispanic communities.

From *Moving toward a "just and vital culture": Multiculturalism in our schools* by B. Bernard, April, 1991. Reprinted by permission of Northwest Regional Educational Laboratory.

Table 6.2

Key Findings From *Prevention Research Update Number Five: Substance Abuse Among Asian American Youth*
- Other than Native Hawaiians, whose drug and alcohol use is more similar to Whites, Asian Americans have low levels of use compared with other ethnic groups.
- Consistent with their low levels of use, Asian Americans suffer less from substance-related problems than do other ethnic groups, and most of these problems are male-owned.
- Drinking in Asian society is governed by social norms that condemn excessive use and encourage moderation.
- The more acculturated Asian males are, the higher their levels of alcohol use become.
- A concern among some researchers and practitioners is that Asian American substance use problems are underreported because of their "model minority" stereotype status and because they do not want to bring shame on their families.
- Prevention efforts should focus on (1) encouraging biculturalism; (2) involving youth in community prevention; (3) providing indigenously owned family counseling and support services.

From *Moving toward a "just and vital culture": Multiculturalism in our schools* by B. Bernard, April, 1991. Reprinted by permission of Northwest Regional Educational Laboratory.

Table 6.3

Key Findings From *Prevention Research Update Number Two: Substance Abuse Among Minority Youth: Native Americans*

- The rates of use for almost all drugs, but especially alcohol, marijuana, and inhalants, have been consistently higher among American Indian youth than non-Indian youth.
- The rate of alcoholism is two to three times the national average.
- Heavy drinking has been called the main reason that one in two Indian students never finish high school.
- Native American adolescents are profoundly alienated and depressed and experience high rates of delinquency, learning and behavior problems, and suicide.
- This situation is the result of persistent and deep sociocultural and economic exploitation, which has made them the most severely disadvantaged population in the U.S.
- The main risk factors for Native American adolescent substance abuse are (1) a sense of cultural dislocation and lack of integration into either traditional Indian or modern American life; (2) community norms supporting use; (3) peer-group support for use; (4) lack of hope for a bright future.
- Prevention efforts must focus on (1) community involvement in community development efforts with youth playing a major role; (2) educational interventions that allow Native American youth to develop bicultural competence, i.e., to develop the skills necessary to be successful in the dominant culture while retaining their identification with and respect for traditional Native American values.

From *Moving toward a "just and vital culture": Multiculturalism in our schools* by B. Bernard, April, 1991. Reprinted by permission of Northwest Regional Educational Laboratory.

Table 6.4

Key Findings From *Prevention Research Update Number Four: Substance Abuse Among Black Youth*

- Substance use is lower among Black adolescents than among Whites or any other ethnic group except Asian Americans.
- While Blacks are more likely to be abstainers and to have lower levels of alcohol use than Whites, they experience more drinking-related *problems,* especially binge drinking, health problems, symptoms of physical dependence, and symptoms of loss of control.
- Compared with Whites, adult Blacks are more likely to be victims of alcohol-related homicide, to be arrested for drunkenness, and to be sent to prison rather than to treatment for alcohol-related crimes.
- At even moderate levels of use, the adverse consequences of substance use are exacerbated by the conditions of poverty, unemployment, discrimination, poor health, and despair that many Black youth face.
- Drug trafficking adversely affects the ability of the entire Black community to function and deal with its other problems.
- Black communities are particularly exploited by the alcohol industry through excessive advertising and number of sales outlets in these neighborhoods.

(Continued)

Table 6.4 *(Continued)*

* Prevention efforts must (1) involve the community in community development efforts that include an active role for youth; (2) facilitate the development of racial consciousness and pride; (3) include public awareness campaigns that counter the alcohol/tobacco industry's advertising; (4) be broad-based, i.e., providing access to a range of social and economic services and opportunities; (5) restructure schools to provide opportunities for academic success.

From *Moving toward a "just and vital culture": Multiculturalism in our schools* by B. Bernard, April, 1991. Reprinted by permission of Northwest Regional Educational Laboratory.

Comparing Latinos/as and Asian Americans

Differences in patterns of use and social attitudes and behaviors associated with drinking and drugs vary dramatically across cultures. To appreciate the enormity of these differences, it is useful to juxtapose the characteristics of two groups—Latinos/as and Asian Americans—by way of comparison. It should be remembered, however, that with acculturation these patterns move toward approximating dominant cultural norms or result in a kind of hybrid behavior. For instance, the use of illicit drugs increases dramatically with acculturation among Latino/a youth. Drug use in comparison to alcohol is much less prominent among more traditionally identified youth. Or by way of example of the interaction, Mexican men tend to drink less often, but more per occasion than U.S. men. After arrival, however, they tend to retain their heavier consumption patterns and also begin to drink more frequently.

Gender differences in substance use among traditional Latino/a youth are far more pronounced than among Whites. Traditional women have very low consumption rates. With acculturation, these rates increase dramatically, reducing the disparity between the genders. Young men's drinking patterns, on the other hand, do not change noticeably with acculturation because drinking is an acknowledged part of male role behavior within Latino culture; it is an aspect of male bonding. For women, American culture gives much more permission regarding drinking behavior than does Latina culture. In comparison to other communities of Color, Latino/a youth are particularly susceptible to peer influence in drug and alcohol use. This is probably related to the high value placed on interpersonal relationships within the culture. In addition, consumption varies with the presence of parental and sibling role models of drinking in the home. The use of dangerous drugs by males also seems related to both a need to escape pain as well as presenting a macho image. Thus, cultural values such as "personalismo" (an emphasis on interpersonal connections as opposed to personal accomplishments), "machismo" (male role characteristics), and "carnalismo" (an emphasis on ethnic pride) play a major role in shaping the way substances are used.

Among Asian Americans, on the other hand, use is more culturally controlled. There is, first of all, evidence of innate biological reactions that discourage drinking. A "flushing" or reddening reaction, which is reported to be rather uncomfortable, is found among some Asian American subgroups. Similarly, there seems to be a physiologically based dislike for the taste of alcohol among some individuals. But these seem to discourage drinking only to the extent that traditional cultural prohibitions are still in place. According to Austin, Prendergast, and Lee (1989), "In accordance with Asian cultural values, Asian drinking is social rather than solitary, occurs in prescribed situations, is usually accompanied by food, is used to enhance social interaction, and occurs within a context of modern drinking norms" (p. 8). Women drink little or no alcohol. Aggressive and noisy behavior when intoxicated is looked down upon. Even when drunk, Chinese and Japanese men are seldom loud or disorderly. Asian philosophies emphasize moderation, order, and social harmony and tend to discourage any practices that compromise these values. Thus, for Asian Americans, alcohol consumption is culturally contained. It occurs as an essential part of religious ceremonies and festive occasions, but only in moderation, and excesses are seen as an embarrassment to the individual and the family.

The Cultural Meaning of Recovery

Substance abuse, though its addictive qualities make it a problem in its own right, is most usefully viewed as symptomatic of other underlying psychological and emotional conditions. From such a perspective, it is believed that individuals use substances to either medicate themselves or to escape inner pain. For People of Color, however, substance abuse and recovery possess cultural and communal meanings as well. I will never forget a talk given by a Native American elder, who had for many years worked as a substance abuse counselor and was himself a recovering addict. "My problem was not alcohol," he emphasized. "It was not knowing who I was and where I belonged. The alcohol was just the way I killed the pain."

Earlier in this chapter, unresolved historic grief was discussed, and it was indicated that its source was not only a history of cumulative traumas, but also the destruction of cultural methods of grieving. According to Duran and Duran (1995), before colonization, alcohol use (as well as the use of substances such as peyote) was strictly controlled by tribal tradition and its use was primarily ceremonial. As Native American culture was systematically destroyed, these controls were eliminated, and with the widespread introduction of excessive drinking as a means of pacifying Native American males, heavy alcohol consumption itself became a tradition on the reservation. Standard treatment methods, based on dominant cultural views of substance abuse, are totally ineffective with Native Americans because they do nothing to change the social and cultural roots of the problem. Only by retrieving what was culturally lost and simultaneously instilling a positive sense of ethnic identity is there any real hope for overcoming substance abuse among Native Peoples. As Duran and Duran pointed out earlier, to subject Native American clients to Western modes of treatment, substance abuse included, that have inherent in them the very processes that undermined Native American culture in the first place is merely to dig the hole deeper.

Duran and Duran argue for the adoption of indigenous views of alcohol abuse, coupled with traditional methods of healing. Traditionally, alcohol was viewed as a destructive spiritual entity that had to be addressed in the spiritual realm if healing was to occur. Healing, in turn, had to occur not only within the individual, but also within the context of the community. More and more, even within the confines of some Western agencies, sweat lodge ceremonies and other spiritual rituals are being introduced as part of treatment. At a more universal level, the idea is that true recovery for People of Color must involve an acknowledgment of the impact of racism as well as substantial clinical efforts to heal its destructive inner effects. In a group therapy session for older African American addicts, I once observed a clear consensus that getting "clean" was not enough. One could never get beyond the "inner prison of drinking or drugging," however, until the "spiritual ghosts" of racism had been laid to rest.

Chapter Seven

Bias in
Service Delivery

The following case study of a Navajo male who was diagnosed psychotic, first described by Jewell (1965), is a classic example of cross-cultural misunderstanding and bias in the delivery of mental health services.

Bill was a 26-year-old Navajo man who had been hospitalized as psychotic in a California State mental hospital for 18 months. Little was known about him on admission. He had been jailed for bothering a woman dressed in white (he had mistaken her for a nurse) on a street corner in Barstow. He was taken for Mexican and placed in the jail's psychopathic ward when he did not respond to the questions of a Spanish-speaking interpreter. He appeared "anguished," kept repeating the phrase "Me sick," was diagnosed as schizophrenic, catatonic type, by the medical examiner, and was eventually sent to the state hospital. There, he was taken to be Filipino, but also did not respond to questions in that language. He appeared "confused, dull, and preoccupied," kept repeating the phrase "I don't know," seemed anguished, and was believed to be hallucinating. He was again diagnosed as schizophrenic, this time hebephrenic type, which was altered back to catatonic 2 months later, when a psychiatrist tested him and found *cerea flexibilitas* (muscular rigidity and lack of movement characteristic of catatonia). He was very quiet, appeared withdrawn and sleepy (there is no mention of the medication that was probably administered), and would arouse himself only for eating and personal care. He would periodically approach staff in broken English and, pointing at his chest repeat: "Me, no good in here." He would also at regular intervals ask: "Can I go home?"

Eight months after admission, Jewell, a psychology intern at the hospital who had been testing Bill, managed to discover his true ethnicity and was able to find a professional Navajo interpreter. Bill talked freely with the interpreter and expressed appreciation for being able to converse in his Native tongue. His answers to questions indicated that he was experiencing no hallucinations, delusions, or other manifestations of schizophrenic thinking, and according to the interpreter who had extensive experience interviewing young Navajos in strange environments, "Bill's behavior and attitudes were not unusual under the circumstances." He was subsequently released to a Native American boarding school, where he adjusted well, later returning to the reservation.

The life journey that ultimately brought Bill to the hospital was not atypical for a young Navajo. He was born in a remote, very traditional, and poverty-stricken area of the Arizona reservation. He was born during an eclipse which spiritually destined him to take part, at different points in his life, in a ceremony that he described as the "Breath of Life" sing. He had participated in it as an infant and at age 6 and was supposed to engage in it once again during the time of his hospitalization. At age 6, he went to live with and assist his grandfather as a sheepherder. He worked for him until the old man's death, when Bill was 17. He reported that his grandfather never talked to him. Bill then got a job with the railroad, which was interrupted by an 8-month hospital stay for tuberculosis. He returned to his previous employment, which took him to several different states. He was always part of a Navajo crew and, thus, never exposed to acculturative influences. After saving a good bit of money and a brief return home to his family, Bill traveled on his own to California in search of additional work. A White man offered to find him a job and, in the process, swindled him out of his savings. Bill returned home, sold some jewelry, borrowed money, and returned to California in search of the man who had tricked him out of his money. He ended up in jail for vagrancy. He traveled with some Navajos who he met in jail in search of employment, picked up a few odd jobs, but his money quickly ran out, and eventually he decided to return home. He thought that if he could get to a hospital, they would send him back to the reservation. That was why he had approached the woman whom he had mistaken for a nurse.

What is most striking about Bill's misdiagnosis is the fact that it was made on the basis of external observation alone. The doctors had never talked with him and, until Jewell took an interest in Bill, did not even know his ethnic origin. He had, in fact, been twice misidentified: first as Mexican and then as Filipino. The doctors first assumed the existence of serious pathology (if he is here in a mental hospital, he must be crazy) and then proceeded to find evidence in Bill's observable behavior. Evidently, they had never felt the need to actually talk with him to make a diagnosis. Equally disturbing was their total disregard of culture and the possibility that cultural differences might have played a role in understanding Bill's behavior. I am reminded of research by Rosenhan (1975), who had himself and colleagues, all mentally fit, checked into a private mental hospital where they merely observed what happened to them and others and took careful notes. Their copious note taking received extensive comment in their respective clinical files: "Patient exhibits excessive writing behavior."

From the perspective of Navajo culture, Bill's behavior made perfect sense and was anything but indicative of the deep mental and emotional pathology that the label schizophrenia, catatonic type, implies. Consider the various symptoms which Bill's diagnosis rested. His "apathetic and withdrawn behavior" was characteristic of how Navajos respond to situations of stress and crisis. Inactivity is their chosen mode of psychological defense. He must have been traumatized by his experiences with the mental health system, not to mention culture shock, and he was also being forced to reside in a hospital, which is a symbol of death in Navajo culture. His unwillingness to talk and his repeated statement: "Me no good in this place" (pointing to his chest) relate to his need to perform the "Breath of Life" ceremony and the belief that he must conserve vocal energy until the ritual is completed. This statement may also have referred to his earlier bout with tuberculosis. The *cerea flexibilitas* was demystified when Jewell learned from the interpreter that Bill held these grotesque positions because he thought that it was expected of him. The most significant symptom of schizophrenia—lack of contact with reality and massive ego disintegration—was never really assessed because that requires talking with the patient.

Bill's experience with the mental health system, though perhaps extreme in its absurdity, is not atypical. In a variety of ways, mental health professionals have repeatedly introduced bias and cultural insensitivity into their work with culturally different clients. Ethnic patients, in turn, have responded by avoiding such services whenever possible and resisting them when they were not voluntary. The result has been the systematic underutilization of services by clients of Color. This chapter delves deeper into the sources of bias in cross-cultural helping. It begins by looking at ways in which attitudes of the provider can shape treatment values and decisions. Next, we inquire as to who the providers are and what skills and preparation they bring to working cross-culturally. Finally, the focus of attention shifts to the helping process itself, and questions are raised as to the relevance of various clinical concepts and practices for interacting with culturally diverse populations. Do concepts such as "helping" or "mental health," especially as they have been traditionally conceived, make sense in all cultures? Has racism or stereotyping played any role in how helping professionals have conceptualized work with clients of Color? Have standard methods of assessment and diagnosis been culture-free, or has their use tended to differentially affect clients of Color? Are the various forms of mental disorder, as defined by DSM IV, found in all cultures, and are their symptom patterns and etiology (i.e., how they develop) the same cross-culturally? For example, do all cultural groups experience emotional states similar to what Western psychology calls "clinical depression," and if so, do they manifest symptoms in the same way? These are the kinds of questions we explore in this chapter.

The Impact of Social, Political, and Racial Attitudes

There is a vast body of research in social psychology that shows how attitudes can unconsciously affect behavior. Rosenthal and Jacobson (1968), for example, looked at the relationship between teacher expectations and student performance. Teachers were told at the beginning of the school year that half of the students in their class were high performers and the other half were low. In actuality, there were no differences between the students. By the end of the year, however, there were significant differences in how the two groups performed. Those who were expected to do well did so, and vice versa. In another experiment, Rosenthal (1976) assigned beginning psychology students rats to train. Some were told that their rats came from very bright strains; others were told that their rats were genetically low in intelligence. The rats were, in actuality, all from the same litter. By the end of the training period, each group of rats was performing as expected. In these two experiments, what the teachers and the psychology students believed and expected was translated into differential behavior, which in turn became what Rosenthal called a "self-fulfilling prophesy." In other words, what we believe (i.e., the attitudes we hold toward someone) shape our treatment of them. Freud called this phenomenon countertransference when it occurred in the clinical setting.

Similar dynamics have been demonstrated in relation to helping professionals. In another classic study, Broverman, Broverman, Clarkson, Rosenkrantz, and Vogel (1970) looked at gender stereotyping and definitions of mental health. They asked a group of psychiatrists, psychologists, and social workers to describe characteristics they would attribute to healthy adult men, healthy adult women, and healthy adults with sex not specified. There was high agreement among subjects, and there were no differences between male and female clinicians. As a group, the clinicians enunciated very different standards of health for women and men; that is, a healthy woman was described in very different terms than was a healthy man. The concept of a healthy adult man and that of a healthy adult with sex not specified did not differ significantly; that of a healthy adult woman did. Compared to men, healthy adult women were seen as more submissive, less independent, less adventuresome, more easily influenced, less aggressive, less competitive, more excitable in minor crises, more easily hurt, more emotional, less objective, and more concerned with appearance. It is probably fair to say that such beliefs about gender differences cannot help but translate into the ways these clinicians work with their male and female clients.

In yet another study, researchers looked at the effect of political attitudes on the diagnosis of mental disorders (Wechsler, Solomon, & Kramer, 1970). Clinicians in the study were asked to rate clients, interviewed on videotape, on the severity of their symptoms. All were shown the same videotapes in which the clients described their symptoms. The only difference was what the clinicians were told about the political activities of the clients. Clients described as being more extreme politically were regularly rated as having more severe symptoms (i.e., as being "sicker" than those who were presented as more conservative). Similarly, when clinicians were told that some subjects advocated violent means of bringing about political change, they too were rated as having more severe symptoms, as were those who were described as having very critical attitudes toward the field of mental health. Again, it is a short step to suggesting that the political attitudes of providers can color their perception and treatment of politically different clients.

Although there is less empirical data on the effect of racial attitudes on provider behavior (probably because of the desire to appear "politically correct" and, therefore, the difficulty in accurately measuring and identifying racist attitudes), some exemplary studies do exist. Jones and Seagull (1983), for example, asked African American and White clinicians to evaluate the level of adjustment of African American therapy clients. He found that White clinicians tended to rate African American clients as more disturbed than did the African American therapists, especially in relation to how seriously they viewed external symptoms and their assessment of the quality of family relations. Other studies show that counselors and trainees tend to think in terms of stereotypes when working with culturally different clients (Atkinson, Casas, & Wampold, 1981; Wampold, Casas, & Atkinson, 1982). In addition, there is much research that shows dramatic differences in the kinds of services that White and non-White clients receive. For example, African Americans are more likely to receive custodial care and medications and are less often offered psychotherapy than Whites (Hollingshead & Redlich, 1958). When they are offered psychotherapy, it tends to be short-term or crisis intervention as opposed to long-term therapy (Turner, 1985). Similarly, African Americans are overrepresented in public psychiatric hospitals (Kramer, Rosen, & Willis, 1972), and African Americans, Latinos/as, and Asian Americans are all more likely to receive supportive versus intensive psychological treatment and to be discharged more rapidly than Whites (Yamamoto, James, & Palley, 1968). In short, there is no reason to believe that racial attitudes are any less likely to affect the perception and treatment of clients than social or political ones.

Who Are the Providers?
Underrepresentation in the Professions

It is well documented that clients prefer helpers from their own ethnic group (Atkinson, 1983). The sense of familiarity and safety that this affords cannot be underestimated. Present statistics do not bode well, however, for potential clients of Color, for the reality is that People of Color are sadly underrepresented among the ranks of helping professionals. This serious lack of non-White providers is often cited as one of the reasons for underutilization of mental health services by People of Color.

A study of membership in the American Psychological Association (APA) in 1979, for example, showed that only 3% of the members were non-White (Russo, Olmedo, Stopp, & Fulcher, 1981). Of over 4000 practitioners who claimed their specialty to be in counseling psychology, under 100 were of Color. A more recent study showed little change, with APA members of Color representing only 4% of the total membership (Bernal & Castro, 1995).

Nor has the situation improved noticeably when one looks to enrollment figures for graduate training programs. As Atkinson, Brown, Casas, and Zane (1996) point out, "the key to achieving ethnic parity among practicing psychologists rests on the profession's ability to achieve equity in training programs" (p. 231). Statistics collected by Kohout and Wicherski (1993) show that African Americans make up only 5%, Latinos/as 5%, Asian Americans 4%, and Native Americans 1% of students enrolled in doctoral psychology programs. These figures represent a decrease for African American students and only a slight increase for the other three groups over the last 25 years (Kohout & Pion, 1990). Although percentages vary slightly depending on the availability of financial aid, programs report an average of about 8% of their new students as non-White. Over the course of training, however, disproportionate dropout rates for students of Color bring their number at graduation close to the 3% or 4% reported for APA membership.

While there is much lip service paid to the need for recruiting more students and faculty of Color, the numbers say it all and remain consistently low over time. In addition to cost, a major deterrent keeping non-White students out of the university (or contributing to their dropout rate) is the Northern European cultural climate that predominates. It is not only difficult for students of Color, especially those who are not highly acculturated, to navigate the complex application and entry procedures that training programs typically require but also difficult to feel comfortable, safe, and welcome in a monocultural environment that is not their own.

An equally critical factor is the number of faculty of Color within these programs. These statistics also continue to be quite low. Atkinson et al. (1996) note that within doctoral training programs in clinical, counseling, and school psychology, African Americans make up 5% of the faculty, Latinos/as 2%, and Asian Americans and Native Americans 1% each. These authors succinctly summarize the current situation as follows: "Although ethnic minorities make up approximately 25% of the current U.S. population with dramatic increases ahead, they constitute less than 15% of the student enrollment and less than 9% of the full-time faculty in applied psychology programs" (p. 231).

Dissatisfaction Among Providers of Color

These numbers will not change until significant diversity is introduced in the helping professions as well as into their training facilities. At present, both remain overwhelmingly White. D'Andrea (1992) documents this fact by pointing to "some of the ways in which individual and institutional racism imbues the profession." He offers the following seven examples:

- Less than 1% of the chairpersons of graduate counseling training programs in the United States come from non-White groups (89% of all chairpersons in counseling training programs are White males).
- No Hispanic American, Asian American, or Native American person has ever been elected president of either the ACA (American Counseling Association) or APA (American Psychological Association).
- Only one African American person has been elected as president of APA.
- None of the five most commonly used textbooks in counselor training programs in the United States lists "racism" as an area of attention in its table of contents or index.
- A computerized literature review of journal articles found in social science periodicals over a 12-year period (1980-1992) indicated that only 6 of 308 articles published during this time period that examined the impact of racism on one's mental health and psychological development were published in the three leading professional counseling journals (*The Counseling Psychologist, Journal of Counseling and Development,* and *Journal of Counseling Psychology*).
- All of the editors of the journals sponsored by ACA and APA (excluding one African American editor with the *Journal of Multicultural Counseling and Development*) are White.
- Despite more than 15 years of efforts invested in designing a comprehensive set of multicultural counseling competencies and standards, the organizational governing bodies of both ACA and APA have consistently refused to adopt them formally as guidelines for professional training and development" (p. 23).

It is not difficult to read between the lines of D'Andrea's examples and sense the enormous frustration of providers of Color with the seeming slowness with which the professional counseling establishment has moved toward actively embracing and implementing its verbalized commitment to multiculturalism. D'Andrea and Daniels (1995) summarize these feelings as follows:

Although persons from different racial/cultural/ethnic backgrounds must continue to lead the way in promoting the spirit and principles of multiculturalism in the profession, it is imperative that White counseling professionals take a more active stand in advocating for the removal of barriers that impede progress in this area. Together we can transform the profession, or together we will suffer the consequences of becoming an increasingly irrelevant entity in the national mental health care delivery system. (p. 32)

Similar sentiments are offered by Parham (1992):

To make the types of changes that are necessary in order that the counseling profession will be able to meet the needs of an increasing number of clients from diverse cultural and racial backgrounds, the profession in general and its two national associations—the American Psychological Association and the American Counseling Association—in particular, will have to learn to share more of its power and resources with persons who have traditionally been excluded from policy-making and training opportunities. (pp. 22–23)

The Use of Paraprofessionals

One strategy that held great promise for dramatically increasing the number of providers of Color was the use of indigenous paraprofessionals. Stimulated by a visionary book by Art Pearl and Frank Reissman (1965) entitled *New Careers for the Poor,* the National Institute of Mental Health committed extensive resources to educating mental health facilities in the use of ethnic paraprofessionals. The idea was a rather simple one. Individuals who were natural leaders within ethnic communities were given training in the rudiments of service delivery (basic assessment, interviewing skills, knowledge of psychopathology) and then hired to act both as liaisons and outreach workers to the community and as adjunct providers working under the direction of professional staff. Often, special satellite centers were established in ethnic communities and staffed by local paraprofessionals. The concept worked exceptionally well for over 10 years. Community members were more willing to bring their problems to paraprofessionals, who were already known, respected, and able to understand their culture and lifestyle. Paraprofessional involvement in mainstream agencies, in turn, gave them a certain credibility that was not afforded when the staff was all White. The strategy also served to inject a large number of entry-level ethnic paraprofessionals into the system. Many, in fact, chose to return to school and became professionals.

Ironically, this strategy was ultimately undermined by the development of a number of academic paraprofessional training programs. Viewing the paraprofessional role not so much as a means of creating more indigenous providers, but rather as a new entry point into mental health jobs, these programs attracted primarily White middle- to upper-middle-class students. Agencies, in turn, received increasing pressure to hire these "professional nonprofessionals." The ultimate result was that indigenous providers were slowly, but systematically, replaced by trained paraprofessionals, and a very functional approach to infusing ethnic community members into the mental health delivery system was undermined.

The Use of Traditional Healers

Another potentially useful strategy for overcoming the lack of ethnic helping professionals is the involvement of traditional healers as part of a mental health organization's treatment team, either on staff or in a consultative role. This is not only a mark of cultural respect, but also an invitation to less acculturated community members, who would not normally avail themselves of mainstream services, to view mental health services (thus more broadly defined) as a resource for them as well. Barriers to including traditional healers usually come from Western professionals who see the use of shamanic healers as unscientific, superstitious, and regressive. Their hesitancies come from conflicting worldviews, although Torrey (1986), for one, has argued that Western mental health approaches work structurally in much the same way as do indigenous healing systems. Both, for example, are afforded high status and power and also depend on clients' sharing the same worldview. Torrey suggests that both be incorporated under the broad multicultural rubric of healer.

Lee and Armstrong (1995), however, enumerate a number of content differences. Traditional healing views human capacities holistically, whereas Western providers typically distinguish between physical, spiritual, and mental well-being. Western healing stresses cause and effect; traditional approaches emphasize circularity and multidimensional sources in etiology. In Western psychology, helping occurs through cognitive and emotional change. In traditional healing, there is a spiritual basis to health and well-being. In Western psychology, helpers tend to be passive in their interventions; indigenous healers are more active and take a major role and responsibility in the healing process itself. In spite of such differences, the only reason for not pursuing cooperation and consultation is ethnocentrism. Such narrow thinking typically goes hand in hand with cultural insensitivity in Western providers because the very spirituality and religiosity of which they are generally critical play a central role in the worldview of most culturally different clients.

One last point needs to be made regarding increasing the number of ethnic helpers. Just because providers have certain racial or cultural roots does not guarantee their cultural competence or ability to work effectively with clients from their group of origin. Making an extra effort to hire providers of Color sends an important social and political message. But to do so without careful consideration of a candidate's experience, skills, training, and cultural competence is merely racism in reverse. No agency would think of randomly selecting White candidates irrespective of their credentials and assume that they will be competent to work successfully with a broad spectrum of White clients. Agencies do, however, on a much more frequent basis, assume that hiring someone of Color will automatically resolve problems of racism and cross-cultural service delivery.

As has been continually stressed throughout this book, ethnic groups are comprised of enormous diversity, and it is dangerous to make assumptions about the characteristics a given individual possesses merely on the basis of group membership. For example, an agency has within its service jurisdiction a small but growing Latino/a population and wishes to hire someone of Latino/a descent to help provide services. Some of the following questions may prove useful in making informed and culturally sensitive choices. Are they bilingual, fluent in both English and Spanish, written and verbal? Are they bicultural, that is, familiar with the traditional as well as the dominant culture? With what specific ethnic subgroups within the broad category of Latino/a culture are they familiar and knowledgeable? What is their knowledge of class, gender, and regional differences in the Latino/a community? Where were they born and how acculturated was their family of origin? Do they have firsthand experience with the migration process? What is the nature of their own ethnic identity? With what other ethnic populations have they worked? And how culturally competent are they?

Cultural Aspects of Mental Health Service Delivery

The chapter has so far looked into sources of bias related to the provider. There are, in addition, aspects of the helping process per se that limit its relevance to clients of Color. In general, these relate to the fact that current mental health theory and practice are defined in terms of dominant Northern European cultural values and norms and, therefore, limit the ability of providers to adequately address and serve the needs of non-White populations. Chapter 4 included a description of four characteristics of the helping process (as it is currently constituted) that directly conflict with the worldview of communities of Color. Here, we explore additional sources of this cultural mismatch as well as describe ways in which the current helping model portrays clients of Color in a negative light, highlights their "weaknesses," and assumes pathology even when it does not necessarily exist. The case study of Bill, a supposedly psychotic Navajo with which this chapter opened, is an extreme example. His behavior, when viewed through the lens of Navajo culture, looked quite normal, but from the perspective of Western psychology, it reflected deep disturbance and psychopathology.

Bias in Conceptualizing Ethnic Populations

There is a long history in Western science of portraying ethnic populations as biologically inferior. Beginning with the work of luminaries such as Charles Darwin, Sir Francis Galton, and G. Stanley Hall, one can trace what Sue and Sue (1990) call the "genetic deficiency model" of racial minorities into the present, carried on by research psychologists such as Jensen (1972). Similarly, Jews have been vilified under the guise of psychological analysis. Jung (1934), for example, wrote a comparison of Jewish and Aryan psychologies: "Jews have this peculiarity in common with women, being physically weaker, they have to aim at the chinks in the armor of their adversary, and thanks to this technique . . . the Jews themselves are best protected where others are most vulnerable" (pp. 165–166). Jung, who also wrote disparagingly of the African American psyche, found his ideas on national and racial character warmly received by the Nazi regime. McDougall (1977), an early American psychologist, offers similar sentiments against Jews in his analysis of Freud's work: "It looks as though this theory which to me and to most men of my sort seems to be strange, bizarre and fantastic, may be approximately true of the Jewish race" (p. 127).

As biological theories of genetic inferiority lost intellectual credibility, they were quickly replaced within social science circles by notions of cultural inferiority or "deficit." While political correctness would not allow practitioners with negative racial attitudes to continue to embrace the idea of genetic inferiority, they could easily attach themselves to theories which assumed "that a community subject to poverty and oppression is a disorganized community, and this disorganization expresses itself in various forms of psychological deficit ranging from intellectual performance . . . to personality functioning . . . and psychopathology" (E. E. Jones & Korchin, 1982, p. 19). These new models took two forms: cultural deprivation and cultural disadvantage. In relation to the former, non-Whites were seen as deprived (i.e., lacking any substantive culture). Disadvantaged, on the other hand, a supposed improvement over the term "deprived," implies that, although ethnic group members do possess culture, it was a culture that has grown deficient and distorted by the ravages of racism. More recent and acceptable are the terms "culturally different" and "culturally distinct." But as Atkinson, Morten, and Sue (1993) point out, even these can "carry negative connotations when they are used to imply that a person's culture is at variance (out-of-step) with the dominant (accepted) culture" (p. 9).

Psychological research on ethnic populations has also tended to be skewed in the direction of finding and focusing on deficits and shortcomings. This body of research, which E. E. Jones and Korchin (1982) refer to as part of a "psychology of race differences tradition," has been widely criticized for faulty methodology. "Studies typically involved the comparison of ethnic and white groups on measures standardized on white, middle-class samples, administered by examiners of like background, intended to assess variables conceptualized on the basic U.S. population" (p. 19). But even more insidious have been two additional tendencies. First, researchers have chosen to study and compare Whites and People of Color on characteristics that culturally favor dominant group members. Thus, intelligence is assessed by measuring verbal reasoning. Or schoolchildren are compared on their ability to compete or take personal initiative. In other words, research variables portray White subjects in a more favorable light and simultaneously create a negative impression of the abilities and resources of ethnic subjects. Second, where differences have been found between Whites and People of Color, they tend to be interpreted as reflecting weaknesses or pathology in ethnic culture or character. Looking at such studies, various researchers have asked why alternative interpretations stressing the creative adaptiveness or strengths inherent in ethnic personality or culture might not just as easily have been sought. Hampden-Turner (1974), for example, writes the following about the "Moynihan Report," which attributes various African American social problems to deterioration of the Black family and has been soundly criticized both for blaming the victim and pathologizing to the exclusion of other possible explanations: "Moynihan's accusation of 'pathology' . . . is an excellent illustration of the mental health paradigm in political use . . . If we regard the social oppression of blacks by whites as a total dynamic, why is the black end of this dynamic more pathological than the white end . . . And how does one distinguish a 'pathology' from an 'heroic adaptation to overwhelming pressures'" (p. 83). Inherent in Hampden-

Turner's critique is a most important point: These negative portrayals and stereotypes of People of Color serve as justification for the status quo of oppression and unfair treatment and, thus, serve political as well as psychological purposes.

An interesting and provocative example of the psychological mystification of ethnic culture and cultural traits is offered by Tong (1981). Tong argues that the psychological representation of Chinese Americans as the model minority—that is, "passive, ingratiating, reticent, non-complaining and self-denying" (p. 3)—is more a survival reaction to American racism than a true reflection of traditional Chinese character. He goes on to suggest that there is within traditional culture a "heroic tradition" that portrays the Chinese in a manner very different than the uncomplaining model minority: "Coexistent with the Conventional Tradition was the 'heroic,' which exalted a time-honored Cantonese sense of self: the fierce, arrogant, independent individual beholden to no one and loyal only to those deemed worthy of undying respect, on that individual's terms" (Tong, 1981, p. 15). Tong calls to task fellow Chinese American psychologists for perpetuating this myth through their research and writings and thus for confusing psychopathology with culture:

> Timid and docile behavior *is* indicative of emotional disorder. If Chinese Americans seem to be that way by virtue of cultural "background," it is the case *only* to the extent that white racism, in combination with our heritage of Confusion [sic] repression, made it so. The early Chinamans [sic] *consistently* shaped themselves and justified their acts according to the fundamental vision of the Heroic Tradition. Their stupendous feats of daring and courage, however, remain buried beneath a gargantuan mound of white movies, popular fiction, newspaper cartoons, dissertations, political tracts, religious meeting minutes, and now psychological studies that teach us to look upon ourselves as perpetual aliens living only for white acceptance." (p. 20)

Tong calls this mystification of the Chinese American psyche "iatrogenic." *Iatrogenesis* is a medical term that means sickness or pathology that results from medical or psychological intervention and treatment.

A final difficulty with contemporary psychology's model of helping is its theoretical narrowness and inability to acknowledge different cultural ways of looking at and conceptualizing mental health as valid. I once worked as part of a team whose task was to create a mental health service delivery system for recent Southeast Asian refugees. This is an at-risk population that has suffered serious emotional trauma as a result of war, migration, and rapid acculturation in the United States. The first problem we encountered was that there was no concept within their culture for mental health per se, nor was there a distinction between physical and mental health. Problems were not dichotomized, and as we were to learn later, what we considered mental health problems were generally presented in the form of physical symptoms. In time, however, it was possible to discern certain patterns of physical complaints that seemed to indicate emotional difficulties, (e.g., depression and PTSD). But the symptom patterns for these disorders within Southeast Asian populations looked very different than those presented in the DSM IV, which is normed primarily on Northern European clients. In addition, the Western concept of helping (i.e., seeking advice, help, or support from a professional stranger) made no sense to our Southeast Asian clients. In most Asian cultures, one does not go outside of the family, let alone to strangers, for help. The acknowledgment of emotional difficulties brings shame on the family. What is expected of individuals is quiet acceptance of their condition. From a Western perspective, this is denial or avoidance.

As a general strategy for intervention, we decided to train paraprofessionals from the community to serve as outreach and referral workers. Not only did our paraprofessionals (who were young adults and among the most acculturated individuals in the community) have great difficulty grasping, understanding, and using the mental health concepts and simple diagnostic procedures we tried to teach them, but there was also a problem in their being accepted by older community members as legitimate resources for health providers. This was largely because of age. As long as we approached the community from a Northern European perspective, we were destined to fail. We had pushed the model of training with which we were familiar as far as it could be stretched and were still unable to accommodate major aspects of Southeast Asian culture. What does one do when the very concept of mental health makes little sense within a culture? Or when the very notion of helping as conceived in Western terms is irrelevant because it is considered shameful to share one's problems with complete strangers? I came away from that experience realizing that if we were to continue, we would have to start from scratch and create a new helping model that was not merely an adaptation of mainstream helping practices, but rather, specifically tailored to the cultural needs of Southeast Asians.

Bias in Assessment

In no other area of clinical work has there been more concern raised about the possibility of cultural bias than around psychological assessment and testing. This is because People of Color have for many years watched their children being placed in remedial classrooms or tracked as retarded on the basis of IQ testing, and loved ones diagnosed as suffering from serious mental disorders because of their performance on various personality tests. Serious life decisions are regularly made on the basis of these tests, and it is reasonable to expect that they be "culture-free"; that is, scoring based on what is being measured and not differentially affected by the cultural background of the test taker. In reality, there probably is no such thing as a culture-free test, and it has been suggested, and supported by some research, that ethnic group members tend to be overpathologized by personality measures and have their abilities underestimated by intelligence tests (Snowden & Todman, 1982; Suzuki & Kugler, 1995).

Reynolds and Kaiser (1990) list a number of factors that can contribute to cultural bias in testing. Test items and procedures may reflect dominant cultural values. A test may not have been standardized on populations of Color, only on middle-class Whites. Language differences and unfamiliarity or discomfort with the client's culture can cause a tester to misjudge them or have difficulty establishing rapport. The experience of racism and oppression may lead to groupwide deficits in performance on tests that have nothing to do with native ability. A test may measure different characteristics when administered to members of different cultural groups. Culturally unfair criteria, such as level of education or grade point average, may be used to validate tests expected to predict differences between Whites and People of Color. Differences in experience in taking tests may put non-White clients at a disadvantage in testing situations. In short, it is very difficult to assure fairness in psychological testing across cultures, and practitioners should exert real care in drawing conclusions based exclusively on test scores. They should, as a matter of validation, gain as much nontesting collaborative data as possible, especially when the outcome of the assessment may have real-life consequences for the future of the client. They should also be willing not to test a client if it is believed that the procedure will not give useful and fair data.

Having raised all of these cautions, the fact remains that much culturally questionable testing still takes place. Clinicians tend to be overattached to psychological tests as a means of gaining client information. When they do try to take into account cultural differences, it is done not by creating new instruments, but rather by modifying existing ones: adjusting scores, rewriting items, or translating them into a second language. In general, this merely creates new problems in the place of old ones. The MMPI and TAT, probably the two most widely used personality assessment techniques, provide excellent examples.

The Minnesota Multiphasic Personality Inventory (MMPI) is by far the most widely used instrument to measure psychopathology. Historically, it has been administered without reservation to racial and ethnic minorities. Concerns about cultural bias were first raised because it had been normed (i.e., standardized as far as cutoff scores reflecting normal vs. psychopathological behavior) exclusively on White subjects and second because it was being used extensively to make decisions about hospitalizing patients, a disproportionate percentage of whom were people of Color. Cultural differences and the possibility of bias are most evident in differential scoring patterns. African American test takers (from normal, psychiatric, and inmate populations alike), for example, consistently score higher than Whites on three scales: F (a measure of validity), 8 (a measure of schizophrenia), and 9 (a measure of mania). In addition, 39% of the items are answered differently by African American than by White subjects. Of these, a third are not clinical scale items, which implies that differences are related to culture as opposed to pathology. There is also evidence that MMPI items are neither conceptually or functionally equivalent for African Americans and Whites; this suggests that they neither mean the same thing nor fulfill a similar psychological purpose for the two groups.

As a means of dealing with these problems, Costello (1977) developed a Black–White Scale, which adjusted African American scores so that they might be interpreted similarly to White scores. But Snowden and Todman (1982) are critical of this procedure:

> The Black–White Scale may be useful in the short term for making interpretive adjustments to allow for known differences, however it must be seen as a stop-gap measure. In the long run, it leaves unanswered all the pertinent questions raised by both cross-cultural and environmental psychologists alike . . . The Costello Black–White Scale does not ask these questions; it merely corrects for them. The logical extension of this scale could very well be the following: If one subtracts a factor of x from the score of a black male, his profile is then "as good" as if it were of a white. One can conclude with confidence that the MMPI has never established its validity as a diagnostic or assessment instrument with blacks. (pp. 210-211)

The MMPI-2, a revision of its predecessor, was tested initially on both African American and Native American samples. The resulting research has been so confusing, however, that Dana (1988) and Graham (1987) both conclude that it is best not to use the test with ethnic group members.

The Thematic Apperception Test (TAT) and the Rorschach are the most widely used projective tests for assessing personality and psychopathology. The TAT involves showing clients drawings of people in various situations and asking them to tell a story about the picture. Scoring involves both the kinds of themes that are generated and the style of responding. Questions about its use with non-White populations were raised early because the stimulus figures on the cards were White, and there was the obvious question of whether African American clients, for example, could identity with these figures or would instead inhibit self-disclosure because of them. To test this, Thompson (1949) developed the same cards redrawn with African American figures and used them with African American clients. Though he showed that his cards generated more responses than did the original White cards, all the questions about cultural comparability raised by Reynolds and Kaiser (1990) still remain unanswered. For example, TAT scoring generates impressions about unmet needs within the client. Who is to say that such needs or motivations are equivalent across cultural groups or that the stimulus pictures, irrespective of the race of the figures, have equivalent cultural meanings?

Finally, there is a question about the use of projection with non-White groups. Generally, it has been found that Blacks are less responsive, less willing to self-disclose, and more guarded about their participation in the TAT testing situation than members of other groups. Snowden and Todman (1982) suggest that this guardedness may be culturally determined and the result of a long history of dealing with racist institutions. Yet in spite of all of these questions about the cultural validity of the TAT, it continues to be used cross-culturally. There is, in fact, now a Latino/a version as well as one specifically designed for children with cards showing animal characters instead of people.

Bias in Diagnosis

According to Gaw (1993), culture shapes and affects the very essence of how clinical work is done. This includes how problems are reported and how help is sought, the nature and configuration of symptoms, how problems are traditionally solved, how the origin of presenting problems is understood, and what appropriate interventions involve. Each culture, in short, has it own paradigm of how these processes occur, and there is enormous variation. Difficulties emerge, however, when practitioners superimpose their own cultural worldview onto the life experience of culturally different clients and then make clinical assumptions or judgments from that perspective. This is where things stand today vis-à-vis Western mental health service delivery and the desire to serve other cultural groups. Most practitioners tend to be far too narrow and ethnocentric in their thinking to acknowledge and accept other versions of clinical reality. Rather than trying to redesign the "puzzle" and broadening their perspective, providers keep trying to force the "round piece" into the "square hole," and the "hole" keeps objecting.

Cultural Variations in Psychopathology

Nowhere is the limited thinking of Western psychology more challenged by cultural variation than around the question of what psychopathology is and how it is diagnosed. This is also where misdiagnosis of those who are culturally different most regularly occurs. E. E. Jones and Korchin (1982) summarize the issue as follows:

> Most mental health workers proceed on the assumption of the pancultural (i.e., etic) generality of categories, criteria, and theories of psychopathology originated in Western cultures. Minority clinicians have long objected that standard psychiatric nomenclature does not recognize cultural variation in symptomology. This position is quite consistent with a growing view among cross-cultural psychologists that problems of identifying cases of psychopathology in clients from different cultures, and comparing incidence and forms of psychopathology across cultures, need to be reconsidered. (pp. 26-27)

Cultural Attitudes Toward Mental Health

Cultures differ dramatically in their orientation and attitude toward mental disorders as well as in their understanding of personality dynamics, what is considered therapeutic, and how help is to be sought. Cultural responses to these issues are shaped by certain key themes that contribute a distinctive Gestalt to how each culture relates to the problem of mental illness. By way of example, I would like to summarize R.G. Lum's (1982) early research on mental health attitudes among Chinese Americans, whose clinical worldview differs substantially from that of Western psychology. Within Chinese American culture, mental health and illness are two sides of the same coin. According to Lum (1982), individuals are considered mentally healthy if they possess:

> the capacity for self-discipline and the willpower to resist conducting oneself or thinking in ways that are not socially or culturally sanctioned; a sense of security and self-assurance stemming from support and guidance from signifi- cant others; relative freedom from unpleasant, morbid thoughts, emotional conflicts, and personality disorders; and the absence of organic dysfunctions, such as epilepsy or other neurological disorders. (p. 183)

Similarly, mental illness involves the opposite: a loss of discipline, preoc- cupation with morbid thoughts, insecurity because of the absence of social support, and distress stemming from external factors. Consistent with this, Chinese Americans tend to externalize blame for mental illness, thus setting the stage for avoidance of unwanted thoughts and feelings. Traditional wis- dom sees value in learning to inhibit and control one's emotions. Defensively, according to Hsu (1949), Chinese tend to use suppression as opposed to repres- sion, which is more common among European Americans. Suppression tends to have an obsessional quality because to use it effectively one must rational- ize, justify, or use other intellectual strategies to blunt the anxiety. Using it, in turn, tends to encourage obsessive-compulsive qualities including extreme conscientiousness, meticulousness, acquiescence, rigidity, and a preference for thinking over feeling.

As patients, Chinese Americans prefer helpers who are authoritarian, direc- tive, and fatherly in their approach. In turn, they expect to be taught how to bet- ter occupy their minds to avoid unwanted thoughts and feelings. Insight approaches tend to have limited meaning, and generally, therapy does not seem to affect Chinese Americans characterologically. Finally, help seeking is limited because within the Chinese community there is a stigma and shame around mental illness. Shame often leads to minimizing the seriousness and frequency of a problem. Patients often feel "ashamed and ambivalent about their illness" and are reluctant to tell others about their emotional difficulties. In sum, the threads that run through the Chinese American worldview of mental health and illness are the importance of controlling emotions and thoughts and their avoid- ance when they become too intrusive or distracting, the necessity of social sup- port as a precondition for healthy mental functioning, the submerging of the self as a means of deferring to family and authority, and mental illness as a stigma that requires the individual to tolerate disturbing symptoms rather than bring shame on the family. These themes translate basic cultural values into behav- ioral prescriptions for living which, in turn, reinforce basic cultural values.

Cultural Differences in Symptoms, Disorders, and Pathology

Cultures also differ as to what disorders are most typically observed, how symptom pictures are construed, and even what is considered pathological. Some disorders (e.g., schizophrenia and substance abuse) appear to be universal, although the exact content is culture specific. Hallucinations, for example, tend to contain familiar cultural material such as voices speaking to the person in his or her native language or visions infused with cultural symbols and motifs. Other disorders (e.g., depression) can be observed across cultures, but vary dramatically in relation to specific symptoms. In Western clients, for example, depression is diagnosed on the basis of a combination of psychological and physical symptoms, whereas among Southeast Asian clients physical symptoms such as headaches and fatigue are more prevalent indicators. There are also culture-specific syndromes or disorders that appear only among members of a single cultural group. E. E. Jones and Korchin (1982) point to two. Ataque, found only among Puerto Ricans, is a hysterical seizure reaction in which patients fall to the ground, scream, and flail their limbs. Largely unfamiliar to majority practitioners, it tends to be misdiagnosed as a more serious seizure disorder. A similar disorder called "falling out" disease is found only among rural, Southern African Americans and West Indian refugees and is regularly misdiagnosed as epilepsy or a transient psychotic episode.

The same symptom can have very different meanings depending on the cultural context in which it appears. Mexican Americans, for instance, view hallucinations as far less pathological and more within the realm of everyday (normal) experience than do Whites. Hearing voices is, thus, more culturally sanctioned and often associated with deep religious experiences. Meadow (1982) has shown that hospitalized Mexican American patients report significantly more hallucinations, both visual and auditory, than do Whites. The question all of this raises is exactly where culture ends and psychopathology begins. Meadow (1982) attempts to sort it out as follows:

> Some Mexican-American hallucinatory experiences may simply reflect a cultural belief and occur in persons completely free of psychopathology. In other cases Mexican-American hallucinations may have the same significance as those reported by Anglo-American patients. There exists an intermediate group of Mexican-American patients in which the hallucination may be interpreted as a symbolic expression of a wish fulfillment or as a sign of a warded-off superego criticism. For these patients the hallucination is a symptom of psychopathology, but it does not signify the serious break with reality that would be implied if it occurred in an Anglo-American case. (p. 333)

The Case of Suicide

The same mental health problem can be configured very differently both as far as its sources (etiology) and frequency (incidence) across cultures. A classic example is suicide. According to the Group for the Advancement of Psychiatry's Committee on Cultural Psychiatry (1984), suicide rates differ substantially across ethnic groups in the United States. By far, the highest aggregate suicide rate (i.e., for all ages and genders combined) is found among Native Americans. The next highest is among European Americans followed by Chinese Americans and Japanese Americans. The lowest aggregate rates are found among African Americans and Latinos/as. Practitioners are often surprised by the relatively low rates among People of Color. Why? Because stereotypically, many equate non-Whites with violence. It is also useful to note, as pointed out previously, that as ethnic groups assimilate, their relative position in the hierarchy increasingly comes to approximate that of European Americans. Thus, with acculturation, it is expected that African Americans, Latinos/as, and Asian Americans will increase their aggregate suicide rates.

Looking at peak rates across ethnic groups provides even further insights, especially since it is reasonable to assume that suicide rates reflect periods of optimal stress in a group's life cycle. For European Americans, suicides tend to occur three times as often for men as for women. In addition, peak rates tend to increase with age. For men, the highest rates are in those over 65, and for women, rates are highest in the early fifties. The picture is very different for the communities of Color. First, suicide occurs most frequently among young males in African American, Native American, and Latino cultures. Japanese Americans show a similar trend, but less pronounced. Chinese American young males are a notable exception. These high rates most likely result from the fact that young non-White males are usually "the point men" for acculturative stress. They tend to be the ones who have the closest, most sustained contact and least positive interactions with White institutions, usually through schools and then work. High rates of unemployment and underemployment are certainly a contributing factor. Research has also shown that young men of Color who have consolidated a positive ethnic identity and attachment to tradition are less likely to be at risk for suicide than those who have become marginalized from their culture. The same is true for other self-destructive behaviors such as substance abuse and violence.

A second major finding is the extremely low suicide rates among African American, Native American, and Latina women when compared with ethnic males and majority group members combined. The one exception was Chinese American women, who showed a peak incidence in later life. There seem to be two reasons for these low rates. First, because of traditional sex roles, ethnic women have less exposure to the stressful effects of acculturation. In addition, they tend to experience much lower rates of unemployment and underemployment and can also derive personal satisfaction from alternative roles in the home. The higher suicide rate among older Chinese women is probably due to the interaction of several factors. They tend to be traditionally identified and, as such, separatist in their orientation toward majority culture. As they lose their nurturing role in the family with age and their children acculturate, they tend to grow even more isolated and lack support for their traditional orientation. In addition, many experience poverty without support from their family, and they are unable or unwilling to seek help from majority social agencies. Finally, there are especially low rates of suicide among older African Americans, Native Americans, and Latinos/as in comparison to younger ethnic group members and majority group members combined. It is likely that these individuals have learned to cope with the acculturative stress. They tend to be revered in their communities and supported by strong community institutions that they likely helped found. The fact that older Asian Americans were not included in this statistic may reflect the effects of greater acculturation, which would lead to greater isolation of the elderly as is more common in mainstream culture.

Given such cultural relativity in defining mental health and psychopathology, an interesting question arises as to the appropriate criteria to be used in assessing psychopathology. From what cultural perspective should deviant behavior be judged? And within any particular cultural perspective, what makes a behavior deviant or psychopathological? The problem is made difficult by the fact that ethnic group cultures exist within a broader framework than is usually identified and defined culturally as Northern European. From a clinical standpoint, individuals' behavior must be judged in accordance with the values and criteria of their own group's culture. Thus, "to justify an interpretation of behavior as an instance of psychopathology, it must be established that there is intersubjective agreement among members of the culture that the behavior in question represents an exaggeration or distortion of a culturally acceptable behavior or belief" (E. E. Jones & Korchin, 1982, p. 27). If one applies this maxim to the case of Bill, the institutionalized Navajo with which this chapter began, it is clear that he was acting within the bounds of culturally acceptable Navajo behavior and that his diagnosis as catatonic, his assessment as psychopathological from a Western psychological perspective, and his institutionalization were all inappropriate.

Chapter Eight

Critical Issues in Working With Culturally Different Clients

We have so far focused on a variety of conceptual issues related to working with culturally different clients. Earlier chapters have defined cultural competence, explored the meaning of racism, especially as it impacts clients and providers, and defined culture and worldview as well as the cultural limits of the helping model that has shaped most provider's thinking. In addition, we looked at a number of factors unique to the experience of ethnically diverse clients. These included child development and parenting, differences in family structure, biracial/bicultural families, potential areas of psychological difficulty (conflicts in identity development, assimilation and acculturation, stress, unresolved historic grief, and alcohol and drug problems), and sources of bias in cross-cultural service delivery. We now change direction and focus more fully on the process of actually working with culturally different clients. This involves describing some general guidelines that maximize a provider's initial contact with clients in this chapter and then providing culturally specific information useful in working with clients from the following groups: African Americans, Latinos/as, Asian Americans, Native Americans, and Whites and White ethnics (Chapters 9–13).

Preparing for Cross-Cultural Work

The previous chapters have highlighted the kinds of life experiences that impact culturally different clients as well as areas of professional functioning that the reader may consider modifying or adapting to work more effectively cross-culturally. No amount of preparation, however, can totally allay the anxiety that is typical of providers who first contemplate work with culturally diverse clients. Students regularly ask: "But what do I do when I find myself sitting across the desk from someone who is culturally different? I'm afraid I will panic or draw a blank and not know what to say." My usual answer is: "Just do the same thing you do with any other client—begin your work." The anxiety and hesitancy reflect a basic discomfort with cultural differences and the fact that most providers have grown up in a racist society separated from those who are different from them. They are afraid because of their ignorance of not knowing enough about a client's culture, of making a cultural faux pas, or of missing something very obvious. They are, in addition, anxious and uncomfortable due to feelings of guilt over the existence of racism or embarrassed because of past indifference, the racist behavior of family and friends, or feelings of personal privilege or entitlement. It feels like very dangerous territory, and after reading chapter after chapter about the complexity of issues in working with diversity and how easily cross-cultural communication can breakdown, the prospect of facing someone from a different culture and providing them with useful help must strike the readers as rather daunting.

At such moments of doubt, it is important to remember several things. First, as a provider, one is already, or is in the process of becoming, a skilled professional. Becoming culturally competent does not mean starting from scratch or learning everything anew. Rather, it means further honing skills one already has, broadening clinical concepts that are too narrow in their application in the first place, and gaining new cultural knowledge about clients with whom one will be working. Culturally competent providers are, in general, more competent professionals because they must remain more conscious about what they are doing to be vigilant as to the cultural appropriateness of tasks, methods, and perspectives that others may routinely overlook. In a certain sense, one might say that every client carries his or her own unique culture, and it is the professional helper's task to discover how to respectfully gain entry into that culture and offer services that are sensitive to its rules and inner dynamics.

Second, the clients with whom one will be working are, above all, human beings, and this is the ultimate basis for connection. They, too, are anxious about coming to see someone new, especially if that person is culturally different. More than likely, they have had experiences that make them mistrust the kind of system in which the provider works. The initial task, then, is to set clients at ease in a manner that has meaning for them. Helping is, above all, a human process. It is bound to fail, however (with all clients, not just culturally different ones), when that awareness is lost. Unfortunately, in the process of teaching people about cultural differences, there is a tendency (that must always be guarded against) to objectify and stereotype clients by seeing them only in terms of their differences. By attending to these too fully, one can easily lose sight of the person sitting across from the provider. Focusing too heavily on differences, and thereby overlooking basic human similarities, can turn cross-cultural work into a mechanical process. For example, with Asian Americans, you must do this, be aware of this, assume this, and so forth. Nothing could be further from the truth. Cross-cultural interaction must be based on the shared humanity that exists between client and provider. That is the one place where both are similar and can most easily join. Kroeber (1948), an early anthropologist, pointed out that there were three kinds of human characteristics: those that one shares with all other human beings, those that one shares with some other human beings, and those that are unique to each individual. It is in relation to the first that cross-cultural communication and helping are made possible. A sensitivity to the second and third allows for the defining of human differences and uniqueness once a basic connection has formed. Again, it is through the very human capacities of caring, having sympathy and empathy for others, and identifying with the basic joys and predicaments of being human that differences can best be bridged.

How Is Cross-Cultural Helping Different?

There is general agreement among practitioners that cross-cultural helping is more demanding, challenging, and energy-draining than work with same-culture clients. According to Draguns (1989), for example, it tends to be more "experiential, freewheeling, and bilateral" (p. 17). By "experiential," he means that it is more likely to directly and emotionally impact the provider. Draguns likens it to culture shock, where providers are immersed in a foreign culture in which familiar patterns of behavior are no longer useful and new means of acting and relating must be discovered. It has also been described as more labor intensive and more likely to result in fatigue.

"Freewheeling" refers to the fact that the helping process must be continually adapted to the specific cultural needs of differing clients. As suggested earlier, the only constant is the shared humanity. Standard approaches are overwhelmingly culture-bound and Northern European in nature, and even efforts to catalog cultural similarities among racially related ethnic groups must be tentative and ever mindful of enormous intragroup diversity. To this end, Draguns suggests:

> Be prepared to adapt your techniques (e.g., general activity level, mode of verbal intervention, content of remarks, tone of voice) to the cultural background of the client; communicate acceptance of and respect for the client in terms that make sense within his or her cultural frame of reference; and be open to the possibility of more direct intervention in the life of the client than the traditional ethos of the counseling profession would dictate or permit. (p. 16)

Finally, "bilateral" implies collaboration. By the very nature of cross-cultural work, the provider is more dependent on the client for help in defining the process itself. Though it is common practice, for example, for providers to collaborate with clients in setting treatment goals, in cross-cultural work it is even more imperative. Providers need direct and continuing client input on what is culturally valued so that what is created is culturally appropriate, useful, and minimizes ethnocentric projection. Since provider and client begin at very different cultural places, it is reasonable to expect some mutual movement in the direction of the other. Culturally competent professionals adapt and adjust their efforts to the cultural milieu of the client. At the same time, by entering into the helping process, culturally different clients cannot help but gain some knowledge and insight into the workings of mainstream culture.

Assessing Culturally Different Clients

A good culturally sensitive assessment provides different kinds of valuable information. It gives insight into the problem as conceived by the client and a sense of any barriers that may have stood in the way of seeking help. It can suggest what clients expect to receive from the helping process and their notions of what the process will involve. It can also provide a reading of how acculturated they are, how comfortable they would be with a more mainstream approach, how much the process needs to be adjusted, and whether any special preparation of clients is necessary prior to treatment. On the basis of answers to these questions and impressions gained during early contact, decisions about how to proceed can reasonably be made.

Collecting data about the client's cultural history and lifestyle is an excellent place to start. The following list of specific items to be explored is repeated from Chapter 1: Place of birth. Number of generations in America. Family roles and structure. Language spoken at home. English fluency. Economic situation and status. Amount and type of education. Amount of acculturation. Traditions still practiced in the home. Familiarity and comfort with Northern European lifestyle. Religious affiliation. Community and friendship patterns. Together, these items provide a good initial basis for understanding the client ethnically and culturally.

Grieger and Ponterotto (1995) suggest six additional areas of assessment that should be useful in deciding how the helping process must be adjusted in relation to the cultural needs of the client. These include (a) the client's level of psychological mindedness, (b) the family's level of psychological mindedness, (c) the client's and the family's attitudes toward helping, (d) the client's level of acculturation, (e) the family's level of acculturation, and (f) the family's attitude toward acculturation. If a client's or family's worldview precludes "conceptualizing one's problems from a psychological point of view and having the construct of emotional disturbance as a part of one's interpretive lens" (Grieger & Ponterotto, p. 363) and their levels of acculturation are low, several alternatives to insight approaches are possible. One is to work with the problem as defined by the client (irrespective of whether the provider sees underlying psychological issues). For example, the authors describe a case where a Chinese student presents with academic problems and an underlying depressive disorder. In such a situation, it is possible for the helper to work directly with the academic problems, perhaps via improving study skills, time management, and so on, without raising the issue of the depression. Behavioral types of intervention for the depression (that don't require psychological insight) offer a second alternative. A third possibility involves trying to educate the client vis-à-vis psychological mindedness. The choice between the three approaches is, however, an ethical, not a clinical, one. Similarly, low acculturation and negative attitudes toward it tend to mitigate against general insight work. It is also likely in such a situation for the family to serve as a force against the client seeking help.

Pinderhughes (1989) offers the following series of questions which further pinpoint and define the cultural dimensions of the problem being presented. All are worth exploring in depth:

1. To what extent is the problem related to issues of transition such as migration and immigration?
2. To what extent is the client's understanding of the problem based on a cultural explanation, for example, "evil curse," "mal ojo," and so forth?
3. Is the behavior that is a problem considered normal within the culture or is it considered dysfunctional?
4. To what extent is the problem a manifestation of environmental lack of access to resources and supports?
5. To what extent is the problem related to culture conflict in identity, values, or relationships?
6. To what extent is the behavior a consequence of psychological conflict or characterological problems?
7. What are the cultural strengths and assets available to the client such as cultural values and practices, social networks, and support systems? (p. 149)

Combining all three sources of information—that is, the basic demographics with the more specific questions raised by Grieger and Ponterotto (1995) and Pinderhughes (1989)—provides a good beginning for understanding the life situation and presenting problem of the culturally different client.

Establishing Rapport and the First Session

In working with culturally different clients, the first session is especially critical. Research has shown that up to 50% of all clients of Color do not return for a second session (Sue & McKinney, 1975; Sue, McKinney, Allen, & Hall, 1974). This suggests that these clients either did not feel safe with the provider or concluded, based on what had transpired during the first session, that their needs were not going to be met. Sue and Zane (1987), it will be remembered, argue that culturally different clients must come away from early sessions with both a sense that their problems are understood from their own perspective and that they will soon receive concrete benefits from their work with the provider. Thus, goals for the first session should include establishing good rapport, gaining an understanding of the client's problem and what he or she expects from the helping relationship, communicating clearly what the provider can reasonably offer, providing the client with the experience of being heard and understood, and (if possible and appropriate) hope that the process into which they have entered can offer some immediate help. The following general suggestions are offered as a means of better approaching these goals:

- Be warm, sincere, and respectful in your manner.

- Mutual introductions are very important. Northern European American culture is unusual in its desire to "get down to business." Other cultures are more personal in preceding business matters with introductions and inquiries as to health, family, and the like. Introduce yourself by the title and name you wish the client to use. Refer to adult clients as Mr. or Miss or Mrs. initially. (It is usually most appropriate to address the oldest family member present if it is a family session.) Be sure to inquire as to whether you are pronouncing their name correctly and how they wish to be addressed. Also ask by what name or names they wish you to refer to their ethnic group. If you are comfortable doing so, share with them some personal information (e.g., family data, where you reside, etc.) along with your professional credentials. Most cultures do not view others in terms of their social roles to the extent that European Americans do in regard to professional behavior.

- If you feel anxious about your lack of knowledge about your clients' culture, do something about it by way of research prior to meeting with them. At the same time, it is not realistic to expect that you can become an expert on their culture and all of its diverse aspects. Exhibiting such a position about another person's culture is, in fact, likely to be taken very negatively: as haughty, presumptuous, or even demeaning. It is far better to be open about one's lack of knowledge and ask questions. For example, "I have not worked with many clients from your community and feel I do not know as much about your culture as I would like. I would appreciate your help in explaining certain things I may not understand as you refer to them." Your sincere openness and desire to learn is not a hindrance but rather a matter of respect for them and their culture. At the same time, it is necessary to point out that many People of Color (e.g., African Americans) may react negatively to being expected to educate Whites about their culture. "If you want to learn about me, read a book." Anger at such expectations reflects a historical experience of People of Color which involves both an attitude on the part of Whites that it is the responsibility of People of Color to deal with racism and injustice and the feeling that the desire to "learn about us" is not really sincere. I would suggest asking the client if he or she is comfortable playing such a role.

- Give a brief and nontechnical description of the helping process, its purpose and the specifics of how often you would like to meet, for how long, when, where, and so forth as well as any other relevant information such as where and how to contact you. Describe what is expected of them and what they can expect from you. Be sure to discuss confidentiality and what happens to the information they share with you. Remember, this may be their first experience with a professional helper and that such roles may not formally exist in their culture.

• Have clients describe in their own words the problem(s) for which they are seeking help. Feel free to ask questions and get as much clarification as necessary. Then, summarize for them what you heard and ask if your summary is accurate. It is critical that you truly understand what they are communicating and similarly that they are aware that you understand. Also ask what kind of help they need most immediately, how other family members view them and the problem, and whether family members or significant others are willing to participate in future sessions. Throughout this phase of the process, try to determine what the client expects vis-à-vis gaining help with the problem.

• On the basis of the information you now have, share with them what you believe can be accomplished both in terms of more immediate and longer range needs. It is important that you describe possible goals in collaborative terms (but at the same time do so in a manner that continues to emphasize your skills and knowledge) and indicate that if they choose to proceed, the specific goal setting will be done jointly. Also discuss what might be some of the consequences of successfully achieving the goals.

• Clients should be asked if there are any aspects of the helping process, as it has been described and experienced so far, that may be difficult for them. Similarly, if you notice anything that already seems problematic, it would be good to raise your concerns at this point.

• The session should end with a formal good-bye and concrete plans for what will transpire next: another appointment, a referral, a call to the client with some additional information at which time you will discuss continuing, and so on.

These general suggestions must be altered and adjusted in relation to the individual circumstances and personal characteristics of each client.

Additional Suggestions for Preparation and Support

Finally, there are a number of preparations that create support or allay some of the natural anxiety that may be felt as one contemplates or actually begins cross-cultural work.

As suggested in Chapter 2, the development of cultual competence is a lifelong pursuit. This book is only a first step. The more you can learn about the general topics of racism, culture, diversity, cultural competence, and cross-cultural service delivery as well as the specific knowledge about individual groups and their cultures, the more comfortable and conversant you become. Since the late 1980s, in fact, there has been an explosion of good material in this area and a dramatic increase in the availability of excellent training opportunities. You should take advantage of these whenever possible.

• Prepare for work with clients from a particular ethnic group by doing personal research on that group's culture, history, and health care issues. This can include not only academic and professional reading, but also novels, biographies, social histories, travel accounts as well as movies, videos, theater, art exhibits, lectures, and so forth.

• A most valuable supplement to such cognitive learning is varying degees of actual immersion in the client's culture. This can range from attending celebrations, cultural events, political rallys, eating regularly at ethnic restaurants, and patronizing community businesses to more sustained contact such as volunteering in the community, learning the language in programs in the community, and traveling to countries of the clients' origin.

• It is also an excellent idea to have someone such as a professional who is indigenous to the community with whom one will be working to consult with on a regular basis. As a beginner to cross-cultural work, it is particularly useful to discuss all cases, especially early in their development, with someone who is knowledgeable about the workings of the client's culture. With more experience and comfort, one might feel the need for consultation only in more difficult or problematic cases. Agencies should also establish ongoing consulting relationships with indigenous cultural experts from all groups that they serve.

• One might also consider establishing a study/peer supervision group with other providers who are involved in cross-cultural service delivery. Regular meetings can involve discussing shared readings, presenting cases, having guest experts, and the like. Such a group can provide opportunities to share resources and knowledge, receive supervision and support when helpful, and remain focused on the cultural dimensions of cross-cultural service delivery.

• A final suggestion is to join local ethnic provider groups and networks. Often, providers who work extensively with a specific population join together as a means of sharing information and resources, advocating for the needs and rights of clients, and keeping knowledgeable on current research and trends in providing services to the population of interest. Active participation in such a group is an excellent way to learn more about a client population, connect with other providers who might serve as valuable resources, and demonstrate interest and commitment to cross-cultural service delivery as a career focus.

Avoiding the Stereotyping of Individual Group Members

The chapters that follow are organized according to ethnicity—that is, each focuses on working with a different ethnic community. Chapters 9–12 deal with clients of Color: Latinos/as, Native Americans, African Americans, and

Asian Americans. As described in greater detail at the end of this chapter, each is written in conjunction with a professional provider from that community. Chapter 13 addresses working with White and White ethnic clients. In writing it, I have drawn on my personal and clinical experiences as a Jew. Although adopting such a general "cookbook" approach (i.e., the enumeration of stock formulas or "recipes" for understanding and dealing with a certain group of people) is a convenient way of summarizing a good deal of culturally specific information, it does present certain pitfalls. To begin with, the division of America's non-White populations into four broad racial categories, although a common practice within majority culture, is artificial and serves to mask enormous diversity. For example, Americans who have immigrated from Asian countries do not generally identify or call themselves Asian Americans. They may self-identify as Chinese Americans, Chinese, of Chinese descent, or even according to more regional or tribal groupings. Some may find being called Asian American offensive. The term is, in fact, bureaucratic in origin, developed by the U.S. Census Bureau. It is used here, as elsewhere, for convenience, but should not be assumed to imply sameness. In actuality, as Atkinson, Morten, and Sue (1993) point out, the term Asian American refers to "some twenty-nine distinct subgroups that differ in language, religion, and values" (p. 195). The important point here is that such broad categories subsume many different ethnic groups, each with its own unique culture, and to lump them together on the basis of certain common geographic, physical, or cultural features merely encourages an underestimation of their diversity and uniqueness.

Thinking about People of Color through such categories also serves to encourage stereotyping. Such thinking tends to be most common among inexperienced providers who find the prospect of cross-cultural work, at least initially, anxiety producing. Stereotyping, in turn, is an effective means of reducing what might be experienced as unpredictability in the behavior of culturally different clients. Thus, less experienced providers often project the same cultural characteristics onto all individuals they identify as belonging to a specific group. If I can be sure that all clients will act similarly, I can more easily develop a general strategy of how to deal with them in session and, therefore, feel more in control. If I believe, for example, that all Native American clients are reticent, I can prepare myself to be more active in seeking information, or if I know that all Asian Americans are taught early to suppress emotions, I can be on the lookout for more subtle forms of emotionality in their presentation. Similarly, descriptions of what approaches have been most successfully used with a given client population can be misread by those wishing to limit complexity as the only approaches to be adopted. In sum, then, taking the material that appears in the following chapters too literally (i.e., as some sort of gospel) limits provider creativity and adaptability and at the same time suppresses sensitivity to intragroup differences.

Instead of assuming unanimity among clients from the same group, a far better way to proceed is to treat all guesses about what is going on with a culturally different client as hypotheses to be verified clinically. I may know, for example, that alcohol abuse is a very common problem in Native American communities. If I inquire about it and the client says he is not abusing alcohol,

I must consider the possibility that his statement is true rather than suspect massive denial. Or in contemplating work with a recent immigrant Latina woman, I should not assume that she is experiencing serious conflict with her culture's traditional role for women, even though that often occurs. Perhaps she is, but then again, maybe she is not. It is clearly best to hold off making such judgments until one has carried out a thorough cultural assessment to check out the hypotheses that the following chapters can help generate.

Introduction to Chapters 9–12

What follows are four in-depth interviews, each focused on working with clients from one of the four communities of Color. Each is written in conjunction with a provider from that community who is a human service professional with extensive experience working with clients from his or her respective group. All were asked to answer the following general question: "What do you think is important, or even critical, for a culturally different provider to know in relation to working with a client from your community?" Their responses are presented according to a number of distinct topics that provide the structure for the interviews. Included are (a) professional and ethnic autobiographical material, (b) demographics and shared characteristics of their community, (c) group names, (d) history in a nutshell, (e) help seeking behavior, (f) family and community characteristics, (g) cultural style, values, and worldview, (h) common presenting problems, (i) socioeconomic issues, (j) important assessment questions, (k) subpopulations at risk or experiencing transition, (l) tips for developing rapport, (m) optimal therapeutic style, and (n) a short case study.

The text of each chapter was generated through an interview format in which the provider summarizes his or her thinking about the general characteristics that community members share. This is not an easy task given the fact that each racial category in essence represents an array of ethnic groups that are quite diverse. Each interviewee tried to speak broadly enough to fairly represent the cultural and psychological characteristics shared by the majority of the ethnic group he or she is representing. At the same time, they tried to make distinctions between subgroups where necessary. Since no single provider can claim expert knowledge or experience working with all of the subgroups or divisions within any racial category, the interviewees were asked to discuss specifically and draw examples from subpopulations with which they are most familiar. Answers to the various questions in each interview have been left close to verbatim to retain their personal and cultural flavor.

Chapter Nine

Working With Latino/a Clients:
An Interview With Inez Souza

Latinos/as will soon be the largest racial minority in the United States, numbering over 20 million according to the 1990 census. According to Soriano (1994), they are projected to reach 29 million by 2000, which will represent 10% of the total population, and by 2050 they will surpass African Americans as America's largest racial group. As a collective, they are quite diverse, including individuals whose roots are in Mexico, Cuba, Puerto Rico, and South and Central America. The vast majority are Spanish-speaking and Catholic and share a strong emphasis on family as well as certain general cultural characteristics. There are, however, as many differences as similarities. Klor de Alva (1988) points out that: "Different Hispanic groups, generally concentrated in different regions of the country, have little knowledge of each other and are often as surprised as non-Hispanics to discover the cultural gulfs that separate them" (p. 107). Latinos/as are predominantly city dwellers, and most work in unskilled and semiskilled jobs. Compared to non-Hispanics (a census term rather than an identity of choice among most group members), Latinos/as tend to be younger, poorer, less educated, and more unemployed. A unique set of factors related to their entry and circumstances in the United States puts Latinos/as at high risk for physical and psychological difficulties. Included are pressures around bilingualism, immigration and rapid acculturation, adjustment to American society, poverty, racism, and the loss of cultural ways. As we shall discover from our expert guest, Dr. Inez Souza, a central factor in understanding the psychological situation of most Latino/a clients is their experience or the experience of their family in migrating to the United States.

Inez Souza, PhD, is assistant professor in the PsyD Program, John F. Kennedy University, Orinda, California. She has also served on the teaching faculty of The Wright Institute, Berkeley. She has a private practice in psychotherapy working with adults who are predominantly Latino/a immigrants. She is also a third-year candidate at the Lacanian School of Psychoanalysis and research fellow at the University of California, Berkeley, Anthropology Department, where she is examining the impact of gender and class on the immigration process of Brazilians.

The Interview

Author: Could you begin by talking about your own ethnic background and how it has impacted you and your work?

Souza: I am Brazilian. I was born in Rio de Janeiro. My bicultural life began when I was 6 and came to this country for 4 years while my dad was going to school to get a doctorate in civil engineering. I went back home at the age of 10, when he had completed his studies, but returned 10 years later—I was 20 then—to go to the University of California. My heritage? I believe I have some Indian as well as Portuguese, which is representative of the Brazilian population. I don't know if I have any African in me, but that could be possible.

My migration to the United States was somewhat disguised in the sense that I never made the decision to migrate. I sort of came and never left. But the one thing that stands out is that I was not aware that I was an "other." Of course, I knew I was different and saw myself as a foreigner, and that went with me everywhere. But it was only much later that I realized there was something also "other" about me. So I think I actually was in denial about experiences related to discrimination and racism for a long time. I only began to see myself differently as I realized that others perceived me as such. Actually, I can pin down the exact day it happened. When I was an alumna, I received a letter addressed "To Person of Color." That wasn't a label I was familiar with. I didn't see myself that way. I remember showing it to my husband and asking, "Are you sure they mailed it to the right person? Maybe they have somebody else in mind." And of course, my name was right there, so it hadn't been a mistake. It was just that I was being lumped together with others in a certain way that I hadn't been used to or familiar with.

Other experiences I went through that really stand out? It is mostly around my immigration rather than ethnicity or race. My immigrant status has colored my life, permeated it entirely. That has been a characteristic of mine that I have found others insensitive to or very ignorant about. What is it like to be an immigrant? What is it like to miss one's home? What is it like to have to negotiate two worlds at all times? What really struck me was other people's ethnocentricity. How come you don't love it here? How come you miss home? This is the best place on earth. How come you still refer to "back there"? You get that a lot. And then I would feel some uneasiness, especially professionally, when I was around groups where I was the only immigrant. And there was no one else who could in any way relate to that facet of life for me.

Author: Who are the Latinos/as and what characteristics do they share as a group?

Souza: What I would like to say about Latinos/as is that they are a very heterogeneous group. It's very important to remember that we're referring to Mexicans, Puerto Ricans, people from Central and South America with that term. Many people prefer the term Latino or Latina to Hispanic because of its reference back to the Spaniards, and they don't really identify with them. Others refer to themselves based on their nationality, such as "I'm Chilean" or "I'm Argentinian" or "I'm Puerto Rican." In addition to geographic diversity, there is also a lot of variation in terms of socioeconomic class as well as people coming from rural versus more urban areas. These are all important variables to consider when thinking about Latinos/as and their experience as immigrants. Class differences can at times be even more noticeable among Latinos/as than cultural differences, and this can also be true of other ethnic groups.

There are many general shared characteristics as well. Even though the United States is not usually thought of as a collective society, Latin and Central Americans share a lot of collectivistic traits. What I mean by this is that there is a lot of interdependence among nuclear families, extended families, and in the community as a whole. This connectedness sustains life for its individuals and is very important to the fabric of Latino/a society. From the perspective of a more individualistic society, such dependency tends to be pathologized or seen as negative. Thus, Latino/a families might be viewed as being enmeshed or as there not being enough separation and individuation. Members of collectivistic societies also tend to feel limited by the perceptions of other. So, for example, there may be a lot of hesitancy in seeking out mental health services because the community is so tight: "What will others in the community know?" In short, being so interconnected is wonderful. It provides a great support system. On the other hand, it sometimes can be an obstacle.

Religiosity is an important aspect of Latino/a culture. There are usually a lot of Christians, primarily Catholics, among the population. There's also a significant number of individuals whose beliefs represent a blend of African religious rituals with Catholicism. So you find a lot of the African cults that are blended in. Such blending goes back to the time of slavery, whereby slaves could continue to practice their beliefs in a manner that would not be out of line with the Catholic faith. These cults exist especially in Cuba, Haiti, and Brazil and have various names and customs depending on the tribes that came over from Africa. Thus, one finds variation in religious practice across socioeconomic class and educational status. Often, people will come to psychotherapy via their clergy, and in so doing, the clergy make it legitimate in terms of, "You're not crazy; it doesn't mean that there's something wrong."

Without wanting to be too reductionistic or referring just to stereotypes, there is the tendency toward similar sex-role behavior across Latino/a groups: of the "macho Latin male" and the more martyr-like wife or female. The man tends to have a lot of power in the home. This is especially true if he is an immigrant and lacks power in terms of his work environment. Under such circumstances, he is more likely to assert that power at home. Often, there is a lot of domestic violence also. To the extent that he is exploited and oppressed outside and cannot protect or assert himself against it, he may likely take out his frustrations at home on his wife and children. The women tend to be more submissive and subservient, and the whole dichotomy between Madonna and whore still exists in many psyches, not only for the men but for the women as well. Of course, not all women and men fall into these patterns.

Latinos/as generally think of themselves and their culture as being warmer and more spontaneous than Anglo or European culture. People are regarded as more lively, real, and well-rounded. Affect, emotion, and feelings are constantly being expressed. Interactions are highly valued. The individual is seen as the center of communication. It is going on at all times. A conversation could strike up between two strangers at a bus stop and could continue through the course of their trip together. Human contact, in short, is highly valued and sought after. It is my perception, however, that these traits also tend to be infused with a certain sadness, at times a profound melancholy. I see it more in some groups than in others; there is a kind of denial of that sadness. Brazilians, for example, would fall into that category, where sadness is played down, and there is a more happy-go-lucky, hedonistic outlook on life. "Tomorrow will be a better day; life will bring better solutions to some of the problems." Conflict is underplayed, and there is more of a tendency to escape into pleasure-seeking behaviors and activities. Nevertheless, it is evident in the music, songs, poetry, and religion: frequent references to loss, homesickness, longing, and unfulfilled desires. In fact, there is a word in Portuguese that exists in no other language, *saudade*, that refers to that longing. It's a noun which describes what you feel when you are homesick or when you miss or long for someone or something. It permeates the music and the culture. No one escapes it, because there is always something that has been lost, even if it's just childhood, youth, and other losses inherent in life.

Author: Could you talk about the various names that different Latino/a subgroups use to describe and identify themselves?

Souza: This is very important because such terms are rich in underlying assumptions about where a person has come from and how they define, identify, and see themselves. For many years Hispanic was the term of choice, especially among acculturating and more affluent individuals. Its primary reference was to Spanish speakers. Many, however, refuse to use it because of its reference to both European origins and the role Spaniards played in the colonizing of the New World. Many people are profoundly bothered by the exclusive use of the term Hispanic in U.S. census taking. They might be Indian or of European descent but not necessarily of Spanish origin. Many complain: "There's no representation of me here," which is true of my case as well. Brazilians are not Spanish-speaking, so the term Hispanic would not apply.

The terms Latino and Latina, which refer to Central and South America and to anyone born there, are currently in the forefront of usage. Many prefer, however, to refer to themselves according to their country of birth. The term Mexican, for example, refers to people who were born in Mexico. But it's important to remember that a good part of the Southwest of the United States used to belong to Mexico. So we have Mexicans who were born in the United States and who nevertheless call themselves Mexican and identify primarily with the term Mexican as opposed to Latino/a or Hispanic. The first and second generations of Mexican immigrants refer to themselves as Chicano/a.

If you do not know where someone is from, it is important not to assume that they are Mexican or Puerto Rican, for example, just because the majority of Spanish speakers in the United States come from these two countries. What I usually tend to do is wait and see what clients tell me about themselves. If it doesn't come up, I might ask them where they are from. Or I might ask them how they see themselves—as first generation or an immigrant—because that will give me a sense of their level of acculturation, how they're negotiating the two worlds, the losses as well as the gains from the new world. Their self-description will also give me an important sense of their subjective group identification—what community they feel themselves a part of and what group they have an affinity with.

Let me use my own case as an example. I view myself more as a foreigner than as a minority, even though others here would place me in the category of minority because my foreign-born status coincides with an existing U. S. minority group. But I personally identify with the term foreigner because it reminds me and the rest of the world that I am an outsider. The term minority would bring me in more, as if I had grown up here, which is not the case. I have really resided as an adult in two different cultures.

It is also vital to be aware of geography. A lot of immigrant clients complain that dominant culture members are very ignorant of geography and will often make ghastly mistakes in terms of thinking that Buenos Aires is in Africa and that Peru is a country in the Middle East. We are talking absolutely horrendous mistakes that Latinos/as live with on a day-to-day basis. Often, this leads to a sense of superiority over "gringos," because gringos, with their ethnocentrism, don't have a clue as to who makes up the rest of the world.

Author: Having talked about some of the cultural characteristics and identity issues that Latinos/as have in common, could you next describe some of the shared history that they bring with them to the United States?

Souza: Most of Central and South America was colonized by the Spaniards (except for Brazil, Guyana, Suriname, and French Guiana, which were colonized by the Portuguese, British, Dutch, and French, respectively) so we are speaking of the history of a colonized people. There is also the important influence of the assimilation of Native Indians as well as Africans who were brought to the colonies as slaves on Latino/a cultures, an influence that is still very predominant and important to this day. Some countries value this aspect of their ancestry more than others. To illustrate, there is substantial Indian pride in Mexico; it is primarily lacking in the case of Peru. An important facet of history for those of Mexican descent is the fact that a good deal of Mexican land was lost as a result of the war with the United States. Out of avarice or greed, Anglos took what is now Texas, New Mexico, Arizona, and California—a lot of the Southwest—for their own. Feelings about this still run high among certain segments of the Mexican population. "How can Americans speaking out against the Chinese occupation of Tibet remain so quiet about what they've done in terms of the Mexican territory?" It is also important to remember that many countries in Central and South America have been victims of war and military dictatorships. Those fleeing these circumstances arrive here as refugees, which means that they are involuntary immigrants. Their return home is an impossibility. Many have also had to contend with a history of torture and persecution as well as flight into exile.

Author: Let's switch focus somewhat and begin to look at issues related to help giving and treatment. First, could you talk about factors that influence how Latinos/as go about seeking help?

Souza: It's important to remember that Latino patients usually find their way to therapy through a referral: either from a physician, priest, or friend who has been a client. Typically, the first attempt to address a problem is either medical or religious. Then, with much reassurance that no, they are not going crazy, and no, there is nothing stigmatizing or embarrassing about seeking help, they'll make their way to the mental health system. So it's important to remember that a lot of reassurance is necessary. Often, the wife will come first. The husband usually has long work hours, and the wife might be the one that is most motivated to seek help. Often, the husband ends up needing treatment more than the wife due to a serious drinking problem or violent behavior, and so on. But if he finds his way, it will be via the wife. Also remember that if he does come, this represents a financial loss, since he will be missing work to come to treatment. The wife, then, will need to do a lot of footwork both in regard to finding a referral source and in convincing the husband that it's an okay thing to do. This is especially true since there is a cultural tendency to rely on the community, the extended family, and the church for help.

In general, a woman may present with a more submissive style and tends to come in expressing more somatic complaints. She will refer to it as, "Oh, it's a disease," or "It's a problem of the nerves," or "It's nervousness." She will present it in physiological terms that will seem to her more concrete, legitimate, and less stigmatizing. Dizziness or faintness might be another complaint. Remember also that there is always a potential for the husband to feel very jealous of the clinician. If, for example, he is in the waiting room, it is important that the therapist introduce himself or herself, shake his hand, and make some kind of connection so that he will not feel excluded. It is also important to include him at other points if and when relevant. Be aware also that as the wife improves and her behavior changes in the outside world, not just in therapy, there may be greater risk of her dropping out and leaving because the husband might feel terribly insecure or threatened. This is particularly true in the case of a wife being treated by a male therapist.

Author: What are the common problems that clients bring to you? I would assume, from what you said earlier, that many of them relate to experiences with the migration process.

Souza: What brings people into therapy? Substance abuse and alcoholism, especially cocaine; there are many immigrants that are cocaine addicts or involved in drug dealing; that's one common problem. Marital problems, domestic violence, depression, work inhibition, acculturation issues, and posttraumatic stress disorder. It must be remembered that a lot of immigrants from Central and South America have been tortured, were political prisoners, and are exiles.

You are certainly right that many of the conflicts Latinos/as face result from their immigration experiences. I would like to talk about this in some detail. Two important variables in this regard are clients' degree of acculturation and their reason for being in this country. Is the goal for them to send money back home? Is it to advance economically? Are they seeking social mobility or do they hope to acculturate and remain in the United States? Therapists should keep this as a point of reference: Are they oriented toward the old country, "back home," or are they moving toward something new? Circumstances vary across subgroups. With the Mexican Chicano population, for example, geography is such that they can come back and forth very easily. When you think of Central American refugees, however, going back is not an option. Their migration is permanent, and that poses a whole new series of issues and problems. Many Mexicans do tend to send money home, to think of their stay here as temporary, with the hope that they will some day move back permanently. With refugees from Central America, the direction is reversed. They see their migration here as permanent and will invest a lot more energy in acculturating and attaching to their new home. With South Americans, there's always the ongoing wish that some day one will move back, that this is only a temporary migration, but it may take many years for this to occur.

Another critical issue to be aware of, which is not always volunteered, is a client's legal status here. Are they legal or not? What kind of visa are they on? What preoccupations and concerns might they have as a result of all this? With the constant changes in the immigration law, many feel terribly persecuted and fearful of being discovered, caught, deported. Also related to this is their occupation. They usually work odd jobs, where papers are not required or too many questions asked. Here, too, there is always the fear of being discovered or caught. But there are differences between the kind of work men and the women find. The men tend to work in construction, repair, and delivery jobs. Often, the occupations they find involve serious health and injury risks. But because of their immigrant status, they're not able to apply for disability or openly confront dangerous working conditions. So they continue to expose themselves to serious health problems and continue to work in spite of injuries, often in extreme pain. Many are at risk of abusing pain medication and of becoming addicted, which they in turn need to conceal or they won't be able to get work.

In most of their jobs, however, men tend to have peers and extensive social contact. Women, on the other hand, find work in child care, elder care, and housecleaning, which are very isolating occupations. They may go a whole day with minimal, if any, interaction with another adult. In treatment, they talk a great deal not only about their loss of social and occupational status as a result of migration, but also about their deep isolation. Remember, too, that for all of them, English is a second language—one that has been learned at great cost — and this even furthers their isolation. The external world with its discrimination, racism, and exploitation is not a very safe place, and so many of the frustrations that the men feel, especially from their job, will then get expressed at home, where it's safe to do so, where it's safe to answer back or assert one's authority or be able to express some of the aggression, anger, and rage that is held in all day long. It will often get expressed to the wife and children, and a perfect situation is set up for problems of domestic violence, of child abuse, of drinking and alcoholism.

For first-generation Chicanos, the isolation and alienation are of a different kind. They don't feel a part of, or feel that they belong in, the American culture into which they were born and yet feel completely alienated from the "old world" Mexican culture as well. There's a lot of conflict in terms of, "If I identify with the 'new world,' am I being disloyal to my parents and my cultural heritage?" On the other hand, the old world is an unknown so, "How do I get to belong or fit or be a part of it?"

Another important dynamic for the immigrant is a kind of splitting that occurs between the old country and the new, where one place is idealized and considered to be paradise and the other denigrated and devalued. The split is most intensely felt in the beginning of their migration experience, but seems to be ever present in some form or other. It doesn't

really seem to matter which country is being idealized and which is denigrated. What is important, according to Grinberg and Grinberg (1989), is
that this split is absolutely necessary so that the immigrant can organize
his or her world. If they are about to leave, for example, the country that
they are migrating to becomes the paradise and El Dorado. In order to be
able to live and create for themselves a new life in a new place, they need
to denigrate the old one. It is as if doing so makes it psychologically possible to go on or else be paralyzed by the enormity of the loss. So it's
important to listen to how well the client has integrated the two worlds.
How capable is the individual or family group to create a new world for
themselves, a new "potential space," to use Winnicott's term, which
brings together elements of both to enrich it? So you always want to
know how they manage the split. Is it very extreme or more or less well-
integrated? Is it peripheral or is it absolutely in the forefront of the person's existence. One of the clues that will speak to this is how they treat
and speak of those left behind. Where is their point of reference? In what
direction are they moving? Are they interested in burning bridges or not?
Related to this is the delinquent behavior that is sometimes observed just
prior to returning home. It usually has the quality of getting even or feeling like, "I felt exploited, so I'm going to take all that I can," even if it
involves criminal behavior. But for those whose immigration patterns are
going back and forth or who have relatives and friends who will be
remaining here, one sees very little of such acting out.

Finally, something should be said about the children, who are always
involuntary immigrants, for there is always someone else in authority
making the decision to migrate. Because children are very adaptable and
resilient, there is a tendency to forget the enormous impact that the
migration has on them. They're losing not only their friends, extended
family, and community from the old world, but also the "nonhuman"
environment that is so important to them: their school, their room, their
home, the streets where they played. They are also in a delicate position
in their new world. Since they acculturate more rapidly and easily than
adults, they often have major pressures placed on them. Sometimes they
are called upon to translate between family members and the English-
speaking world at large. Sometimes parents feel threatened by their
child's ability to acculturate. Sometimes parents push the child to acculturate, depriving them of their native tongue, encouraging them to
always speak English, and depriving them of a continuity between the
cultural present and past. Immigrant children tend to have a very high
school dropout rate. They also experience a set of unique problems related to language such as not being as fluent in English as they are in
Spanish and having to contend with all of the fluctuations and mixed
feelings about bilingual education and English-only schools. Finally,
children rely a great deal on their family, and to the extent that immigration has created any dysfunction within the family system, they are
placed at risk.

Author: You've spoken a lot about the psychological dimensions and difficulties associated with migration. How does socioeconomic class affect these
dynamics?

Souza: As far as the socioeconomic issues, it is important to remember that in
their country of origin immigrants may have had a much higher status
socially, professionally, occupationally. They may have been employed in
professional jobs that they might never be able to do in this country. So
for many, this may lead to an enormous sense of loss and downward
social mobility and in turn the shame and embarrassment that goes along
with being reduced to a lower status. But it's important not to assume
that this is always the case. I've heard some explain, "Well, here I'm a janitor, I make a lot of money, I don't care if people back home know I'm a
janitor because look what I have accomplished for myself." Or: "I've
been able to survive in another country." Just that alone is a monumental
accomplishment. But for most, there is a lot of embarrassment and shame
in having to begin from scratch without any kind of acknowledgment
or recognition for what they were in their country of origin. There are
some gender differences here as well. For many women, this is the first
time they are able to earn what seems to them substantial amounts
of money. At times, in a couple or family, the men want to go back and
the women do not as a result of what they've been able to accomplish
here economically.

What I have noticed across Latino/a subgroups is that those coming
from lower socioeconomic situations have less conflict around their
migration. The reasons for that are many. For one, they seldom come with
the goal of really acculturating. They will come here and live under very
difficult circumstances, for example, in crowded apartments where there
are eight or ten people living. They work incredibly long hours, they're
homesick, but very clear as to what their purpose is. So there's little conflict. They're here to make money, to save money, to send money back
home, and once they've accomplished that goal, they will go home.
They're not interested in learning English, in acculturating, in creating a
life for themselves here. Now, with the middle class, it's a completely different scenario, especially when they believe they have nothing to show
for the years spent abroad, no accomplishments to be proud of, since they
have been working at odd jobs.

I'm talking about those who come possibly without ever making the
decision to stay. What I would call a more disguised migration. They end
up staying here 4, 5, 10, 15 years and feel that they have nothing to show
for their time. They feel that they haven't advanced their lives in any way.
They have not adequately learned the English language; they have not
made progress toward any kind of professional endeavor; there's been no
upward social mobility. What you see is an enormous amount of shame
over the lost years of one's life as well as an inability to return because of
that shame. I have had patients refer to it as follows: "It's a very serious
thing to 'play' at being an immigrant. There's time and a place for that.

It's fine when you're young, or if you do it for a very short amount of time, a maximum of 3 years." They refer to themselves as having "gotten dumber, poorer, older and that it's been a complete waste of time." Underlying it all is a deep sense of loss, of shame, of regret, of ambivalence over acculturation, and of having to hide the shame when they go back to visit, of feeling like they've got to keep up a façade, especially in front of those left behind. In the case of some, feelings can reach a point where there is an intense dislike for everything that is American because it has grown too desperately familiar.

Author: Could you talk a bit about issues of identity and belonging in the different generations of Latinos/as?

Souza: One's identity will differ greatly depending upon whether one is first generation or an immigrant. With Chicanos, for example, there is initially a great deal of conflict feeling that they don't fully belong to either world and not yet knowing how to be more of a member, how to belong more, to either or both. At times, the confusion and wish to really belong get channeled negatively, such as into drug dealing or joining a gang in adolescence. For many assimilated adults, there is a deep sense of loss and feeling that they have been deprived by their parents' desire to acculturate them, and they focus too much on American traditions at the expense of their own native culture. Some want to take the time and learn Spanish as an adult, to get more familiar with the culture, and to incorporate some of its traditions. For the immigrant, in some ways, it's less conflictual, but that's not to say that there are not enormous feelings of sadness or loss. Their losses, however, are very palpable and real in a way that is not the case for the first generation. What's important in their identity struggle, as mentioned earlier, is the "split" and to what extent they rely on it to organize their experiences and attribute meaning to them versus an ability to integrate the two and speak freely to the advantages and limitations of both worlds.

For new immigrants, the sense of emerging identity depends very much on the existence of an intact ethnic community in the United States. For those who are lucky enough to have such a community to integrate into, there is less likely to be a sense of "otherness" and not belonging. As a foreigner, I've always envied those communities that were already in place. For example, there's a huge Mexican community. So I've always imagined that for a Mexican immigrant it would be a lot easier. However, it is not uncharacteristic for some people to be distrustful of those existing communities. You hear that a lot, certainly in my patient population. "I will not date a Brazilian. I will not associate with a Brazilian." One can almost feel the split. One's fellow "nationales" are denigrated. "You should be suspicious of them, slightly paranoid; they can't be trusted." So even when cultural networks do exist to facilitate migration, they're not always explored to their fullest or even acknowledged as valuable. One can also sense in this dynamic the extent to which some immigrants have been able to acculturate and take advantage of mainstream resources, but the amount of distrust they have of coming too close to the old world is quite noticeable. I believe it reminds him or her too much of their losses. So one takes a step back and avoids taking advantage of what still exists traditionally. This process speaks to one's sense of pride, or lack thereof, and where one stands as far as that identity process is concerned.

Author: Could you now discuss some of the factors that you see as important in assessing a Latino/a client?

Souza: Wherever possible, it is best to use the language that the person brings in—that they use to describe their symptoms. It is equally important to not assume that there is a shared language between the two of you. If they talk about being depressed, try to get a clear sense of what that means to them: How do they come to that label and what does depressed behavior look like for them? There is an old therapy adage that tells us "to be astonished and learn afresh with each person." In cross-cultural work, it is especially necessary to try to enter the worldview of the client, and this is particularly true in the case of somaticizing and bodily symptoms. What is the person's theory of why they have those symptoms? Is it fate? Is it a religious punishment? Is it destiny? Is it hereditary? What does it mean for them, if anything? Also be sure to get information as to what physicians have told them. This can help you see the extent to which they're able to be insightful about symptoms and problems, curious about their meaning, and work on a more symbolic level.

I also want to again stress the importance of understanding the impact of the migration experience both on the individual and subsequent generations. So during assessment, it is vital to get in as much detail as possible, a lot of information regarding the migration, even with first-generation clients. How did they or their family originally come to the United States? Was it a chain migration in terms of there being a relative, friend, or someone in their community already here who enabled or facilitated their coming? Did they migrate alone? Was it just an individual migrating who later brought the rest of the family? How does the client feel about the migration? What's their legal status? When someone comes in with a very particular problem and migration issues do not seem to be on the forefront, I will not immediately introduce the topic. I will keep an ear out for it, but respect the person's timing as to when he or she is able to speak about it.

There is a danger here in working with migration issues that I would like to address. It's very important that the therapist not pathologize the enormous reactions to loss that the immigrant may experience. At the same time, therapists should be very mindful of their own ethnocentricity in terms of misunderstanding the feelings of loss and the intense desire to go home. Such feelings are viewed as normal and healthy within Latino/a culture even though they may be seen as unhealthy from a mainstream American perspective. I have heard Latino/a patients complain, over and over, that their strong emotional attachment to "home" as well as their interconnectedness to family and community are downplayed and pathologized. They also describe an enormous push on the part of some therapists to get them to individuate, separate, and move out of the family home. There are major cultural differences in this realm, and it is vital not to assume that things that are done differently are somehow psychologically suspect. For example, adult children may still be living in the home of their parents. This is not an unusual occurrence in a Latino/a home. It could be for no other reason than simple economics.

It's very important to tease out pathology from culture and to not assume that something is cultural, especially if one doesn't know too much about the culture just because it is different. Individuation and separation are a good example. Although in Latino/a culture it is considered acceptable and even healthy to remain much closer to one's family as an adult than is true in mainstream White culture, there are extremes in such behavior that would be considered abnormal. For example, a parent not allowing adult children to individuate, to have a life of their own, but rather demanding that they live at home and help support the family indefinitely is all done in a way that really curbs the adult children's own development. This would be considered unhealthy from both cultural perspectives. One way of teasing out these differences that I have found helpful and at the same time nonintrusive is the following. When a problem or complaint is reported in therapy, I ask the client if what they describe is generally how things are done in their culture or group. Would your uncles be responding the same way? Would the community at large be addressing this issue in this manner? In this way, I can get a better sense of whether the practice or behavior in question is unique and idiosyncratic to this family or a cultural norm or traditional value. In other words, is it culturally "syntonic" or not?

Author: Next, I would like to ask you about suggestions you might have for providers about developing rapport with Latino/a clients.

Souza: As far as developing rapport, it's very important to remember that Latinos/as coming to therapy will tend to see the clinician as an authority. They will expect or anticipate that the clinician will take a more active role, will participate, will educate them, will give them information, and will share knowledge with them. That knowledge will in turn be seen as particularly valuable since the therapist's authority gives them special credibility. This does not mean, however, that one needs to be extremely active or use a highly structured approach. What it does mean is that rapport seems to develop more quickly, especially initially in therapy, when the provider is more engaging. This can be done by asking for information, by being empathic, by offering explanations. What is important is to go beyond just reflecting back feelings and to add something, to contribute something, to make a connection for the person, to legitimize their somatic complaints and at the same time raise questions as to their psychological repercussions.

As far as taboo or delicate topics, sexuality is certainly one. One should be aware, if one is a male therapist working with a married woman, the potential of jealousy on the part of the husband. I think that sexuality in general is a delicate subject that needs to be approached with a lot of tact and sensitivity. If I'm working individually with someone, I will wait to see if they introduce it into our discussion. If it hasn't been introduced after some time, and I can easily relate it to whatever topic we are currently discussing, I may do so gently and see how the client responds. The same is true for couples. I will not, during the initial stages of treatment, ask a lot of questions regarding one's sexual history. I might wait and do that later, after rapport has been established, especially when working across genders. After rapport has been established, I do not run as much of a risk of scaring the person out of treatment.

Other delicate topics include domestic violence, substance abuse, and of course, incest. With the Latino/a population, conflicts with in-laws often exist, but they are not necessarily taboo. It's something one might be able to talk openly about in time. Of course, as I mentioned earlier, it's very important, when working with families and couples, to not alienate the other spouse, to really include him or her, to frame treatment in such a way as to find something they can gain as well. Another topic that is especially difficult for most Latino/a parents and families is homosexuality. In spite of being in the United States for many years, homosexuality is still a very unsettling and stigmatizing topic to confront within one's family.

After a no-show or a cancellation that has not been rescheduled, I tend to pursue Latino/a clients more actively than I do with majority group clients. If someone seems to have dropped out of treatment, I make an effort to connect with them over the phone or via a letter, letting them know that should they ever want to pursue therapy again, I am available to them. It is my hope that contacting them will allow them to talk with me about whatever problem or conflict stands in the way of them continuing and, if possible, remove their source of resistance. Latinos/as, like other minorities, have a particularly high dropout rate from treatment and thus tend not to benefit as fully from it as they might. So I want to make every effort possible to ensure that they're seen, if they want to be, either by me or someone else.

Author: In addition to developing rapport, what else is important to know about working therapeutically with Latino/a clients?

Souza: Once clients are in therapy, it is important to educate them as to the value and benefits of the process: what the work involves and how it can be beneficial to them. After this is accomplished, I subscribe to Stanley Sue's notion of "the gift," although I don't particularly like the term. What he is referring to is the need to give clients, especially minority or immigrant ones, something back in the initial hour, something that makes it worthwhile for them to continue in treatment. It might be an empathic stance or an explanation that really resonates with what they're going through and gives them a new insight at the same time. Something like this needs to happen in order for the client to see the relevance of therapy and for it to be something with which they can emotionally resonate. Once they have gotten the sense of what it is about and how it works, it is very surprising just how capable of working symbolically on an analytical level they are. It is my experience, in fact, that Anglo patients generally do not take to the analytic process as well. Latino/a clients are able to work within the realm of the symbolic, often showing incredible insight and sophistication. They're capable of drawing symbolic connections for themselves. They really take advantage of techniques such as free association. They're very curious about dreams, symbolic meanings, and their importance. I have found this to be true across class and regardless of how well-educated one is, even though such a stance is generally unavailable to someone of more rural or poorer background. What's really interesting about this is that, as first-generation groups become more and more acculturated into the dominant culture, they tend to lose this ability. They become slightly more limited as far as how and at what level they are capable of working in treatment.

Latina women in particular tend to be very psychologically sophisticated as well as curious, even in regard to their somatic complaints. So even though the somatic presentation offers a way of permitting oneself to be in treatment, once they're beyond that, they're able to work at a very high level. Often, the wife is the moving force in couples and family therapy, helping the husband make progress by modeling how to be a good client.

Another important issue is the importance of language, given that patients are bilingual. It is critical that such clients be seen by someone with whom they can work in their native tongue whenever possible. A lot is lost in the second language. It is easier to become defensive in one's second language, which doesn't have the same emotional resonance as one's first tongue. I have found that a client is able to work at a deeper level if one is able to have a therapist that speaks their first language. I have had Spanish-speaking patients specifically seek me out, aware that I too was a non-Spanish-speaking immigrant, but not wanting to work in Spanish as if there was too much emotional pain to be processed, as in the case of those who have experienced torture in their native countries. For some immigrants, also, being able to carry out the treatment in English means that they have mastered the language, and there's a lot of pride in that.

It's very helpful to follow the lead of the individual in regard to language. If they're speaking in English, I will always speak in English. If they feel free mixing both languages, I usually do the same. If they don't, I really watch myself so that I don't mix the two languages. I also do not switch language unless the client does so first. There have been accounts where the therapist has done that, and it's had enormous psychological repercussions for the client. In short, I tend to follow as opposed to taking the lead because it is actually very psychologically significant what language they use. I find it very useful to observe when they do shift, whether there are certain topics they're unable to speak about in their native tongue, others they can only speak about in their acquired language, and so on.

Another interesting issue is that of time. Remember that in Latino/a cultures one has a lot more leeway and time is more flexible and fluid of a concept. Chronic lateness is not unusual. One might be chronically late for everything by 10 or 15 min. It might even be considered rude in certain circumstances to be right on time. If this is a problem with a client, I gently explore it, talk about it, explain the 50-minute hour so that the person is aware of how I will work with them. You can gently educate clients to the importance of the frame of time in treatment. What should be avoided, however, is to assume that their lateness is resistance or indicative of ambivalence. It might very well be, but it might also be a reflection of cultural style. Once it is addressed, the client might be able to arrive more on time, and when they don't, then it might be clearly something worth exploring. But in any case, begin with the awareness that with this population there is a cultural tendency of being late for everything.

Time is just one of many aspects of therapy around which some education is necessary for those who have not grown up with a familiarity for the process. Most basic is explaining and outlining the aspects of therapy that are specific to them: how long the session is, telephone calls in between, ending the session, beginning on time, cancellation policies, who can come, who you're working with because you don't want to run the risk of them bringing a spouse and then being surprised by their request for couples therapy. On the other hand, it's important that you not exclude children if they don't have child care, especially if you would like them to use you as a whole family resource, as someone who is available to the community at large and to the extended family as well. If you are not comfortable with this expanded role which culturally makes more sense to traditional clients, then it might be useful to educate them as far as the benefits of them having a separate couple therapist or a separate therapist for their child or adolescent. On the other hand, there might be reasons to work with just you if, for example, you are able to work in Spanish or Portuguese, in their native tongue. So it's important to weigh all of the pros and cons of each one of these scenarios.

Finally, you should be aware that clients may very well invite you to important events in their lives: weddings, graduations, other significant family gatherings. They may want to talk with you more than other patients usually do if they run into you on the street. I personally feel it's legitimate to answer questions such as where you're from. I typically get that question as early as during the initial phone call, before they've even discussed anything else. With this population, it is especially important to be more flexible about answering questions such as how long have you been in the United States. During a vacation, it's very possible that they will ask you if you are going back home. It is not so much that they're

being disrespectful of the frame or that they want to know personal information about you. Such questions are usually very selective in nature and
relate back to them and their issues of living abroad. If you're married, do
you have experience raising children? Do you have other relatives here?
It's more in the realm of attempting to connect with you on that level.
Being distant or only willing to explore rather than answer periodic questions will likely alienate Latino/a clients. A way of responding might be
to answer some of the questions that seem acceptable to you. If they don't
seem that relevant or the client is being very pushy about it, you might
explore their motives a bit. "What did you have in mind?" or "What does
that mean to you?" There may have been other questions or anxieties or
concerns behind the question that I may not have addressed, even though
I answered the question. They also may need a lot of ongoing reassurance
about being in therapy—that it will not reflect negatively on them. So just
be aware of that.

Author: Having shared all of this rich information with us, would you finish
by presenting a short case to show how these various strands come
together?

Souza: I worked with a 26-year-old single mother. She came here alone with
a daughter in an attempt to follow a boyfriend. She comes from a lower-
middle-class family in the northwestern part of Brazil, close to the capital.
She worked as a house cleaner, which meant she was alone a good part of
the day. Our work together focused a great deal on issues of immigration,
especially an enormous desire and ever-present longing to go home. This
theme emerged in every session and was reflected in her dreams as well.

"How long will that take?" "I've got to save money; I've got to be
able to find a way to make it happen." "How can I do that and at the
same time create a life for myself here: learn English, acculturate, be a
part of the world in the United States?" "But, if I do that, will I be compromising my desire to go home?" These kinds of conflicts permeated
every session. She vacillated between the idea of making money here, but
being happier there.

The patient's presenting problem was actually depression. But it was
atypical in that it did not get expressed in terms of being down or sad,
hopeless or helpless. Instead, it took the form of almost catatonic behavior
and an inability to get involved in life, whether it be tending to her
daughter, cleaning houses, or even how she related to her homesickness.

A second issue that emerged for her was the question regarding her
sexual orientation. Within my clinical experience (and there are few formal statistics here), a lot of immigrants will use leaving home as an occasion for coming out. It's safer here. They're removed from their culture of
origin, where it is a much greater stigma, and can get more support and
validation in the general culture of the Bay Area, where being gay or lesbian is far less stigmatized. Being in a new environment affords an opportunity to build a new identity and develop a new community. For this
patient, it was a matter of facilitating this process, which was filled with

doubt, confusion, and conflict. We first worked on self-acceptance and how to integrate it with the rest of her life: friends, her new world in general, and especially her old world. "How can she ever go back now that this is a part of her life?"

A third issue that this young woman presented with was seizurelike behaviors. Our work around this issue involved trying to discern whether these were purely organic in nature or involved a more hysterical component. This in turn fed back into her immigration issues and where she could get free medical help. She was an illegal immigrant. If it was confirmed that she was having organic seizures, how could she drive? How would this impact the rest of her life here, especially her legal status?

She eventually decided to go home and has been back in Brazil for 3 years now. Evidently, some of her issues have been resolved in that she has not become one of those immigrants that goes back and forth. One thing that this case illustrated for me about working with Latino/a clients was the importance of developing a resource list of low fee and Spanish-speaking clinics and services for legal advice, medical treatment, information about schools, and so forth. This is a vital resource in helping clients integrate into the community here.

Chapter Ten

Working With
Native American Clients:
An Interview With Jack Lawson

The only word that adequately captures the horrors that befell the Native Peoples of this continent at the hands of the White majority is "genocide." According to Churchill (1994), the population of Native Peoples in the United States fell from 12 million to 237,000 during the first 400 years of this country's history. During that period, almost 98% of their lands were expropriated (a fancy word for legal theft) by the American government. Today, 2 million survive, but are riddled by debilitating alcoholism, high suicide rates, unresolved historic grief, economic hardships, and loss of cultural ways. They represent a true American tragedy.

Unlike other Peoples of Color, Native Americans have found it impossible to assimilate upward in American society. While the other communities of Color struggle to increase their underrepresentation in the ranks of the middle class, in professional and white-collar job categories, in higher education, and so on, Native representation in these groups is all but nonexistent. Why these great disparities? First, if one were to construct a continuum of cultural differences with White Northern Europeans at one end and plot other cultural groups in America along that line, Native culture would most appropriately be placed at the far extreme. The radical differences between their ways and those of mainstream White culture set the stage for what was to occur. Their notions of stewardship of the land, fair play, honor, and dignity paled in comparison to mainstream values of capitalism and "might makes right" and made them easy victims in a clash of cultural systems. Second, so horrendous were the actions against Native Peoples that the victims needed to be silenced. To accomplish this, Native People were turned into stereotypes: savages of the frontier, drunken Indians, Pocahontas, mascots for sports teams, and emblems

for automobiles. Regarding the latter, Kivel (1996) suggests various mechanisms of denial such as minimizing estimates of the number of Native Americans who lived here, questioning the vitality and stability of their culture,
picturing the genocide as a natural process with a life of its own, and attributing their demise to biological inferiority. Third, for generations, the government systematically destroyed Native culture and alienated individuals from
their traditions and customs. Our guest expert, Jack Lawson, describes their
loss of identity and disconnection from tradition as the source of all contemporary Native woes.

Jack Lawson has worked in the field of alcohol and drug treatment, primarily with Native People, for over 22 years. Currently, he provides treatment
services to Native inmates in the Oregon State Prison System, is lead trainer for
the Oregon State Alcohol and Drug Office's cultural diversity training program, and works as a counselor in a wilderness treatment program for the
Siletz tribe in central Oregon. Ethnically, he is a member of the Creek Nation.

The Interview

Author: Could you first talk about your own ethnic background and how it has
led to your work in alcohol and drug treatment?

Lawson: I am a Creek. My family is originally from Oklahoma. I was born in
California and moved to Oklahoma when I was about 6 years old, and
then moved back to California when I was 10 years old, where we continued to live. While in Oklahoma, I remember attending ceremonies and
gatherings. Feasts, singing, and dancing are part of my memories of that
time. After returning to California, I lost contact with my relatives in
Oklahoma. As a consequence of moving back to California, I was separated from my Native culture and traditions. I attended public schools all
my life, and for the most part, the information I received about Native
Americans has been negative and based on stereotypes. Most western
movies portrayed us as drunks, heathens, violent, and dirty, which supported the information I received in the schools. I knew I was a Native
American, but I didn't have any way of accessing positive information
about who I was racially and culturally. Growing up in a situation where
I was not exposed to my own culture and traditions left me lost as to who
I was and open to accepting what others said about Native people. One of
the first signs of oppression is when you start believing other people's
version of history about yourself. I seemed to have only numb feelings
about my Native identity back then.

Both my mother and stepfather were alcohol dependent. After their
separation, my stepfather died in a fire. My mother remarried when I was
about 16 and has quit drinking. During high school, I developed an alcohol addiction. I took to alcohol like birds to flight. In retrospect, I realized

what I was struggling with was issues of internalized racism and, as a result of it, a variety of self-destructive behavior. I received my first message about recovery from a couple of Native Americans who were active in Alcoholics Anonymous while serving in a military jail. After a couple of false attempts at sobriety, I was able to catch onto the program. My first 2 years of recovery were made possible by strict attendance at AA meetings. Several years later, I had the opportunity to attend my first sweat lodge ceremony. Experiencing it seemed to make all the difference in the world for me. It directed my recovery in a way that would not have been possible without access to my culture and identity as a Native person. It was through exposure to the traditions of my People that allowed me for the first time to develop long-term relationships with others and good connections with my community. As a result of this experience, I began to understand the influence of culture and identity in the recovery process and the influence of people who can teach these cultural ways and traditions to us. My own recovery experience taught me what has to happen for other Native People. It has been a real blessing to be exposed to people knowledgeable in the ways of our culture and traditions, who could and did teach me about myself, about who I am, and where I came from. Having those mentors in my life, with their understanding of Native ways and identity issues, has allowed me to access areas of my life that otherwise would have remained invisible to me. I would have been left with a substantial void inside. Learning how I, as well as my People, reacted to being oppressed by oppressing others and losing ourselves in destructive behavior and thinking has made it possible for me to bring that understanding to the treatment process and to others who are still suffering from mental health and addiction problems so that they, too, can transcend those barriers for themselves.

Author: How would you define Native Americans or Native People as a group and what characteristics do they share?

Lawson: Native People comprise over 350 different tribes and languages that are unique to this continent. We are both very different and very similar. There is not, for example, one monolithic religion that belongs to all Native People. We have many languages, cultures, and many religions. We understand these differences, as we always have. But today, we are focusing more on our commonalities, on those things that pull us together. Paramount among these are historical experiences. As a group, we have all been systematically subjected to colonization, to the effects of losing our language and our culture, and to governmental policies that have been destructive to our People and eventually led us to a variety of social and health problems. These, in turn, have divided us in relation to ourselves and into differences in levels of acculturation. There are people that range from very traditional to fully assimilated, and differ enormously in how they relate to their culture and identity.

Differences among Native Peoples are small in comparison to those things that set us apart from members of the dominant culture. I think we stand apart both because of a value system that is qualitatively different and a set of historic experiences that cannot really be understood by dominant culture. When I take a look at the behavior of Native People, the first thing that strikes me is that we keep to ourselves, are very insular and private, especially in comparison to members of the dominant culture. Some of this is certainly dictated by culture. But for Native Peoples it is also a matter of self-protection. This is because of a shared sense of historical oppression and victimhood. The historical experiences of genocide and culturicide have left a deep mark upon our thinking and feelings, which is all the more tragic because our only "crime" was being on this land first. Everyone else that is in America today has come from somewhere else, but as Native People, this is the land from which we originated. We believe that we were created here. This is where our People have come from. It is an intricate part of who we are: how we define our communities and our mental health. When we view many of the problems that have arisen in our communities, we know they arise because of the loss of our land and our way of life that is so tied to the land. And of all the peoples in America today, we have been the least welcome.

The process of becoming an "American" for most citizens involved willingly giving up one's cultural heritage or identity in order to assimilate into the dominant culture and its values. This has been a very damaging process for Native People. We did not ask to be part of this process; it was forced upon us. Native People experienced enormous and longstanding traumas in their lives as a result of the assimilation process. And it is not an experience that many dominant culture people can really identify with: having your religion outlawed, having your language outlawed, and living in a world that has devalued your very existence. And that brings about feelings of justified anger that are present in our Native communities. Anger is everywhere, and it plays itself out in different ways as our People respond to both historical and ongoing oppression. It comes out in the form of self-destructive behavior, alcoholism and drug addiction, suicide, and homicide. We have become very different as a result of our historical experiences in "America," and these differences have to be paid attention to in the counseling setting. Our mental health issues involve the forced imposition of the dominant culture's value system over our indigenous value system and have resulted in vast conflicts and misunderstandings as well as much resentment and mistrust that exist in our community.

Culturally, Native People tend to be nonintrusive and nondirective. They let people make up their own minds. If people come and seek advice, it will be given, but not offered. Life is experienced as an interconnected entity. Nature, the People, the community all intertwine and depend upon each other for meaning and existence. We also tend to be very spiritual in our orientation, and the underlying force of our spiritual beliefs comes from the geology of the area from which we come. That spirituality infuses the community and becomes its base. It is central to the identity of each person and gets expressed through various religious and cultural practices. The creation stories of each people, for example, are set in the geographic area from which they came. The Navajo and the Hopi believe that they came up through the center of the world, and that center is located in their sacred places. For the Modoc people of central Oregon, their creation story is built around the lava beds of northern California, and they believe that humanity enters the world through the creation center which is located there. All things come from our ties to the land, and all Native People are joined in their commonality with the Turtle Island, as we refer to the continent.

Author: Could you describe some of the names that have been used historically to describe and identify Native Peoples and the general process of naming within the culture?

Lawson: In regard to names, there are the names that we call ourselves, and then there are the names that other people have given us. Most familiar to dominant culture is the term Indian. It is actually a misnomer. It comes from the time that Europeans first landed on this continent. Christopher Columbus mistakenly believed he had landed on the coast of India, and hence, we got tagged with the name Indian, which has over time taken on a pejorative meaning for us. In spite of the fact that the term has been prevalent in describing us, it carries no significance in our world. At some point, we as a People decided to take control of how we identify ourselves. The process began with the term Native American, which signifies that we come from this continent. But then, because we predate the naming of this continent and the Americas, we have begun to look at ourselves as the Indigenous People or First People of this land.

Outside of these more political distinctions, we also have names which we prefer to use and with which we more closely identify ourselves. There are tribal names and affiliations, such as Creeks, Choctaw, Crow, and so on. There are often clan names within the tribes, and then there are individual names: how we identify ourselves personally. Many of us have a Christian name that was given to us. But we also have personal names that are received through ceremony, a spiritual name that is often kept secret and used only for special occasions. It is important to realize that Native People vary greatly in which of the various terms they prefer, and to some extent, our choices say something about where we stand politically and culturally. Some of us still refer to ourselves as Native American, and others prefer Indigenous People. Sadly, there are still many who do not care or feel anything about who they are.

When first making contact with a Native client, it is perfectly appropriate to ask where they are from, what their tribal affiliation is, and how they prefer to identify themselves. I think we get into trouble when we don't do that and start making assumptions or just randomly use a term without being respectful enough to ask.

Asking about this information is probably a good way to begin contact. In mainstream America, people are identified primarily by what kind of work they do. We don't ask people what they do for a living. Instead, we ask each other, "Where are you from?" or "Who are your people?" This is because we come from a relationship-based culture, and our relationships are defined by our communities, our relatives, and our tribal affiliations. We socially locate ourselves by our human connections, not by our activities or jobs. Two last points. Spiritual names are sacred and private, and used only during ceremonies. It is considered inappropriate to inquire about these names unless they are spontaneously offered. In addition to Christian names, nicknames are very commonly used in Native communities. One might go an entire lifetime calling someone by a nickname and never know their given name.

Author: We have already talked some about history. Could you give us a nutshell version of historical events of which a provider should be aware?

Lawson: Historically speaking, Native People have suffered greatly at the hands of governmental policies and the actions of various religious groups. The experience of colonization is not just historical, but is still happening in our communities today. Loss of our culture, loss of religion, loss of community, and loss of family cohesion are contemporary realities. And these patterns, which are the consequences of oppression, continue to play themselves out emotionally and psychologically in the lives of our People. They are major issues that concern us deeply because they involve nothing less than the loss of our identities and integrity.

The boarding school experience is a particularly destructive example. Until the mid-1980s, many Native children were taken from their natural families and communities and forced to reside in boarding schools, where they were isolated from Native culture and ways, and then immersed in the dominant culture and Christian values. In these institutions, children were punished for speaking their Native tongue or practicing traditional ways. The motto of the time was, "Kill the Indian, but save the man," and its purpose was to eradicate all traces of Native culture and identity. Once accomplished, the child could be molded as desired, which meant shaping them into White Christians with mainstream values and attitudes. To make the task easier, the government outlawed our religion.

Perhaps most insidious about this practice was its effect on the Native family and its cohesion. When the children were taken out of their families, they were separated from their grandparents, parents, extended family, aunts, uncles, community, and so on. For generations, many Native American children were robbed of the nurturing of their families, deprived of the opportunity to learn parenting skills and other cultural lessons that would have enabled them to raise healthy families of their own. These children were forced to reside in institutions that were harsh and brutal. Some of our elders believe that our many social problems stem from the boarding school experience. Many of the children, as adults, remained isolated from families, no longer able to communicate because their language had been beaten out of them. They felt no comfort returning to their communities and were generally left alone to deal with the many internal issues that had been created as a result of growing up in the schools: low self-esteem, negative feelings about being Native, and a deep self-hatred. We can now see very clearly how generations of such experiences have impacted our communities and made them into what they are today.

We have begun to look at the consequences of the loss of our culture and realize that some Native People have come to internalize the stereotypes Whites hold about them. As a result, they have become those stereotypes: the subtle ones and the not so subtle ones, the "drunken Indian," the "lazy Indian." How can all those negative stereotypes not affect us? I am thinking of one of my uncles. He once told me that during high school, he very much wanted to go on to college. He went to see a school counselor and was strongly discouraged from going on. "Native People tend to be better with their hands," he was told and encouraged to pursue a trade. And so, with that advice, he didn't go to college, but went on to a trade school. He also went on to become alcoholic and drug dependent, and has since been in recovery. He attributes a lot of his problems to that stereotype and how believing in it changed his life. So for some of us, it is all too easy to live down to the stereotypes and to begin thinking about ourselves in self-deprecating terms—that we are not very smart or that we are only good with our hands and that we are destined to become alcoholic. These issues—residual effects of the boarding schools and stereotypes—are still being played out in our present-day experience. But fortunately, there has been a growing movement among many Native Peoples to regain our self-identity, to regain cultural pride, to regain our self-respect, and to learn about the traditions of our families, tribe, and People.

Author: Let's switch focus and begin to look at issues related to help giving and treatment. What factors influence how Native People go about seeking help?

Lawson: When Native People become involved in treatment programs, it's usually because of some external motivating force. That is, they are mandated either because of trouble with the law, family problems, child protective services, or the like. Generally speaking, that's how most people will come to be involved with outside agencies. Sometimes the tremendous anger and mistrust that Native People feel prevent them from seeking help outside of their community. Sometimes it is discrimination against them that serves as a barrier to accessing treatment. When you do find Native People coming into your agencies by themselves seeking help or assistance, they often are assimilated or bicultural—those who are more familiar and comfortable with White institutions and practices.

As a result of these patterns, there is a movement among various tribes to develop mental health and addiction services within our own communities so that people no longer have to choose between White services or no services at all. The hallmark of this trend is the creation of culturally relevant services. Culturally relevant means that the treatment process is infused with Native cultural values, that treatment goals make sense to Native sensibilities, that the need and value of developing positive ethnic identity are acknowledged, and that services are relevant to the lives and daily existence of the people being served. It also means that services are provided in a manner that is culturally comfortable to Native People. This trend is extremely important because the fact is that Native People usually experience less success in programs designed for mainstream White clients. Cultural barriers are a major obstacle to successful treatment in any program.

Author: Are there any other things you would like to say about the nature of family, community, and culture among Native People that have relevance for human service providers?

Lawson: Family structure in Native communities is very different from the nuclear family that predominates in dominant culture. Among Native Peoples, extended families are more typical, where an aunt may also act in the role of the mother or the grandparents raise the children or an uncle is the primary teacher for a youth or cousins are treated as brothers and sisters. Traditionally, responsibility for child care is communal. Also included in the family structure are clans, which are determined by kinship, and bands, which are people living in the same locale.

There are and have been many obstacles for the Native American family. As mentioned previously, the boarding school experience left many people devastated. Many of our social problems stem from them. Having been forced into these institutions, children were separated from an environment where they would have been socialized and reared culturally by parents, grandparents, aunts, and uncles and placed in an often harsh environment which did not recognize Native American beliefs as having any value. Today, alcoholism is our number one health problem with 100% of all Native Americans affected, either directly or indirectly. In the age group of 16 to 21, we lead the nation per capita in suicides and higher than national rates of diabetes. Currently, our average life span is 45. These statistics attest to the problems faced in the Native American community and more privately by family members, and most of these are linked to the destruction of the cultural family.

Other disruptions for the family come from state children services agencies that routinely adopt our Native children out to non-Native homes. Often in conjunction with religious organizations or acting on stereotypical beliefs about Native American families, these agencies disregard the critical importance of Native culture for these children. There are many horror stories from the past of White people coming into Native American communities and removing children. Fortunately, this is a practice which has been stopped by implementation of the Indian Child Welfare Act of 1978, which reestablished tribal authority over the adoption of Native children. Even though our rights have been reinforced, we are constantly struggling with agencies who are working to undermine the law. By these few examples, it is obvious how there has been a basis for the development of mistrust of social service agencies, a feeling that continues today.

Oppression has had a significant effect on our family structure. Some Native People have decided not to teach their children about the culture, language, or traditions because they do not want their children to experience the same treatment of degradation and rejection from the outside world. Others have successfully made the transition into dominant society, taking on mainstream values and religious beliefs and living happily. There are also many who have managed to hang onto and practice cultural traditions and beliefs, learning from elders who have been able to share their wisdom with a younger generation. Some families mix traditional and dominant cultural ways. Clearly, we are a community in transition, adjusting to significant changes in social structure and identity, with much from the past to set right. But in spite of the historical and contemporary obstacles, our Native community is healing itself. We have weaknesses and strengths within the Native families. We have oppression and discrimination to overcome. We have social problems with addiction and abuse. But our People are making a comeback in pride and dignity by reclaiming indigenous family values and recovery.

Author: What are the kinds of problems with which a Native client might present?

Lawson: One hundred percent of Native People are affected either directly or indirectly by alcoholism. Underlying this are a host of complex problems related to the loss of culture, identity, and disruption of the family unit, all symptomatic of a long history of genocide and oppression. There are also a lot of anger and anger-related issues, depression and hopelessness, health problems, and unusually high rates of suicide and homicide, especially among the young. There has also been a serious increase in the diagnosis of HIV in our community, mostly related to IV drug use. Among Native People who are incarcerated, alcohol and drugs are a major contributor to their incarceration.

Author: Does class or other socioeconomic issues play any role in these various problems?

Lawson: Definitely. Unemployment rates can be astronomical on a reservation, and the same is true for Native Peoples living in urban areas. The Relocation Act of the 1940s was one in a series of efforts by the government to encourage Native Peoples to leave the reservation, move to cities where jobs are more plentiful, and become part of the American mainstream. That was the ultimate goal. However, the reality was not quite as simple as that. Although some did relocate successfully, many found the experience traumatic. In the move from reservation to city, many traditional ties were lost. Kinship ties weakened with distance, and some people became disassociated from their relatives and community. Many ended up living marginal existences in the skid row areas of cities, and those who followed them from the reservations would tend to migrate toward these same enclaves. What the logic of the Relocation Act did not envision was the reality that most of these people, familiar with a very different kind of existence, did not have the dominant cultural tools to survive successfully, let alone prosper in such a foreign environment where they were met with substantial discrimination and rejection.

The move to the city was also instrumental in cutting off many from traditional cultural ties to their People. In addition, certain patterns of connection between the reservation and urban settings began to emerge. First, it was not uncommon for individuals to move back and forth between the two, and for many, this became a lifelong pattern. Second, animosities and various conflicts developed between people from these increasingly divergent lifestyles, with each looking down on the other. In general, some people in the urban centers may tend to view those on the reservation as backward, their ways antiquated, rustic. Those on the reservation in turn tend to see the urban dwellers as having lost their way, as suffering from the same malaise as the White man. Today, increasing numbers of Native People are returning to their traditions and culture in both locations and striving for unity.

There is an important cultural point here as well. In mainstream culture, success is measured in economic terms, and socioeconomic success implies a certain lifestyle that depends on having sufficient monetary resources, accumulating wealth, regular employment, living according to a certain style, and so forth. Our traditional cultural values are very different from this. Our wealth is located in the richness of our culture, tradition, ceremonies, and in the richness of our lifestyle. Difficulties arise when a person tries to live by a cultural value system that is not based on material economic gain within a broader culture that is so absolutely dedicated to it. These are not value systems that are easily integrated. Such clashes set the stage for Native Peoples losing our lands and having our language and culture outlawed in the first place. Today, we struggle with a similar conflict around remaining attached to our traditional way of life that cares little about accumulating economic wealth. It comes down to the question of divergent value systems. Those who are bicultural know what they would need to do to be successful, and that would be to eliminate their culture and perform accordingly, but that would go against their beliefs, which are based in indigenous culture and tradition. The integration of two such diverse value systems is difficult, to say the least.

Author: In making an initial assessment, what kinds of information do you feel it is important to collect from a Native client?

Lawson: Before getting too specific, I want to say something about cultural perspective and worldview. During any assessment process, it is vital—I can't emphasize this enough—that counselors and other human service providers be aware of their own cultural values, biases, and barriers, and understand clearly how they themselves have been influenced by culture. All behavior is derived from a cultural context as are treatment programs. If one is going to assess a client whose worldview is culturally different from one's own, then it is likely that, if the client displays culturally relevant behavior, it may well be labeled as "deviant" or "abnormal." For example, in dominant culture, a firm handshake is seen as a sign of honesty, sincerity, and straightforwardness, whereas if one encounters a person of traditional Native beliefs, a firm handshake is avoided because in our culture it is sometimes seen as being intrusive, rude, overbearing, and impolite. However, someone assessing that behavior from a dominant cultural perspective might construe it as reflecting dishonesty, nonassertion, withdrawal, and evasiveness. When working with people from different cultures, it's always important to validate their experience and existence in terms of their own cultural perspective. In order to do this, we as service providers must be aware of our own culture and how that culture affects our lives.

Assessments must be carried out within the framework of the client's own culture. It is important, however, to not let the client be your only source of information about their culture. This information needs to be balanced with information from their community as well. It's necessary that you reach out to our communities and listen to the people. It has been my experience that the more you learn about another's culture, the more open they are to you. Learn as much as you can. You get that information from the community through developing relationships. Go to the communities and events and develop relationships. This doesn't mean that you have to give up your own cultural values or beliefs. It does mean that you should to be able to understand and respect beliefs of others and evaluate their behavior from within their cultural context.

Perhaps the most important piece of information to gain about Native clients is where they fall on a continuum from assimilated to traditional. People that are assimilated will often feel uncomfortable around their own People, not knowing the behaviors and what is expected of them. They appear to be Native and possess all the physical features of being Native, but internally they're different. They may feel uneasy because of their lack of knowledge of traditional ways and may feel unaccepted because of it. Assimilated individuals tend to act differently than those who live by traditional values and possess a traditional belief system. The assimilated person may appear more talkative and open, even though there might be distrust. They will be the ones who know the rules of the program and of society in general. In short, they will have learned what one needs to do within dominant culture to survive. Traditional Native People present themselves as more reserved and quiet. But rather than being indicative of withdrawal, it comes from a cultural value of respect, nonintrusiveness, and honor.

What kind of information should you seek from a client? There is all the standard assessment material. Who was a person raised by? Family structure? Religion? But with Native People, what is important is to interpret this information through the filter of how they see themselves culturally. This would include identity development, involvement with the community, involvement with family, how family views its situation, whether or not traditional beliefs are practiced. Again, the distinction between assimilated and traditional is important because treatment methods may differ according to where a person falls on that continuum. By way of example, there was a doctor in Seattle who noticed that Native People weren't recovering as fast in the hospitals as he felt they should. They regularly spent longer periods in the hospital. One of the things he did was go to the elders of the Native community and started incorporating medicine people and traditional healers as part of the treatment process in the hospital. And recovery times shortened dramatically.

Author: Are there subgroups within the Native community that are particularly at risk?

Lawson: I believe that all Native People, especially children, are at risk for developing alcoholism or some other form of dependency. There are physiological issues—social, economic, and emotional ones as well. They have been passed down from generation to generation, and together create a "lump sum" of a risk for us as Native People. At one time, it was prevalent in our communities to accept alcoholism as a way of life. That is how we tended to cope with oppression and the discrimination in our lives. It became part of our continual grieving process. Although in many places this is still the norm, there are many of us who are beginning to take more control over our lives and find recovery.

Author: What suggestions can you give regarding developing rapport with Native clients?

Lawson: I believe we have to be aware of our own prejudices and biases and the way we regard people who are culturally and racially different from us. It is not a matter of learning to say or do the right things. Instead, we have to be aware of ourselves and the underlying issues that affect our clients. It's not about having to learn all the in's and out's. We are dealing with a very diverse population. It's impossible for me to say: "Well, this is the one thing you will need to say, or this is the one thing that you do in order to develop rapport." I would be merely creating a new stereotype. We are all going to make mistakes, and mistakes are a common thing in working with diverse cultures. But if one really comes from a place of acceptance and respect as a care provider, then that is going to translate into developing rapport with clients. As helpers, we all have a goal in mind: helping to develop a therapeutic relationship so that clients can heal themselves. But there is more than one road we can travel to get to the same place.

In order to develop rapport with Native clients, one has to learn to not be afraid of their anger. You can be sure that there is going to be mistrust and anger that may very well be directed toward you personally as a White provider. But if you can tolerate it, not be frightened by it, and just allow it to be expressed as honest communication, you will be on the road to making a connection. There is the possibility the client will see you as part of the White establishment and, as such, unlikely to be of any real help. Remember: Historically, Native Peoples have had their feelings discounted, been patronized and demeaned, and chronically abused by the system. You may be witnessing justified anger running rampant. In short, you may be stereotyped and lumped into this category of the enemy. The only way to get beyond this is to acknowledge your Whiteness and the feelings they are likely to project onto you as well as your general understanding of what they have experienced as a people. But be clear, the walls are not going to come down overnight, but only with time and patience. In addition, becoming aware of the effects oppression has on a people will aid in understanding self-destructive behavior, such as addiction being systemic to oppression.

Author: What else is important to know about working therapeutically with Native clients?

Lawson: I have provided services to both White and Native clients, and there are clearly some important differences. In the White groups, traditional counseling methods are effective. I am more direct and confrontational here, and the clients tend to respond positively. I use a very different approach with Native clients. We sit in a talking circle, but it is the issues we talk about that are important. The issues have to do with Native culture, identity, how they see themselves as Native People, the effects of stereotyping, justified anger, positive identity development, and ceremony. And we use ritual objects and ceremonies as part of the process: eagle feathers and pipes, smudging, sweat lodges, and so on, introducing our culture into the treatment process and acknowledging what they are going through ritually and with ceremonies. Such a process fits naturally with our cultural understanding of health and sickness. We also discuss the effects of oppression, while at the same time addressing the issues around denial, relapse prevention planning, and recovery maintenance.

As far as therapeutic styles with Native People, you will most likely be working with those who either know nothing of their culture or are bicultural. In both cases, I find that traditional counseling methods generally prove effective, but with the incorporation of cultural material. My approach with Native Americans is to use culture as an avenue to recovery because loss of culture and identity is the most basic problem that Native People face. In this regard, I assist clients in identifying their culture, how it has influenced them, how they came to lose touch with it, and how they may become reconnected to their culture. I also have them identify where they stand along the continuum between traditional and assimilated. At times, I come across clients who hide their issues behind culture or try to use it to get something for themselves. They use it as a "front," as a means of not dealing with treatment issues. The value of culture and community is not about what it can get you, but who you can become because of it. The challenge for non-Native service providers is to know the difference between clients using culture as a defense and when the Native culture is genuine.

I provide culturally relevant treatment services for the Native Americans incarcerated within the Oregon Department of Corrections who are dealing with their addictions. As a part of those services, I conduct a week-long alcohol and drug workshop and ongoing treatment groups that focus on Native American spirituality, ceremony, and recovery. As a part of the workshop, we utilize the talking circle, drumming and singing, sweat lodge ceremony, smudging with sweet grass or sage, use of eagle feathers and other sacred objects, and discuss issues which are relevant to their recovery. Through this service, many Native inmates have been given their first positive encounter with Native American culture and tradition. I believe this is an important thing to offer them: to be able to get in touch with their culture and to be able to have some experience with their traditions. Again, I see that as critical to recovery for Native American clients. But there are some diverse opinions about this within our communities. Some of our elders say, "They never sought out the culture while they were in the community. Why should we go to the institutions to provide them with anything cultural? When they get out of the institution, let them come to us." That's a valid point. But at the same time, I feel that it's important for a person's recovery to develop some cultural awareness. The issue of them learning it in the institutional setting is that often much of the learning comes from other inmates. So, information can get contaminated inside institutions.

Similar dynamics can occur in treatment in general, and that's why it's important for non-Native providers to have connections and resources in the Native community. It is clearly not productive for providers to exclusively learn about Native culture from their clients. Contact with the community will also give you a certain credibility. In working with our People on a regular basis, you just have to get out of your office and make contacts. We are a relationship-based culture.

Author: Finally, could you present a case that brings together the different issues and dynamics about which you have been talking?

Lawson: I am thinking of a client I'll call Joe. Joe came to a program that I once worked called Sweathouse Lodge. It was an inpatient alcohol and drug treatment program which focused heavily on traditional Native modes of healing. We used sweat lodges, brought in traditional people to speak, brought in medicine people, hosted spiritual gatherings, took clients to powwows, and did a lot of resocialization work. When Joe entered the program, he was 25 and very angry and mistrustful, not only toward the system, but toward the program as well. He had developed a severe alcohol and drug problem by the age of 17. His family had a long history of alcoholism. His parents knew nothing about their culture and traditions, and although he had a grandfather who was very traditional, he had only limited contact with him. Joe was mandated to the program by court order and was initially very resistant to treatment. While in the program, he experienced his first sweat lodge ceremony. It was a very positive experience for him, and he reported that during the ceremony, he felt for the first time some connection with his Native heritage and the value it might have for him. This motivated him to seek out further information about his own culture and traditions. In group therapy, he revealed harboring prejudicial and destructive thoughts about being Native. As a result of growing up in an alcoholic home, he had learned to equate being Native with being drunk and violent, as these were the only role models he had.

Through continuing positive contact with Native culture, both in the form of ceremonies and positive role models, he was able to begin to distinguish between what was truly cultural and what was internalized from negative stereotypes of Native People and culture. This in turn enabled him to develop a more positive cultural self-image, something which was totally lacking before coming to the program. He increasingly took pleasure in attending sweat lodge ceremonies, learned to drum and sing, learned more about Native values, and in time began to work at incorporating these values in his treatment plan. He became more open to attending AA and NA meetings and eventually involved himself more and more in the Native community. As part of treatment, he received a lot of very direct feedback from other Native clients and staff. He found it very helpful to hear others who had gone down a similar path of alcoholism and dysfunction "call him" on his self-destructive behavior, attitudes, thinking patterns, and lifestyle.

The eventual result was better feelings about himself, an emerging ethnic identity, and a positive sense of belonging to the Native community. During group therapy, he was able to make the connection between his own self-destructive ways and the lack of culture and traditions in his life. In short, participation in the program forced him to experience a powerful identity crisis and reformation, and it gave him an outlet and place to experience feelings that he thought were unique to him. After completion of the program, Joe continued to seek out sweat lodges and remained actively involved in community events. He has begun to take on some communal leadership roles and actively strives to encourage others to find recovery through their culture and traditions.

Chapter Eleven

Working With
African American Clients:
An Interview With Jimmie Turner

The term African American subsumes a diverse array of peoples including African Americans born in this country, Africans, and individuals from the West Indies and Central and South America. The trauma of slavery and a long history of racism have shaped and defined the African American experience in the United States. It is impossible to understand the African American psyche without keeping these two events clearly in mind. Kivel (1996) states the facts of slavery quite succinctly: "From 1619 until slavery ended officially in 1865, 10–15 million Africans were brought here, and another 30–35 million died in transport" (p. 121). The magnitude is staggering and even difficult to conceive. But that is not even the full story because there was also the systematic destruction of African culture and identity by the slavers and slave masters, the tearing apart of families, the creation of myths of inferiority and subhuman status to justify what was being done, and an entire nation that benefited greatly economically and socially from this cruel institution.

Racism replaced slavery as a vehicle for the continued exploitation of African Americans as well as a justification for continuing to deny them the equality guaranteed by the U.S. Constitution. As a People, they survived, grew strong, and fashioned a new culture in America, but continue to this day paying an awesome price for the color of their skin. Hacker (1992) argues that the United States is functionally "two nations," black and white, and that there is an enormous disparity in the access that these two groups have to the resources and benefits of this rich nation. The long list of statistical inequities—from average salaries to unemployment, from incarceration figures to education levels, from teenage pregnancies to poverty statistics—is staggering. African Americans have in turn been the "point men" for the struggle that has been waged against the inequality and social injustice that continues to exist in this country. Through the Civil Rights and various other social movements, they have been the voice of conscience in America, not allowing it to forget the grave injustices that are still very much alive. As Kivel (1996) suggests, they have been the "center of racial attention," and all other oppressed groups have learned from and modeled their fights after that of African Americans. But it is little wonder, as our guest expert Jimmie Turner points out, that African Americans mistrust and avoid seeking help from established White agencies and institutions. Their motives and agendas, throughout history and into this day, have just not proven to be trustworthy.

Jimmie Turner, PhD, is a clinical psychologist who has practiced in the private and public sectors for the past 25 years. He works in the Department of Psychiatry at Kaiser Permanente Medical Center, Oakland, California, and is a member of the core faculty at John F. Kennedy University's PsyD Program, Orinda, California. He has also taught at the Wright Institute, Berkeley, and the California School of Professional Psychology. He serves as a community consultant to various African American agencies and clinics as well as to the African American community in general.

The Interview

Author: Could you begin by talking about your evolution as an African American psychologist and what meaning that term has for you?

Turner: My training as a clinical psychologist began in graduate school at the University of California, Berkeley, after several years of volunteer community work in the late 1960s. My development as an African American psychologist was stimulated early by an internship at Mt. Zion Hospital's Department of Psychiatry in San Francisco. The department was psychoanalytically oriented, predominantly Jewish, and located in the heart of the Black community. I cannot imagine a more challenging way of beginning my training than the diversity of the Western Addition of San Francisco, the radical politics of the University of California, Berkeley, and Freud.

Following Mt. Zion, I joined the staff of an all-Black agency, Pacific Psychotherapy Associates, that was started by Drs. William Grier and Price Cobbs, the coauthors of *Black Rage*. Many of the all-Black agencies of that time didn't survive the Proposition 13 cuts and all of the economic changes over the years. That early experience highlighted a struggle that continues for me today, and that is trying to understand the relevance of fairly traditional psychotherapy theories for the African American community and for the communities of other oppressed people in general. The opportunity of working in an all-Black agency directly confronted me with the question of how to work with Black families and how to think about the cultural implications of diagnosis and treatment. Following Pacific Psychotherapy Associates, I treated children at Pacific Children's Center in Oakland, and then to Kaiser Permanente Oakland, an HMO, for the last 18 years. That's what I have done professionally in addition to teaching graduate students and private practice. The one thing I would add is that as an African American professional, my activities are not confined exclusively to what I do in the office or classroom. I'm often called upon to consult on community-related issues. I'm often involved in projects related to the public schools and issues that are confronting our young people today. I also speak at workshops on the problems confronting African American youth, particularly Black men. This is both by choice and a requirement of a community-focused African American psychology. To remain a creative and relevant psychologist in the African American community of Oakland requires a great deal more than just the traditional roles that I might otherwise play.

Author: How would you define African Americans as a comprehensive group and what characteristics do they share?

Turner: When I think of African Americans, I think of the wonderful evolutionary way that the whole issue of naming ourselves has emerged in our community and the various subgroups that are a part of the diversity of the African American community. African Americans are comprised of people who are almost completely African and those who have a great deal of European. The variations in skin color, body size, and physical characteristics are often extreme, ranging from very dark complected to individuals who are practically white. Friends and colleagues who have traveled to Africa have reported that Africans would say, "Oh, you're from the Ivory Coast," because you have the body type and/or physical characteristics of that region of Africa.

The African American community contains several distinct levels of social class. Some social scientists argue that there are only two classes: the middle and above and the underclass. The underclass is made up of people who dropped out of the mainstream due to alcoholism and drug addiction, major mental health problems, psychological casualties of the Vietnam War, homelessness, and others who have just worn out in the face of unrelenting racism and oppression. The working poor are those African Americans who strive to maintain family-centered values and traditions, but are not economically prosperous enough to enjoy the resources of the middle class. Acquiring a good education remains of high value to the working poor Black community. Class status in the African American community is often dubious and unpredictable and vulnerable to political economics and discrimination. Blacks can work for 20 years at companies like Standard Oil and General Motors, command an income of nearly six figures per year, only with downsizing to find themselves slipping into a lower class existence in a very short period of time. This has often been the plight of African Americans who are part of the "middle class" without graduate education and who work at the post office, public transit systems, or in corporate America. Many have done reasonably well rearing their children, purchasing homes, and so forth.

The upper middle class is what I would call the "Black bourgeoisie" of today. Following the Great Depression, there were only two distinct classes of Blacks: the Black bourgeoisie and the poor. The Black bourgeoisie are primarily educated Blacks who do not identify with the working class. They aspire to have their children attend the best colleges, marry within their privileged group, and maintain a professional career-oriented existence. The very rich (professional athletes and entertainers) are in a class by themselves. They are very prominent role models for youth in the African American community. On the whole, African Americans tend to be socioeconomically overdependent on the general economy. If one loses his or her job, that could negatively impact their economic plight for the rest of their lives. This is not usually the case for people with greater access to economic resources in general. Youngsters who are involved in the rap counterculture glorification of the gangster hip-hop, "player fast life" can be found in all class levels in the Black community. Likewise, the church and religion command a presence in every subgroup of the community.

Other demographics? African American men are still dying at 59 and in their early 60s. Thirty or forty years ago, African Americans lived predominantly in the South, but now we are living all over the United States. There is now a movement back to the South, especially to Georgia, Florida, and Alabama. Demographics shift according to the economic opportunities for African Americans. Finally, there is the whole issue of migration from the suburbs to the inner cities, the inner city preponderance of African Americans, the attempts of the middle class to move outside of the city, and now the return to the city, as they are finding their way out of poverty. These shifts are as much a part of the African American migration as they are a part of this country in general.

Author: Let's turn to the question of names. What names or terms do individuals within the African American community use to describe and identify themselves?

Turner: Group names? In my lifetime, I was clearly colored; Negro when I got to school, first grade; we were Negroes, but in the community—I grew up in Arizona—we were called colored people. In school, because they taught the three major races—the Negroids, the Caucasoids, and the Mongoloids—we were Negroes. Then, in the beginning of the Black Pride movement, we became Afro Americans, and finally Black. Black was a much stronger statement about power. Afro American was the beginning of the Pan Africa movement and in some way was intertwined with the Black Pride movement. There was a big intellectual discussion about being Afro Americans, and the people who favored that term were mainly intellectual, college students, who were honoring our connections with Africa. On the streets, in the communities, when James Brown sang "I'm

Black and I'm Proud," Black became the identification of the people, the group name. As the Black Pride movement dissipated and as we've moved more toward diversification, African American has become the current way that the community is naming itself. There are many people who struggled during the Civil Rights and Black Pride movements who use Black and African American interchangeably and don't apologize for Black. Black is not considered a negative term. African American is the most contemporary, but naming is as diverse and changeable as the community itself. I can remember when Black was beautiful, many of the older generation were not comfortable with being called Black. They never got comfortable with it, and probably aren't terribly comfortable with being called African Americans either. There are a lot of people who feel White, who had a great deal of biracial White blood, who were quite comfortable with being called colored, and still are. Politically, the issue of naming takes on a very different function than what's happened socially and what's part of the cultural community norms. As far as working with members of my community, I think the term African American is most appropriate. I think it's important for a counselor to know what is the most respectable political name.

Author: Can you highlight for us key historical events in a nutshell? What historical experiences should providers be aware of in relation to the African American community and African American clients?

Turner: I think it's important historically to recognize that Africans came from all over the African continent. If you read *Before the Mayflower* and other historical accounts of slavery, it is well documented that slaves were captured throughout the continent of Africa, transported to Northern and Western Africa, put on ships, and brought to this country, the Caribbean, and so on. There were different languages, spiritual practices, customs, and experiences on those slave ships during the Middle Passage. From the beginnings in America, African Americans were quite diverse but thrown into a common experience. It was probably the strength of the diversity that determined who survived and what part of African American culture that has continued to exist. Certainly the "peculiar institution" of slavery—the need to treat us as property, to be used as servants and to work in the fields, the whole economic aspect of slavery—is very important. In counseling people, the reality of slavery is often forgotten. We see the kind of behaviors that people currently bring to us and have no sense of what I call "carryovers" from the slavery experience. The whole issue of whipping children and corporal punishment are probably carryovers from slavery. We report people and call corporal punishment "abuse" without having any sense of the roots and meanings of that behavior.

What else is critical? The whole experience of freedom and emancipation and the fact that African Americans were not all freed at the same time. The "Juneteenth" phenomenon occurred in Texas and in Oklahoma. People didn't get the news that the Emancipation Proclamation had been signed until the 19th of June. So some people were free while others were still slaves, and for years, Oklahoma and Texas maintained illegal forms of slavery because of the way in which freedom was delayed. The whole promise of Reconstruction following slavery looked a lot like the War on Poverty programs of the 1960s. People were offered 40 acres and a mule and an opportunity to go to school. There were Black folks in Congress, and many Black-owned businesses developed. Then came the emergence of lynching and the withdrawal of Reconstruction, the prominence of the Ku Klux Klan, racial oppression, violence, and destruction. Recall the Rosewood lynchings which destroyed early efforts of that African American community to thrive after slavery and the beginning of the whole concept of the miseducation of Black youth. Finally, the Great Depression was a major event in the lives of African Americans as well. To be poor and discriminated against in a time when the whole country was struggling to feed itself was no small matter and required heroic challenges to survival.

The Black Renaissance of the 1930s is an important piece that people need to understand because so much of the literature and art, the emergence of jazz, all the creative aspects of the Black community are embedded there. It continues to inform creativity today. The literary contributions: Richard Wright, James Baldwin, Chester Himes with the whole mystery writing, Langston Hughes, the Black poets. All of that period is very exciting.

After the Great Depression, the Civil Rights movement spearheaded by the Southern Christian Leadership Conference, the Student Nonviolent Coordinating Committee, the NAACP, and the whole relationship of Blacks and Jews struggling to fight for civil rights are all very important parts of African American history. Similarly, the Black Pride movement and the emergence of the Black Panther party here in Oakland and throughout the country along with the war in Vietnam and the disproportionate number of African American men who were drafted must be given serious consideration. I recently saw the movie *Glory* again and was reminded of how Black men were segregated in the military: the Tuskegee Airmen, etc. And finally what has happened post-Vietnam and post-Black Pride movement: the blight in the community with drugs and alcohol, the miseducation that's occurring, and the decimation of the community that we're seeing now. People working with African Americans need to have an appreciation for all of this. I would particularly recommend the works of Larone Bennett, Jr., his historical landmark accounts of Blacks in America.

Author: I would like to switch focus and look at issues related to treatment and seeking help. Could you discuss some of the factors that influence the ways African Americans go about seeking mental health services?

Turner: The health and the mental health care systems have traditionally been mistrusted by African Americans. Early on, psychologists in particular saw slaves as the embodiment of mental illness. The earliest diagnostic categories for African Americans appeared during slavery. One diagnosis, for example, suggested that African Americans were inherently unable to survive without the care and benevolent protection of slavery. When freed, slaves were expected to develop an inability to cope or function. Such logic obviously served to justify the institution of slavery. For years, the only experience African Americans had with mental health was when someone became psychotic or had a violent outburst, received heavy doses of antipsychotic medication, and was placed in a mental institution. Similarly, the experience with health care in general has been painful. Dentists were prone not to use painkillers to pull African American teeth, and extractions were often the only dental care that was permitted. The Tuskegee experiments were perhaps the most dramatic example of systematic abuse of African Americans by the health care system: the withholding of treatment for syphilis while pretending to perform worthwhile research. It was not until the beginning of the community mental health movement and the prevalence of more African American health care providers that African Americans became more willing to accept these services. In general, people just avoided health care unless it was absolutely necessary, and life expectancy statistics certainly reflect the consequences.

There are also cultural attitudes that operate against help seeking. One is that you don't share your personal business outside of the community or even outside of the family, especially with someone from another ethnic group. If it becomes absolutely necessary, you only share enough to get the issue settled or the job done. African Americans are not likely to come to psychotherapy for free association. It's not safe nor is it part of the community's norm to free-associate. Free-floating fantasy has historically met with the whip because it was a mark of idleness and lack of focus and purpose. In short, we are focusing on a group of people for whom it has not been in their best interest to be "good patients." Often, African Americans are mandated to mental health facilities by the courts for substance abuse, domestic violence, and child abuse. Obviously, forced treatment affects the motivation and willingness to participate openly and freely.

There is also a belief in the African American community that many problems can be handled spiritually and/or religiously. If you go to church, live a "good" Christian life, and turn your life over to God, then issues of substance abuse, marital disharmony, difficulties in child-rearing, depression, and alienation, will go away or at least be handled in the context of the church. For many African Americans, church is where their mental health needs are met.

During the Black Pride period of the 1960s and early 70s, it was a symbol of health that an African American would request a Black therapist if mental health services were needed. The Community Mental Health Act of 1963 had made readily available, for the first time, services in the community provided by people from diverse backgrounds. Home visiting teams and community advisory boards were actively involved in preventive mental health services. African Americans were beginning to see psychology and their lives as not completely separate entities. A number of adults began thinking about the value of talking to someone about their problems, conflicts, and concerns. They would request a Black therapist because it was the correct social-political thing to do. This was somewhat of a renaissance for African Americans and mental health services. Today, if African Americans insist on only seeing a Black therapist, it usually reflects a lack of trust of non-Black therapists and severe trauma and woundedness emotionally. African Americans who are open to mental health services, especially from the middle and upper middle classes, are generally sophisticated enough to get their needs met regardless of the race of the therapist. They tend to be less concerned about the race of the therapist and more about the accessibility and affordability of services.

There is community pressure to solve problems on your own and to stay as far away from the mental health facility as possible. It is believed that you ought to be able to help yourself. "How can you trust others to take care of you when it's been the system that made you ill in the first place?" Depression, stress, and trauma are part of everyday experience. A person is prone to go to mental health services when it's been their experience to seek help for such problems. But if the community norm is that solutions to traumatic life experiences are part of community life, then you are not likely to go and see an outsider for help in dealing with difficulties, especially in regard to racism.

Author: You have already made a number of references to family and community and their centrality in African American culture. What do you think a potential provider of services to African American clients should know about family and community issues?

Turner: When I think about the African American community, I am immediately aware of the importance of the Black family. The importance of family is probably one of those values that came over with slaves and was strengthened by segregation. Family ties have been important to survival in restricted and confined quarters and protection against the outer world. But family represents a highly complex system in the African American community. There can be family members who are very significantly bonded but have no biological kinship ties. These are often referred to as "play brothers and sisters" as well as godparents.

African American families are also very diverse. Some are single-parent-headed households, with elders residing in the home and young people staying well into their late twenties until it is economically feasible to move out. There are any number of different configurations of extended families in the African American community. In the South and more rural communities, family members often purchase homes in close proximity and practice rituals like getting together on Sundays for large family dinners, celebrating births and deaths, and commemorating other important events like Juneteenth celebrations and Kwanzaa. Education is highly valued and commands a prominent place in family rituals. Graduations from elementary, junior high, and high school can command as much attention as graduating from college in some African American communities.

The sense of community differs greatly in rural and urban Black communities. Urbanization has undermined the more rural customs that added to the richness of the Black family. The family structure has been injured by generations of welfare recipients, public housing, and the institutionalization of poverty. The stress on individualism to cope with the competition of city life constantly challenges community attachments. The community has become more important as a resource in urban America than the traditional family. This is largely because small family units are not supported by community and at times have undermined the more rural customs that provided some of the richness of the Black family. We see more individual existences in the cities and a sense of a lack of community attachment. The community has become more important as a resource than the family itself in urban America. This is because small extended family units are not supported by the community and at times are under attack. A grandmother living in public housing is not permitted to bring her grandchildren for extended visits. She would lose her place in public housing. So there are many ways in which the experience of the Black family in urban America is very different than the rural, and that tension continues to build and grow.

When I think about the value of the community and the family, I am reminded of the cultural belief that life is determined by chance, fate, and luck. Although spirituality helps to maximize one's chances and to determine one's fate, still in large measure, life is a gamble and one's community a base. Things are just not necessarily based on the traditional Protestant work ethic. One thus has to be far more creative in tolerating the groupings, the family, and the rituals of the community. It doesn't matter how far you have transcended the group or culture; you're always considered a part of it. You never get terribly far away. Whether you've been highly educated or moved from the South to the North, you are encouraged to maintain a presence in the community and in the culture as well. A different side of this same feeling finds expression in the empathy, acceptance, and support African Americans feel for other oppressed groups. There's sort of a kinship among oppressed groups and an identification with the underdog. We see it in sports, where the Dallas Cowboys have become the traditional "America's team." Even though they have some great African American players, African American fans can really get passionate about someone beating them, say, the Denver Broncos. "Kill 'em!"

Author: Next, I would like to ask about the kind of problems that are most commonly brought by African Americans into treatment.

Turner: African American patients suffer from the same forms of mental illness and stress as anyone else. I have seen symptoms ranging from classic obsessive-compulsive disorders, to paranoid schizophrenia, and so forth. But the majority of African Americans seek mental health services for problems in living and a preponderance of life stress issues. Many come to treatment because stress issues are affecting their jobs, families, relationships, and/or their children are having difficulties in life. That's going to be the majority of African American patients that come to any treatment facility. Instead of viewing these patients as merely externalizers of deeper internal problems, I prefer to see it as an opportunity to introduce people who aren't necessarily psychologically minded to psychotherapy and address their emerging issues in that context.

African American patients often somaticize their problems. They come in with any number of aches and pains as a way to talk about their depression. Depression is certainly a major issue in the African American community, but it's often not viewed as such because chronic fatigue, headaches, back pains, and other forms of somatization are considered normal complaints. Certainly, chemical dependency is a major problem in the African American community. Often, African Americans seek treatment for chemical dependency because it affects their jobs, families, and kids, not because it's a common way of coping with the stress that has gotten out of hand. In general, it is not something that is done voluntarily. More typically, people are mandated to come and, once they're there, are able to benefit from chemical dependency treatment.

The whole issue of eating disorders and how African Americans relate to them is an interesting one. Generally, they don't seek professional treatment for eating disorders. The concern for getting enough sustenance is probably so tied to slavery, the Great Depression, and discrimination that people don't often see overeating as a disorder, but sometimes as a mark of prosperity. When you are working with an African American obese person, you've got to be clear that they identify their size as a problem, or you may discourage their participation in treatment.

What I am seeing a lot more of is suicide and homicide among late adolescent African American youth. Most don't seek treatment. A Black psychologist developed the concept of *quasimorticide.* This is the notion that if you look at vehicular manslaughter involving young Black people, you'll often find a suicidal intent in what appeared to be an accidental death. Or if you look at some of the shooting and killing of gang members, you'll find that someone stepped out in front of an Uzi as if to say, "Shoot me! Because I am ready to die." This phenomenon of quasimorticide, which often gets labeled and disregarded as just another instance of gang violence, is part of a growing problem of adolescent suicide in the Black community. Tupak Shakur was clearly a suicidal young man who eventually got himself killed. He'd been shot multiple times on five separate occasions and continued to put himself in danger until his eventual death.

Author: Could you talk about issues of identity and group belonging as they affect members of the African American community?

Turner: Boy, this is one that has gotten a lot of attention—the whole notion of
role models in the community and how many homes in the Black community are headed by single parents. Do you necessarily need both parents to provide the models that are needed for healthy child development? Black families, and especially extended families, often have a male
figure in single-parent homes, whether it's a boyfriend, uncle, grandfather, or some other male that carries that role model function for both
boys and girls. We've seen the importance of a male figure for girls as
well as for boys, but especially for boys. So the question comes down to
the following: Who are the role models, what is the actual kinship relationship, and how available are they in the community? There's a tremendous movement in the Black community toward mentoring programs for
Black boys from the fourth grade on. Some feel that there has been an
ongoing conspiracy to destroy Black males, and the mentoring programs
have been developed to minimize this trend. They target fourth grade as
the place that Black boys begin to get lost. They are by then deeply
immersed in educational systems with very few Black men. As challenges
get harder and adolescence sets in, they eventually drop out. A mutual
disengagement phenomenon occurs as they retreat further into their subgroups; society in turn writes them off.

Another piece has to do with who is successful in the African
American community. Who are the role models? Ministers are very
prominent members of the community. Entertainers, sports figures, super-
stars command the respect and identification of lots of the young people
who want to be singers, models, football players, actors, and so on.
Interestingly enough, the police are a very prominent presence in the
community in terms of symbols of power. Traditional models—the educa-
tors, the lawyers, the doctors—are less desired role models. They work
too hard; they're not having a good time; they don't make enough money;
and they're no fun to be with. They represent delayed gratification. They
represent everything the young population is moving away from. Equally
problematic is the status of gays and lesbians. In spite of the fact that they
may represent a prominent aspect of the African American community,
efforts to respect and not oppress them and to make it okay for their identity to grow and develop are slow. But things are beginning to change,
especially among young people who don't carry some of the extreme
homophobia and religious biases that many of the older African
Americans have. I don't think it's fair to talk about identity development
in the Black community without including gay and lesbian youngsters.
But very often, they're just not included.

Author: I would next like to ask you about factors you see as important in
assessing African American clients.

Turner: The profession has attempted to make many of our assessment tools
culturally relevant. I think all of those efforts are positive. Students
should be familiar with them. It's real interesting, however, how people

come to state licensure with little or no knowledge of what psychology has attempted to do with formalized assessment tools.

For African Americans, the presenting complaint is often not the issue that is most problematic. An adequate assessment will accept and honor the presenting complaint, will not diminish it, but rather will use it as an opportunity to open the door and engage in a deeper exploration. Such an approach takes more work. It also takes a different mind-set than most therapists have been trained to adopt. Some of the strategic brief methods of assessment are recommended for everybody. But in reality, they fall short, especially for people who tend to somaticize their complaints, externalize their problems, do not know the rituals of being a "good patient," and define their problems in social rather than psychological terms. For such patients, it is often necessary to engage in an extended assessment of the problem. Sensitivity to the fact that many African Americans aren't going to necessarily self-disclose until there's some sense that a solution can and will be found, even if it's a temporary solution, is essential, or that the therapist cares enough about what they are discussing to really hear them. The issue of being heard is very important.

I don't think that a formal diagnosis can be made without appreciating the cultural context. That involves being able to get sufficient elaboration on the issues that are presented. An assessment is clearly affected by the freedom a client has in choosing treatment versus being mandated to treatment. When people come because they have to be there, that doesn't necessarily mean they won't be good patients or that the prognosis is necessarily negative. Some people can only come if they're forced. Once they arrive, they are able to do some very good work. But how they get to treatment must clearly be noted as part of the assessment. And finally, when you are asking about an individual's life experience, many of the members of the community who may not be viewed as significant may, in fact, have a great deal to offer to the assessment. Do not overlook or discard someone who seems tangential. In an extended family, they may play an important role.

Author: Are there any subpopulations in the African American community you feel deserve additional attention?

Turner: The Black woman has always had a special burden. She has been perhaps the most educated and pushed out there to deal with racism and discrimination. She has had to do both severe physical labor and also take care of the family's domestic needs. She has been raped, abused, and sacrificed in so many ways. The whole issue of the "strong Black woman" is a myth that grew out of an experience that was not chosen but forced upon her. Today, African American women have more choices in the world, and they are choosing alternative ways of interpreting this myth. Self-care and the ability to be cared for are also very important issues for African American women today. Yet, there is tension because the demand to be a strong Black woman is still very much alive today, as is her tendency to carry out that role. This crisis is being articulated in the African American community. Black women are writing and talking about it. They are confronting Black men about it and participating in support groups that focus on this issue. In short, they are very much in transition.

Author: What suggestions might you have for providers about developing rapport with African American clients.

Turner: Rapport? The whole question of how formal one needs to be initially or how casual continues to be an issue, probably for most ethnic groups, but especially for African Americans. Going to the doctor is still a formal experience. It's not something that's taken lightly, not something to be too casual about. Being casual doesn't necessarily develop rapport. Being clear about each person's role can be very relieving. Being clear about the amount of time that's involved and about the expectations can also be quite reinforcing to African American patients. Allowing a client to give you their view of what is going on is very helpful. Sometimes people just need to tell you their peculiar predicament before they're ready to hear you ask all the questions and get the data that you need. There is a common fear among African American patients that they will not be heard, that their own voice will be lost. If that fear does not get allayed, they may never tell you why they came to see you. Some of the things I think one shouldn't do is attempt to be too relevant by using slang or being overly familiar or identifying too strongly with what the patient is going through. These can be as off-putting as being too distant. Most African Americans initially need an interactive style. The distant, analytical approach is too fraught with potential for mistrust and suspicion, and that can initially limit the development of rapport. So, being serious, somewhat formal, interactive, respectful, and clear can make a tremendous difference.

Author: Are there helping or therapeutic styles with which African American clients are most comfortable?

Turner: African Americans can respond to a variety of styles. Clearly, the most problematic is being too distant and noninteractive. A style that stresses questions versus feedback can be equally successful. The nature of the interaction doesn't matter, but there needs to be a sense that the therapist is present, engaged, and interested. It doesn't matter if it's a behaviorist approach versus a more insight-oriented approach. It more depends on whether the therapist is viewed as caring about what's going on and involved. If the therapist is ignorant about important aspects of African American culture, the best way to proceed is to be honest about the lack of knowledge and "out front" about it. "I know very little about the nature of violence among 10-year-olds in grammar school. Can you help me with that?" Or "I know very little about that particular high school and its reputation. Would you take a moment and bring me up to date so that we share the same set of facts?" This is far superior to inaccurately stereotyping or making assumptions that tend to be off-putting because of a lack of knowledge.

African Americans need to feel the sense that the therapist believes treatment can work—that there can be a treatment experience that is useful to the patient. Often, people complain, "He couldn't help me; I didn't think he thought he could help me; I don't think he knew how to help me; so I did him a favor and left his office." There needs to be some sense that it's not an overwhelming task.

Author: By way of closure, could you present a short case that shows how the issues we've discussed about working with African Americans come together?

Turner: I do have a short case study. I treated a 41-year-old, single, African American woman. She was referred and brought to treatment by her parents. The parents contacted me on an urgent basis and sought an immediate conjoint family session. They complained that the patient was discovered a few days ago suffering from amnesia. She did not know who and where she was and did not recognize her parents immediately. After an extensive evaluation at a major medical center for neurological complications, the patient was diagnosed with psychogenic amnesia and told to seek psychotherapy.

The patient is employed as a senior technical engineer at a local military facility. She has worked on that job for the past 18 years since graduating from college. Both of the patient's parents retired from the same facility, but neither had reached the level of engineer. The patient's father had successfully sued the company for racial discriminatory promotional practices. He had been somewhat of a celebrity on the job, especially among the line workers before his retirement. The patient's symptoms presented on the morning of her 2-week vacation. She and her parents had planned a 2-week vacation to the South for an extended family reunion. The patient reported having a major confrontation with a supervisor on her last day at work and came home very distressed. She could not recall any traumatic events over the weekend and was not aware of her parents' concern on Monday morning when they did not hear from her. It is of note that the patient owned a home on the same block as her parents and had lived four houses from them for many years. She had multiple contacts with her parents by phone on a daily basis.

During the conjoint family session, it was clear that the patient had regressed to about age 14 emotionally. Her parents had complete charge of her daily activities. It was clear to me that this family system coalesced around the patient to protect her and was carefully assessing how safe it would be to allow me to enter the system and assist. Because of the patient's amnesia, she had to be driven to the sessions by her parents. It was almost 6 months before the patient became capable of driving and rapidly began to assert her desire to emancipate from parental control. It became clear that the parents were threatened by their rapid loss of total control of the patient's life. They were almost immediately prepared to terminate the treatment but were willing to have conjoint sessions every other week, and I saw the patient individually on alternate weeks.

As it became clear that the patient had reached a plateau in her adjustment both emotionally and with regard to her memory, I requested neuropsychological evaluation approximately 1 year after the original onset of symptoms. The second assessment indicated clear evidence of significant organic impairment. The patient had suffered partial strokelike symptoms due to uncontrolled hypertension and chronic stress not evident during the first assessment.

This case is an example of how African Americans often present with conditions that are severely disruptive to their work and family life. Often, individuals present with the support of their family to protect them from the outside world and the therapist if necessary. It would have been a mistake for me to insist that I see the patient individually from the beginning without her parents. It was tempting to hypothesize any number of traumatic causes for the "psychogenic amnesia" and memory loss that might have argued against ongoing familial involvement. If I had attempted to exclude the family in favor of individual sessions, I would have lost her and the family sessions too.

Chapter Twelve

Working With
Asian American Clients:
An Interview With Dan Hocoy

Asian Americans are the fastest growing racial group in this country, their population nearly doubling in the 1980s. Like the Latinos/as, they represent a diverse collection of ethnic groups with very different languages, cultures, and a long history of intergroup conflict and hostilities. With changes in the Immigration Act of 1965 and large-scale immigration from Southeast Asia, the relative percentages of Asian American subgroup sizes changed drastically. According to the 1970 census, the Japanese were the most populous, followed by the Chinese and the Filipinos. By 1980, however, the Japanese were in third place, with the Chinese moving up to first and the Filipinos to second. Population projections suggest that the Filipinos will eventually surpass the Chinese as the most numerous Asian subgroup. There are also large differences in duration of time spent in the United States. Many Japanese and Chinese Americans have been here for three or more generations, while at the same time, there has been a recent surge of immigration from Asia. For example, 60% of all Chinese in the United States today are immigrants. Early immigrant populations suffered extensively; for instance, the Chinese served as cheap and much maligned labor in the building of the West, and the Japanese were driven from their homes and interned in concentration camps during World War II.

Asian Americans have been described as the "model minority" largely because of their apparent low rates of social problems, educational and financial achievement, and a cultural tendency to defer and not compete openly with mainstream Americans. But this does not mean that there is any less racism or discrimination directed toward Asian American populations or that there are not serious problems within their crowded urban enclaves. At a psychological level, model minority status refers to the general lack of threat that Whites experience in relation to Asian Americans. This attitude has eroded somewhat, however, with increased economic competition from Japan and other Pacific Rim countries and a growing number of Asian American students competing successfully for college and university slots. As we shall learn from our guest expert, Dr. Dan Hocoy, Asian Americans, when they do seek professional helping services outside of their community, tend to present with a variety of problems including value conflicts with parents and family, difficulties regarding identity issues, acculturation, extreme work ethics, and familial obligations.

Dan Hocoy, PhD, received his degree in clinical psychology from Queen's University, Kingston, Ontario, Canada. His dissertation focused on the effects of apartheid and racism on Black mental health in South Africa. He has also carried out research on racial identity and other cross-cultural topics throughout the world, including Chinese racial identity and the psychological impact of racism on Chinese in Canada. He is currently assistant professor in the PsyD Program at John F. Kennedy University, Orinda, California.

The Interview

Author: One of your areas of expertise is racial identity. Could you talk about some of your own experiences growing up Chinese?

Hocoy: Being Chinese has always been very central to my life, although I haven't always been conscious of it. That is to say, I didn't always recognize its influence. I went through various phases of racial identity development. At first, I felt embarrassed about being Chinese. My family was the only Chinese family on the block, and because we were struggling immigrants, I always associated being Chinese with being poor. There was a lot of ethnic self-hate in me at that time. There was also external discrimination. For instance, I was always picked on in school for being Chinese; kids would tease me about the way my eyes, hair, nose looked. I got into a few fights in the schoolyard as a result. During this stage of my racial identity development, I always wanted to be White. This continued into high school. I wanted wavy, more combable hair. I wanted to be taller. I wanted a sharper nose. I always felt inferior. Chinese people were always ugly to me. At the time, I wasn't aware of the influences of having internalized Euro-American standards of beauty. I didn't think I was very attractive. At the height of my racial self-hate, my looks actually disgusted me. Not accepting my ethnicity pushed me toward greater degrees of conformity and assimilation. Yet I never felt I fit into the dominant culture either. Not feeling comfortable in either culture, I found myself marginalized and caught in the middle.

In university, I moved into another phase of racial identity development. Initially, I still didn't like the fact that I was Chinese, but I began to
challenge my negative self-feelings and attitudes toward my people.
Fortunately, at this time, I had an opportunity to visit other cultures
through international development work. It was in Africa that I observed
the psychological effects of colonialism and Western domination.
Witnessing Black self-hatred helped me come to terms with my own
racial self-hatred. This began a process of reclaiming my ethnicity, and
eventually, I would study the impact of racism on Black South Africans
for my doctoral dissertation. I was attending a very Anglo-dominated
graduate school, and it was an especially fertile environment in which to
come to terms with my race. I realized that much of my perception of the
world was based on a lack of acceptance of who I was. I grew increasingly uncomfortable with the feelings of self-hatred and was in time able to
come to terms with them. I wrote my master's thesis on the topic of
racism against the Chinese in Canada, and this was obviously motivated
by a struggle for racial self-acceptance. In time, I developed a great interest in my heritage and started buying and reading books about the
Chinese and, in a variety of ways, immersed myself in Chinese culture.

My training in psychology helped me process what was going on
inside me, both in realizing the effects of my experiences as a person of
Color and in coming to terms with the self-hate. Today, I regard my
Chinese identity as an asset both personally and professionally. As I
became clearer about my own ethnic heritage, I also became aware of the
cultural bias in psychology and the need to redress the systematic neglect
of minorities in both research and therapy. That in turn spawned an interest in multicultural counseling. But the process of racial self-acceptance is
an ongoing one, and I have yet to completely free myself from what Bob
Marley called "the chains of mental slavery."

Author: Let's begin with some definitions. Who are the Asian Americans and
what characteristics do they share as a group?

Hocoy: First, I think it is important to understand that there is a large degree
of diversity among Asian Americans and that they do not conveniently fit
into one categorization or description. There are many shades of yellow,
so to speak, and it is difficult to make global generalizations. Having said
that, individual and subgroup differences are significant, and there do
exist commonalities that Asian cultures share. When I talk about Asian
Americans, I am referring to people with Mongolian and early Chinese
ancestry. This includes the mainland Chinese, Japanese, Koreans, the
Vietnamese, people from Hong Kong, Taiwan, Singapore, Malaysia, the
Philippines, Laos, Thailand, and others from that region. I know this is
not inclusive of all Asians, as it omits East Indians and others, for
instance, but these are the groups with which I am most familiar.

With regard to Asian Americans, it is useful to realize that there are a
number of factors—historical, psychological, and otherwise—that set
them apart as a group in America. First of all, unlike any other minority

group, there is a history of warfare between the United States and many of these Asian countries. You have the Japanese in World War II, the Korean War in which the Chinese and North Koreans were both involved, the Vietnam War, and so on. So for many Americans, there is a visceral resentment and distrust of all things Asian. This is reflected in U.S. culture and media, where Asians were and at times still are portrayed as the prototypical villains. I think the lack of acceptance of Asians in U.S. culture at least partially stems from the fact that Asians possess such a different worldview. For instance, "East versus West" is a common dimension of comparison and dichotomy. Individuals who have been socialized into traditional Asian cultures are likely to possess completely different worldviews, with philosophies, values, and beliefs that are very disparate from Western ones. This major difference, I think, engenders much of the fear and misunderstanding about Asians. Another important factor is that much of Asian culture and society is based on the value of collectivism, which in recent years has been associated with Communism. Such ideas go against the familiar values and traditions of individualism and capitalism that are so basic to American culture and thus threaten many Americans.

The history and treatment of Asians in the United States have caused them to be very closed in terms of their interactions with other Americans. Asians have generally kept to themselves in very small enclaves. For instance, to this day, there are Chinatowns in most large urban areas, which from early times served as ghettos that ensured survival in the economic and political structure of the United States. Another trait Asians generally possess is a tendency to be less overtly militant and politically active than other racial groups. As a result, they have been an easy and frequent target for abuse and discrimination. (Although it should be acknowledged that Asians have historically made significant challenges to the status quo through equity legislation; this has primarily been through the judicial system.) Generally, Asians have been less likely than other ethnic groups to engage in activism toward redress of public policy. Characteristically, this is very reflective of the Asian attitude of not wanting to disturb things. There's a saying among the Chinese: "If you don't know what to do, at least don't do anything." This is very different from the American maxim: "If you don't know what to do, at least do something." This tendency is probably also related to the cultural norm of not showing certain emotions in public. It is very important in many Asian cultures that certain social protocols are followed and that one conforms to the cultural script of not displaying emotions in public.

Recent research findings show that Asians as a collective group are more accepted in America than other ethnic minorities. This, too, seems to be culturally based, with Asians generally perceived as less threatening to the status quo or dominant culture. The Chinese, for example, have survived in America by not having competed economically with Whites. Historically, they have always offered services that were lacking. For

instance, when the Chinese were first brought to California, it was to provide services typically offered by women. California society at that time
was predominantly male. Pioneer men had crossed the flatlands and over
the Rockies looking for land and gold. Their womenfolk had in general
remained behind. So, when the Chinese came to America, they took on
what at that time was considered women's work. They cooked, cleaned,
and did laundry for these pioneers. The Chinese also provided valuable
labor for the expanding railway and picked grapes for the wine industry.
These were services that were needed and desired by the dominant culture, but were not in direct competition with those offered by Whites.
This tendency has generally held true to this day. Thus, in America,
Asians have taken jobs that other Americans have just not wanted, especially those which are tedious and long in hours. Even now, many corner
stores and restaurants are owned by Koreans, Chinese, and Japanese.
These businesses involve excessive work and meager wages, but offer a
means of developing marketable skills and services without displacing
and incurring the wrath of others in the economy.

Author: Could you next talk about the various names that Asian American
subgroups use to describe and identify themselves as well as protocols in
addressing various individuals within Asian culture?

Hocoy: Again, I can speak most confidently about the Chinese. In terms of
racial self-labeling, I think most Chinese regard themselves as Chinese,
Chinese American, or just American. The name or self-reference that one
uses is a useful source of information. Clinically, by asking clients what
they consider themselves or what they would like to be called, you can
get a sense of where they fall in terms of acculturation; namely, assimilation, integration, marginalization, or separation. If they identify themselves as Chinese, this says something very different about their cultural
attachment, as opposed to referring to themselves as American. An integrationist would be more likely to say, "I'm Chinese American," whereas
a separationist is more likely to self-label as Chinese. An assimilationist
would typically use the term American, while someone marginalized
would probably have difficulty identifying with any of these labels. It is
thus quite useful for a provider to ask this question early on and to use it
as an entree into these issues.

Personal names also vary somewhat from person to person. More
recent immigrants and more traditional individuals use their Chinese
name as their legal name. You have the person's family name, preceded
by their Chinese first name. Both would be phonetically translated into
English for purposes of pronunciation. Again, this kind of information is
suggestive of a person's cultural background and degree to which they
had been acculturated. On the other hand, a fifth-generation Chinese
American family would probably have an Anglicized or transliterated
family name, with a Christian first name in addition to a more familiar
Chinese first name that is used only in the home. This is my experience. I
was given a Chinese first name at birth which is known to and used only

by family members. The Chinese practice of naming is similar to the Native tradition. A person is named according to their character at birth, and it is believed that this quality will define them throughout life. My Chinese name is Siao Kee, which translates into "small wonder" to reflect my early curiosity about the world. Many Asians are also given a European name for the sake of convenience in interacting with the non-Asian world.

There are other aspects of naming that are important to know. Within Asian cultures, great honor is given to authority and age, and this is manifest in a general respect for people who are older than you. So, if there is someone in the room of similar age or older than the therapist, it is important to address them formally and with deference, as Mr. or Ms. or whatever is appropriate. If there were several people present, the therapist should address the older person first. Conversely, an Asian client may feel uncomfortable calling a therapist, especially an older one, anything other than Dr., even if invited to do so. I, for instance, didn't call my supervisor by his first name until the 6th year of graduate school, when I was about to defend my dissertation. I didn't feel comfortable referring to him in such a familiar manner until I was of similar academic status. It is also important to be aware that older Asian clients, as a result of their traditional Asian worldview, expect to be treated with a great deal of tolerance and patience by the therapist. Asian culture dictates that elders be treated with an obvious tone of respect and deference, and such an attitude is a necessity for facilitating rapport with older clients.

Author: These sound like some very useful and important suggestions. Let's go back to a topic you alluded to earlier, the history of Asians in the United States. Could you give a nutshell version of this history?

Hocoy: Of the Asians, the Chinese were the first immigrants in the United States. Unlike other People of Color who were either brought here forcibly, such as African Americans, or already here and physically displaced, such as Native Americans and some Latinos/as, they came voluntarily as did the other Asians. The history of Chinese in the United States dates back to the 1840s. Many Chinese American families have roots in California that go back many generations to the time of the Gold Rush. They came mainly for a better life and to escape harsh economic circumstances and a variety of social problems in their native lands. Again, the early presence of Chinese made up for a lack of people willing to do what was considered women's work in California. Their found work in areas which were sanctioned by the dominant culture. From these vocations came the core of the stereotypes of the Chinese laundry, the Chinese restaurant, hiring a Chinese cook, and so forth. They also were instrumental in building a national railroad system through both the United States and Canada. As I said, the Chinese were willing to take the jobs most Americans would not do. They were usually very dirty or involved high risk. There is a saying "not having a Chinaman's chance," which comes from this period. In the building of railroads, it was often necessary to dynamite the sides of a mountain. Chinese workers would be sent to set the dynamite, and often it would go off prematurely or the mountain would collapse on them. Many Chinese died this way, and as a result, the phrase "a Chinaman's chance" was coined. I have also heard the phrase used to describe the already exhausted mine areas which were the only sites in which the Chinese were allowed to look for gold during the Rush.

There is a long history of racial discrimination against Asians in both legislation and public policy. In 1882, Congress passed the Chinese Exclusion Act, which prohibited Chinese immigration for 10 years. It was renewed in 1892 and became permanent law in 1902. This resulted in great difficulties for the Chinese men already here. They were forbidden to bring their wives over, but what they could do was go back and father children, and these offspring were allowed to enter. The result was a very lonely existence: a culture of lonely, hardworking men, isolated from the dominant culture, who kept largely to themselves and lived lives of great hardship and misery. By 1943 immigration restrictions were loosened, and women were allowed to enter. They worked as dressmakers and in sweatshops in the growing Chinatowns, while men opened laundries and restaurants and, as had become typical, took jobs that were of interest to no one else.

And then there are the more recent reminders of discrimination against Asian Americans in the United States: the internment of Japanese during World War II; reactions to the influx of Southeast Asian refugees; reactions to Asian economic success in the United States; reactions to the emergence of Japan and the other "four tigers" as global economic forces; and in the 1990s, talk of quotas limiting the enrollment of Asian American students in U.S. colleges, universities, and specialized professional programs.

There is anti-Asian sentiment intertwined throughout the history of this country, permeating all aspects of U.S. society, some more subtle than others. For instance, with the growing interest in Asian martial arts in the late 1960s, American television producers conceived of a story line about a Chinese Shaolin priest set in the Old West. Chinese martial arts expert and actor Bruce Lee was initially chosen for the role of Cain in the television series *Kung Fu*. When the show was pilot tested, the White audience felt quite strongly that Lee was just too Chinese for the part. A White actor, David Carradine, was chosen instead. Bruce Lee was a hero to many Asians in North America at the time, myself included. One can only imagine the racial affirmation that Lee could have provided for Asians if he had been chosen for the TV series.

Author: Let's change our focus somewhat and begin to look at issues related to help seeking and treatment. First, could you talk about issues that influence the ways in which Asian Americans go about seeking help?

Hocoy: In general, we are talking about very closed and tightly knit communities. They are very insular and cohesive and distrustful of outsiders.

Their survival has depended on it being this way. These enclaves or ghettos—the Koreatowns, Chinatowns, Japantowns—have learned to live on the fringes and construct for themselves self-sufficient alternative social and economic systems outside the dominant culture. As a result of this mentality, Asians can be very distrustful of White people. The Chinese call Whites "ghost people" and consider their ways of life to be strange and sometimes inferior. There is clearly a sense of arrogance here. Both Japanese and Chinese mythologies contain beliefs that view themselves as highly advanced in terms of human evolution. My grandmother described it to me as there being a racial hierarchy according to color. White people reside below the Chinese because they are "pasty and ill-looking" in appearance, whereas the Chinese have a touch of gold in their skin. Another example comes from the name China itself, which literally means Middle Kingdom; the early Chinese were pompous enough to believe that the world revolved around them. The Chinese do bring with them a rich cultural tradition outside of the United States and a long history of inventing everything from gunpowder to eyeglasses, from ice cream to the printing press. When these events were playing themselves out in the East, Europeans were still barbarians. This history engenders much pride among Chinese as well as arrogance and serves to support and justify their isolation.

In times of need, Asians Americans are more likely to turn to their immediate and extended family for assistance rather than to an outsider. There are, however, exceptions, like the family doctor, who may not be Chinese, but who is someone the family has known for years and has learned to trust. With regard to psychological problems, Asian families may just live with the problem, preferring to work it out themselves, rather than going outside for help. Psychological counseling, as a profession, is clearly not an integral part of Asian culture. So, if a client is Asian American, the therapist may have to initially describe and explain the purpose of therapy, the role of the counselor and client, and so on. It should not be assumed that the client understands the nature of therapy. Therapy is a foreign concept in Asian culture. Meditation and self-reflection are traditional ways to self-knowledge, while the writings and sayings of Confucius, Lao Tse, and other philosophers act as guides for human behavior. In addition, one finds extensive informal networks of support within the family and community which provide counseling and advice.

Another thing to be aware of regarding help seeking is the fact that there may be a great degree of shame and stigma associated with someone leaving the community and seeking professional help. The airing and telling of private affairs to strangers are virtually unheard of; it is a concept foreign to the Asian worldview. Part of this has to do with a fear of not being understood culturally by Western counselors. So, building rapport is an important first step to therapy. It is important for therapists to convey, both explicitly and implicitly, a knowledge of Asian culture or at least a respect for it and an openness to learning more. It is also helpful to understand that, given this general taboo, those who do seek out therapy are either very acculturated or desperate and have probably exhausted what resources they had within the culture and feel compelled to go outside.

Author: The discussion of help seeking has led naturally to aspects of the Asian family and community. Could you talk more about family and community and how these shape what happens in therapy with an Asian American client?

Hocoy: To understand Asian culture, it's important to grasp the philosophical traditions and religious influences on the culture. One needs, for instance, to understand the role of Confucian ethics and the Buddhist "middle path" of moderation in life. Asians, in general, come from strong, interdependent family and community bonds; both are very self-contained and self-sufficient. Chinatown, for example, is a microcosm of the greater society in that it contains everything that is needed for life and sustenance. In terms of the family, an important value is the obedience of children. The flip side is respect for elders and their wisdom. These are Confucian values. In the home, there are many token gestures manifesting these attitudes. For instance, in my own family, my grandmother would always sit at the head of the table, even though she was demented in her later years. If there was a big decision to be made, her opinion would always be sought. It was obviously a token gesture, but what was more important was that it was a sign of respect. It's considered taboo to send relatives off to old-age homes once they get old as is common among Anglo Americans. Doing so is almost unheard of and looked upon with disdain in Asian cultures.

Asian culture is heavily based on interdependence; thus, dependence is not necessarily regarded as a bad thing as it is in Western culture, which places prime value on independence. This interdependence is reflected in the Asian attitude toward family relationships. It is understood that children will be dependent upon their parents for caretaking and that these same parents will eventually become dependent upon their adult children in old age. Since the therapeutic situation is a relationship, this value will likely manifest itself in therapy in terms of the client's dependence on the therapist and in terms of the client's goals for life and treatment. It is particularly important to realize that these priorities may not have to do with achieving relational independence.

Much communication in the Asian family is indirect, wherein messages are not directly stated, but instead must be inferred. There's a reticence to talk about personal issues openly. I think the fear is that someone may be embarrassed by what is said. In my own family, certain things are understood. For example, my mother says something without referring directly to it, but everyone knows what she's referring to. The therapist may see some of this reticence in therapy, especially in regard to subjects that are taboo or that the client finds sensitive. Sex might be such a topic.

The therapist may not initially get a very explicit account of the problem. Much may be implied, and clinicians must be attuned to subtle meanings and innuendoes. This is especially true with clients who are less acculturated Again, this indirectness has to do with avoiding embarrassment. Clinicians need to be tactful and equally subtle in identifying the client's problems, being careful to validate the client's experiences, avoiding judgment or confrontation, and gradually honing in on the problem. In treatment, it may initially come down to talking in metaphors and indirectly about a topic in order to make the client feel comfortable enough to name and address it directly. This cultural tendency to imply meaning rather than to speak of it explicitly is very foreign to most Western therapists and counsellors, whose training has focused on the "spoken word" and direct verbal communication. The therapist needs to recognize this difference as a cultural artifact rather than be frustrated by it.

Another Asian value that may result in different therapeutic goals for clients is tolerance for ambiguity and inconsistency in life. In Western psychotherapy, psychological integration is promoted through the achievement of clarity about one's life, consistency in various aspects of one's life, and the resulting decrease of cognitive dissonance. Among Asians, however, the ability to tolerate the ambiguities and contradictions in one's life is considered an aspect of maturity. Thus, striving for complete consistency in or understanding of one's life may not be considered as important, nor a goal of therapy. In general, it is essential for Western counselors to realize that the paradigms and models upon which Western psychology is based are infused with Euro-American middle-class values and may have little application to other cultural groups.

A sense of balance and reciprocity is also very important in Asian cultures. Because the family is such a cohesive unit, individuals are brought up to think of family over self. This basic aspect of the Asian worldview is diametrically opposed to the Western emphasis on self-realization. For instance, research has shown that the concept of "self-esteem" does not exist in Japanese culture. This value difference between the two cultures often becomes a major problem for young Asian Americans who become caught in a conflict of values between generations. The older generation demands obedience and respect; the younger one has been more socialized to the American values of independence and individualism. The result is a conflict of cultures and the need for reconciling two very disparate cultural views and sorting out the confusion as to how to live in both worlds.

Another aspect of therapy with Asians relates to the tendency of Asian cultures to deemphasize the self and a prescription against self-promotion. For instance, one is not supposed to accept a compliment without resistance. If I compliment my mother on her cooking and the preparation of a certain dish, she would never acknowledge that it was deserved. She would probably say instead, "Oh, no. There's not enough salt, and this is actually the worst I've ever made." The implication of this for the clinical setting is that affirmation of the client's self, which goes against cultural norms, may be difficult for him or her to model. A corollary to the lack of emphasis on the self is the avoidance of personal embarrassment. Consequently, direct confrontations and demands on the client to accept personal responsibility for personal difficulties or specific behavior may be problematic for the therapeutic relationship.

Author: What are some of the common problems that might bring Asian Americans into treatment?

Hocoy: Again, I want to emphasize the fact that many Asians in the United States today still retain traditional norms and values; most of the Asian population in America are immigrants. So, only a limited segment of the Asian American community will ever find their way into a therapist's office. Those who do are generally more acculturated and bicultural, often students, as well as those who are particularly desperate for help and have not been able to find it in the family or community. For students, intergenerational and cultural differences are commonly a source of difficulty. Young people who have grown up with Western norms often find themselves at odds with parents who have very different values and expectations of them. One such issue revolves around strong parental pressures on the young person to excel. This can become especially problematic when the parents of their non-Asian peers are saying to their children, "Just relax. Do what you want." In traditional Asian homes, discipline is strongly emphasized as is the demand to be successful academically and otherwise. One symptom that may emerge is depression, resulting from feelings of failure and inadequacy, engendered by internalized, unrealistic family expectations. Also common is a conflict between independence needs and loyalty to family. Excessive guilt can also result from not completely conforming to family demands, as obedience to parents and loyalty are cardinal Confucian rules. In general, holding Western values as offspring of traditional Asian parents is inherently problematic.

A related problem has to do with identity confusion resulting from minority status and the impact of discrimination on personality development. Some young people have a hard time identifying with their Asian heritage because this identity is often disparaged in their non-Asian peer group. Strong pressures to assimilate to Western ways are also likely to be communicated, either explicitly or implicitly. A client might experience "a tyranny of shoulds," pulling in opposite directions. They should be doing this according to the peer group; they should be doing that according to their family. In addition, people may not possess a strong sense of themselves, of who they are, or of what they really want to do. Instead, they may feel caught between two worlds: one side saying, "You should be studying or practicing violin; you shouldn't be going out drinking," and the other countering, "No, no, man. Come on out; you should be getting stoned and having lots of sex in college." It's a very difficult thing to bridge these different worlds. Feelings of being different because of one's ethnicity and not completely fitting in are often accompanied by feelings of alienation and loneliness as well as those of being misunderstood. It is a short psychological step from feeling different to feeling inferior—that there's something wrong with me; that I'm not worthy of love. And there's the depression that comes from wanting to be someone I'm not and will never be.

Many of these characteristics are subsumed in the literature under the title "mismatch syndrome," which speaks to the disparity in values between one's culture of origin and the dominant culture. Common symptoms of this mismatch are self-rejection and low self-esteem, depression, an emphasis on negativity, rigidity in thinking and problem solving, and even attempts to escape reality via addiction and suicide. Also inherent in the mismatch syndrome is active value conflict: traditional versus modern gender role definition, an emphasis on family and community versus self-interest, age status versus youth emphasis, obedience and conformity versus questioning authority and individualism. Self-restraint and formality may lead to a lack of social experience. People brought up in a culture that suppresses the open sharing of emotions may find themselves alienated and unable to make contact with their non-Asian peers, who depend on sharing emotions in order to move toward intimacy. Lack of emotional expression can also lead to the somatization of various ills. Insomnia is a particularly common way in which such problems are manifest.

Other typical problems for which Asian Americans may seek help include compulsive gambling, cross-cultural dating and marriage, overbearing parents, caring for aged parents and other family members, immigrant poverty, extreme work ethics, racial identity issues, and posttraumatic stress in those escaping war-torn countries of origin.

Author: In carrying out an assessment of a new Asian American client, what factors do you think are most important to attend to?

Hocoy: In working with Asian Americans, the first thing I would assess is where a client stands on the continuum of acculturation. It is useful to think of four modes of acculturation. Integration implies that the person equally embraces ethnic as well as dominant culture. An assimilationist tends to neglect his or her own culture in favor of fully adopting the ways of dominant society. A separatist chooses to maintain ethnic ties and traditions, at the same time refusing to take on Western values/culture. Those who are marginalized are caught between cultures, unable to identify as Asian, yet at the same time uncomfortable in the Anglo world. It's vital to make an assessment of where each client stands in relation to these four possibilities and to then identify the social demands that are impinging on them. In my own work, I tend to promote and encourage the integration mode. Research strongly indicates that integration, or biculturalism as it is sometimes called, brings with it the greatest likelihood of psychological well-being, with maximum flexibility, integration, and wholeness. Assimilation, with its rejection of cultural roots, is likely to bring up problems related to self-denial. Separation brings with it difficulties in navigating the dominant culture and can lead to isolation.

Marginalization results in a lack of connection to any group and the possibility of serious mental health problems.

Equally important is assessing the nature of current demands upon the client, particularly from family. There may be serious difficulties both in the situation where: (a) a family tends toward separation and is putting substantial pressure on one of its members to be more Asian, while the member has chosen a more assimilationist direction and (b) a client wants to remain traditionally Asian and must function in an environment that demands conformity to mainstream values. It is the disparity between where a person chooses to be on the continuum and what the environment demands of them that is critical.

Other dimensions that I would assess include language dominance, degree of adaptive behavior, degree of identification with cultural heritage, attitudes toward that heritage and themselves (self-esteem), life history (particularly with regard to events of intercultural significance, like racism), and attitudes toward the dominant culture.

Author: You talked earlier about cultural differences and therapeutic style. What other suggestions might you have regarding establishing rapport and working therapeutically with Asian Americans?

Hocoy: I think something that is essential for non-Asian counselors to do prior to working with an Asian client is a thorough self-assessment of their own competence to work with this cultural group. They must possess sufficient understanding and knowledge about the culture as well as an awareness of what they are bringing to the therapeutic relationship, namely, the assumptions and values of Western psychotherapy, their own worldview, and personal experiences with biases and attitudes toward Asians. This is a critical first step.

As alluded to earlier, it may help to remember that the concept of counseling is foreign to traditional Asians. It's the counselor's responsibility to introduce them to the roles of the counselor and client and explain the process of therapy before any kind of rapport can be established. Counselors have to be perceived as knowledgeable about that client's cultural group right off. That's particularly important for Asians because they may be apprehensive about therapy. Fear of shame and distrust of non-Asians act as potential obstacles to building rapport. Thus, it is critical that the therapist demonstrates clearly that he or she respects and understands the cultural differences that exist and that these differences are not obstacles. At the same time, therapists must be very careful of stereotyping and of recognizing the kind of expectations they hold about Asian clients.

When treating Asian clients, it may be important for Western therapists to be more directive than they normally are with non-Asian clients and to be prepared when an Asian client exhibits what might be considered more than normal dependency in the therapeutic relationship. Western conceptions of psychological health emphasize client responsibility, openness, and personal exploration as well as self-reliance and self-determination in the therapeutic process. Clinical research, however, has found Asians to prefer a more directed and authoritative therapeutic style and to expect a certain degree of caretaking and direction. It is also important for the therapist to be nurturing and to have the therapeutic interaction reflect a familiar family atmosphere: directive regarding instructions, deferential to authority, but also nurturing.

For Asian Americans, few emotions are allowed, and there is generally difficulty with public displays of feelings. Emotionally laden content may not be easily discussed or easily identified by the therapist. The therapist must realize that there may be substantial difficulty with trusting and establishing rapport, given the taboos related to going to non-Asians for help and expressing emotions in public. Similarly, interventions should reflect or be consistent with Asian norms. The alternatives offered should be equally subtle, indirect, and nonconfrontational. There's a risk of Asian clients dropping out early, so it's especially important to build rapport and trust and to intuit any problems and check them out early on. As the client can be rather nonverbal, the therapist may have to ask if there are problems or identify them rather than waiting for them to be reported.

Asians also tend to have a very different nonverbal communication system. Providers need to be aware of this, because unlike the Western therapeutic focus on speaking, much of the communication in Asian cultures is nonverbal. The meanings of facial expressions, gestures, eye contact, and various cultural symbols or metaphors are usually completely different from Western ones. Research has found Asians to be a "low-contact" culture; that is, more comfortable with little physical contact and larger interpersonal distances. Studies also indicate that clients from various cultural backgrounds feel most comfortable with therapists that show similar nonverbal behavior. This "mirroring" of the client's nonverbal communication happens on three levels: proxemics, which refers to physical distance and touch; kinesics, which refers to body and facial movement, gestures, and eye contact; and paralinguistics, which refers to the extraverbal elements of speech, such as rate, tone, pauses, and so forth. It is absolutely essential that therapists pay special attention to the nonverbal dimension of therapy. Research has shown that appropriate nonverbal behavior conveys respect, honesty, interest, and genuineness.

With Asian Americans, the therapist may notice very subtle body gesturing and facial expressions. Large displays of emotion will rarely be seen, even if much is being felt and experienced. In many cultures, emotional states are rather transparent, easily read in the faces and body language of clients. With Asians (traditionally socialized), nonverbal communication is much more subtle. Sometimes all one can discern is a very slight head nod as a sign of affirmation if a question is asked. There may also be a general reticence. Asians are brought up to be indirect and to avoid emotional expressiveness. You probably won't see much gregariousness or strong displays of emotion. Also, as suggested above, nonverbal cues may have different meanings than for non-Asians. For instance, giggling often means embarrassment rather than a sign of humor. This is particularly true for the Japanese. Irrespective of the particular message, it is vital not to assume a commonality between Asian and Western "nonverbals."

The therapist should not challenge or confront avoidance or resistance immediately or in any way single out the client for what might be experienced as criticism. One may eventually be able to address relevant issues through more indirect communication. It is, however, important to lead with regard to the direction of therapy and spell out expectations the clinician has of the client. This is different than being confrontational, which is likely to induce shame and guilt. Again, it's related to "saving face." The therapist can subtly bring up deficits and shortcomings in the person, but not directly. Asians do tend to be familiar with very direct advice giving, but as to how or where they might go or what they might do as opposed to direct commentary on their personality, faults, or shortcomings. For example, if the therapist wants to tell the client the reason he or she doesn't have a very active social life is because of excessive negativity, it must be stated in a way that the Asian client can hear. With Westerners, a therapist can generally be more direct, "I've noticed something and want to give you feedback on it; it seems you're very critical of other people." With an Asian client, it is preferable to be more subtle. For example, the therapist might gently ask, "Do you think there is anything you contribute to the fact that your social life is not so good?" When the concern involves aspects of the client's personality or interpersonal style, it might be shameful, so it's important to be more subtle, indirect, implicit about it. At the same time, Asians tend to be quicker to listen to implicit messages than non-Asians. That's because of Asian cultural emphases on subtleties in meaning.

Finally, it is important to remember that Asian Americans often experience a sense of guilt or selfishness in pursuing their own interests in therapy as opposed to thinking of the family first. The whole act or exercise of going to therapy is an individualistic pursuit. A client may feel some guilt around it. There is also a sense of collective embarrassment to have to go outside the community. It is a capitulation saying, "My community cannot serve me." It may, in addition, be considered a sign of weakness to go outside the community. These are all issues Asian clients might bring with them to therapy.

Author: Could you finally share with us a case that shows how these various themes that you have defined all come together?

Hocoy: When I worked as a university counselor, I'd very often work with Asian students feeling a lot of pressure to excel in school and having difficulty living in two cultures. Terrence is a good example. He was an engineering student who came to counseling because he was getting B's, and there was a strong demand both from his family and from himself to get better, and even perfect, grades. Terrence revealed other difficulties as well. Because he focused almost exclusively on academics, he had developed few social skills and didn't have many friends. During his 2nd year of university, these various factors came together to cause a depression. He found it difficult to concentrate in school and was increasingly losing interest because he was coming to the realization that there was more to life than just school. When his marks deteriorated, pressures from home increased. At the same time, he had difficulty forming the friendships he desired with non-Asians (his primary peer group).

It was obvious from his presentation that he wasn't clear what therapy was about. Nor was Terrence very psychologically minded. He had a low awareness of his own emotions and had difficulty identifying them. He experienced an amorphous bundle of vague, uncomfortable feelings, and he couldn't dissect, label, or identify their source. He initially came in because of slumping marks, saying that he wanted to be able to get A's and that he had problems with concentration. Through joint exploration, we discovered that he wanted to partake in more extracurricular activities. He also wanted to establish relationships with his non-Asian peers and had a romantic interest in a particular young woman (who was non-Asian). However, he knew his parents would not approve of his having a non-Asian girlfriend nor the time he spent away from studying. It was the family's position that school was a time for study and that relationships and hobbies could come afterwards.

It became clear very early that much of his conflict was cultural in nature. He was caught between two worlds: unable to negotiate socially and establish relationships with non-Asians and, at the same time, unable to motivate himself to focus on his schoolwork. He also questioned the expectation that he had to date another Asian. Ultimately, what was at conflict were Asian values regarding the paramount importance of study and maintaining Asian cultural separation versus the value of making friendships with non-Asian peers and spending more time in nonacademic pursuits. He did not feel a part of his non-Asian peers and was increasing feeling unaccepted by his family because of his "failing" grades. In short, he was increasingly becoming marginalized.

We spent the initial sessions helping him discern his emotions; often, I had to make suggestions as to what he might be feeling. With time and effort, a bit more clarity emerged in what he was feeling. He had great difficulty separating his feelings from those of other people's, whether it be his peers or his parents. His emotional boundaries were very blurred, not uncommon in individuals from collectivist cultures. He was eventually able to report feeling pressured by his family to pursue good grades at the expense of social activities and to date and marry someone Asian. These were accompanied by simultaneous feelings of guilt and resentment. He was eventually able to understand that he had internalized the pressure his family had placed on him vis-à-vis academic performance and began to sense that there could be a difference between the demands his family placed on him and what he wanted for himself. It became clearer to him why his studying had become difficult and why he was internally caught between the values of two cultures. He also came to recognize the disparity between the Asian values of academic success and cultural isolation and his desire for relationships with those in the dominant culture and activities outside of school.

I encouraged him to pursue an integrationist path, one that allowed him to maintain his cultural traditions and, at the same time, establish relations outside the Asian community. By this point, he had developed clarity that this is what he wanted to do, but felt uncertain as to how to proceed. I assured him that he could participate in the non-Asian world without compromising his heritage and that, in fact, he could have the best of both worlds. The issue with his parents actually worked itself out as his marks improved because he was able for the first time to pursue the things he wanted to do, including spending more time enjoying himself and establishing friendships with non-Asians.

Chapter Thirteen

Working With Whites and White Ethnic Clients

Finally, we turn to the topic of working with and understanding White clients. What this means in a book on cultural diversity needs some clarification. It does not mean, first of all, an exhaustive description of White culture similar to those in Chapters 9–12. As has been repeatedly emphasized, providers are routinely trained to work with clients of Northern European descent. That is to say, they are trained in a model of helping and service delivery based primarily on the values and cultural style of dominant White America and most appropriately applied to its members. One could, in fact, argue that all books written generically about human services, the helping process, counseling, clinical psychology, social work, and so on are written from this cultural perspective.

In considering issues of diversity in working with White clients, two topics present themselves. First is the nature of racial consciousness in Whites. How specifically do Whites look at and conceive of issues of race and ethnicity and in what ways do such attitudes differ across dominant group members? Chapter 3 spoke at length about what racism is and how it can intrude on cross-cultural service delivery. Here, we look more deeply at the ways in which Whites, both clients and providers, structure and protect their racial attitudes. As part of this discussion, the concept of *White privilege* will be introduced. Second is the situation of White ethnics. As a group, White ethnics exist in a kind of psychological "demilitarized zone." Being White in America, they share the privilege of Whiteness. But concurrently, as ethnic group members from cultures who have experienced long histories of oppression elsewhere, they carry within them some of the same internal dynamics as People of Color. Human services providers working with these groups face the task of helping them integrate and deal simultaneously with these two very different aspects of personality. The second half of the chapter focuses on working with White ethnic clients.

Racial Consciousness Among Whites
White Privilege

In a very heated classroom discussion of diversity, several White male students complained bitterly, "It has gotten to a point where there's no place we can just be ourselves and not have to watch what we say or do all the time." The rest of the class—women and ethnic minorities—responded in unison, "Hey, welcome to the world. The rest of us have been doing that kind of self-monitoring all of our lives." What these men were feeling was a threat to their privilege as men and as Whites, and they did not like it one bit. Put simply, White privilege is the benefits that are automatically accrued to European Americans just on the basis of the color of their skin. What is most insidious about it is that, to most Whites, it is all but invisible. For them, it is so basic a part of daily experience and existence, and so available to everyone in their "world," that it is never acknowledged or even given a second thought. Or at least, so it seems.

If one digs a little deeper, however, there is a strong element of defensiveness and denial. Whites tend to see themselves as individuals, just "regular people," part of the human race, but not as members of a racial group. They are, in fact, shocked when others relate to them racially (i.e., as "White"). In a society that gives such serious lip service to ideas of equality and equal access to resources ("With enough hard work, anyone can succeed in America" or "Any child can nurture the dream of someday being president"), it is difficult to acknowledge one's "unearned power," to borrow McIntosh's (1989) description. It is also easier to deny one's White racial heritage and see oneself as colorless than to allow oneself to experience the full brunt of what has been done to People of Color in this country in the name of White superiority. Such an awareness demands some kind of personal responsibility. If I am White and truly understand what White privilege means socially, economically, and politically, then I cannot help but bear some of the guilt for what has happened historically and what continues to occur. If I were to truly "get it," then I would have no choice but to give up my complacency, try to do something about it, and ultimately find myself with the same kind of discomfort and feelings as the men in my class. No one easily gives up power and privilege.

It is easy, as Whites, to feel relatively powerless in relation to others who garner more power than we do because of gender, class, age, and so forth and thereby deny holding any privilege. As Kendall (1997) points out, one need only look at statistics regarding managers in American industry. While White males constitute 43% of the work force, they hold 95% of senior management jobs. White women hold 40% of middle management positions compared to Black women and men who hold 5% and 4%, respectively. Having said all of this, it is equally important to acknowledge that as invisible as White privilege is to most European Americans, that is how clearly visible it is to People of Color. To them, we are White, clearly racial beings, and obviously in possession of privilege in this society. That we don't see it is, in fact, mind-boggling to most People of Color, for to them race and racial inequity are ever-present realities. To deny them must seem either deeply cunning or bordering on the verge of psychosis.

At a broader level, White privilege is infused into the very fabric of American society, and even if they wish to do so, Whites cannot really give it up. Kendall (1997, pp. 1–5) enumerates several reasons why this is so. First, it is "an institutional (rather than personal) set of benefits." Second, it belongs to "all of us, who are white, by race." Third, it bears no relationship to whether we are "good people" or not. Fourth, it tends to be both "intentional" and "malicious." Fifth, it is "bestowed prenatally." Sixth, it allows us to believe "that we do not have to take the issues of racism seriously." Seventh, it involves the "ability to make decisions that affect everyone without taking others into account." Eighth, it allows us to overlook race in ourselves and to be angry at those who do not. And finally, it lets me "decide whether I am going to listen or hear others or neither."

Peggy McIntosh (1989) offers a number of examples of the kind of life experiences Whites, as people of privilege, can count on in their daily existence. Consider the following:

- If I should need to move, I can be pretty sure of renting or purchasing housing in an area which I can afford and in which I would want to live.
- I can be pretty sure that my neighbors in such a location will be neutral or pleasant to me.
- I can go shopping alone most of the time, pretty well assured that I will not be followed or harassed.
- I can turn on the television or open to the front page of the paper and see people of my race widely represented.
- When I am told about our national heritage or about "civilization," I am shown that people of my color made it what it is.
- I can be sure that my children will be given materials that testify to the existence of their race.
- I can go into a music shop and count on finding the music of my race represented, into a supermarket and find the staple foods which fit with my cultural traditions, into a hairdresser's shop and find someone who can cut my hair.
- Whether I use checks, credit cards, or cash, I can count on my skin color not to work against the appearance of financial responsibility.
- I am never asked to speak for all the people of my racial group.
- I can be pretty sure that if I ask to talk to "the person in charge," I will be facing a person of my race.

- I can take a job with an affirmative action employer without having co-workers on the job suspect that I got it because of race.
- If my day, week, or year is going badly, I need not ask of each negative episode or situation whether it has racial overtones.
- I can choose blemish color or bandages in "flesh" color and have them more or less match my skin. (pp. 10–12)

The opposite of each of these is the experience of People of Color in the United States. What can be done about White privilege? Mainly, individuals can become aware of its existence and the role it plays in one's life. It cannot be given away. Denying its reality or refusing to identify as White, according to Kendall (1997), merely leave us "all the more blind to our silencing of people of color" (p. 6). By remaining self-aware and challenging its insidiousness within oneself, in others, and in societal institutions, it is possible to begin to address the denial and invisibility that are its most powerful foundation. Like becoming culturally competent, fighting racism and White privilege, both internally and externally, is a lifelong developmental task.

A Model of Racial Attitude Types

Two groups of authors have developed frameworks for understanding how European Americans think about race and racial differences. Rowe, Behrens, and Leach (1995) enumerate seven different types of attitudes that Whites can adopt vis-à-vis race and People of Color. They first distinguish between achieved and unachieved racial consciousness. What this refers to is the extent to which racial attitude is "securely integrated" into the person's general belief structure; in other words, how firmly it is held versus how easily it can change. Unachieved racial consciousness can have one of two sources or both. It can reflect the fact that individuals have just not thought about or explored matters related to race and ethnicity or that they have no real commitment to any given position or set of attitudes. Rowe et al. (1995) begin by describing three atti-tude types that are unachieved: avoidant, dissonant, and dependent. *Avoidant* types tend to ignore, minimize, or deny the importance of the issue both in relation to their own ethnicity and that of non-Whites. Whether out of fear or just convenience, they merely avoid the topic. The following sample statement typifies such a position: "Minority issues just aren't all that important to me. We just don't get involved in that sort of thing. I really am not interested in thinking about those things" (p. 228). *Dependent* types hold some position, unlike the avoidant, but merely have adopted it from significant others (often as far back as during childhood). Therefore, it remains unreflected, superficial, and easily changeable. The following is a typical dependent response: "My thinking about minorities is mainly influenced by my (friends, family, hus-band/wife), so you could say I mainly learned about minorities from (them, him/her). That's why my opinion about minorities is pretty much the same as (theirs, his/hers)" (p. 228). The final unachieved type of attitude is *dissonant*.

Such individuals are clearly uncertain about what they believe. They lack commitment to the position they are currently holding and are, in fact, open to new information even if it is dissonant. Their position may result from either a lack of experience or knowledge or an incongruity between a previously held position and some new information or personal experience. It may also reflect a transition period between different positions. The following is typical: "I used to feel I knew what I thought about minorities. But now my feelings are really mixed. I'm having to change my thinking. I'm not sure, so I'm trying to find some answers to questions I have about minorities" (p. 229).

Rowe et al. next define four types of racial attitudes that they consider as having reached an achieved status (i.e., sufficiently explored, committed to, and integrated into the individual's general belief system). *Dominative* attitudes involve the belief that majority group members should be allowed to dominate those who are culturally different. They tend to be held by people who are ethnocentric, use European American culture as a standard for judging the rightness of others' behavior, and tend to devalue and be uncomfortable with non-Whites, especially in closer personal relationships. These are the classic bigots. The following statement is exemplary:

> The truth about minorities is that they are kind of dumb, their customs are crude, and they are pretty backward compared to what Whites have accomplished. Besides that they are sort of lazy. I guess they just aren't up to what Whites are. I wouldn't want a family member, or even a friend of mine, to have a close relationship with a minority. You may have to work near them, but you don't have to live close to one. (p. 229)

A slight variation on this theme is the *conflictive* attitude type. Such individuals, though they wouldn't support outright racism or discrimination, oppose efforts to ameliorate the effects of discrimination such as affirmative action. Where they are conflicted is around competing values: that of fairness, which requires significant change, versus retaining the status quo, which says that I am very content with the way things are:

> There should be equal chances to better yourself for everyone, but minorities are way too demanding. The media is always finding something they say is unfair and making a big deal out of it. And the government is always coming up with some kind of program that lets them get more than they deserve. We shouldn't discriminate against minorities, but tilting things in their favor just isn't fair. White ethnic groups didn't get a lot of government help, and the minorities of today shouldn't expect it either. (pp. 229–230)

Individuals who possess *integrative* attitudes tend to be pragmatic in their approach to race relations. They have a sense of their own identity as Whites and at the same time favor interracial contact and harmony. They further believe that racism can be eradicated through goodwill and rationality. The following is reflective of an integrative attitude:

> Integration is a desirable goal for our society, and it could significantly improve problems relating to prejudice and discrimination if people would

keep an open mind and allow it to work. Race and culture is not a factor when I choose my personal friends. I'm comfortable around minority people and don't mind being one of a few Whites in a group. In fact, I wouldn't mind living next to minority people if their social class were similar to mine. I think we will need racial harmony for democracy to be able to function. (p. 230)

The final attitude type delineated by Rowe et al. is called *reactive* and involves a rather militant stand against racism. Such individuals tend to identify with People of Color, may feel guilty about being White, and may romanticize the racial drama. They are, in addition, very sensitive to situations involving discrimination and react strongly to the inequities that exist in society.

Our society is quite racist. It is really difficult for minority people to get a fair deal. There may be some tokenism, but businesses won't put minorities in the top positions. Actually, qualified minority people should be given preference at all levels of education and employment to make up for the effects of past discrimination. But they don't have enough power to influence the government, even though it's the government's responsibility to help minority people. It's enough sometimes to make you feel guilty about being White. (p. 230)

These, then, according to the authors, are the most frequently observed forms of White attitudes toward race and race relations. The unachieved types are most changeable, by definition, not having been truly integrated into the person's worldview. The four achieved forms are more difficult to change, but under sufficient contrary information or experience, they can be altered. When that does occur, it usually involves a process of change during which the individual looks a lot like those who are in the dissonant mode.

A Model of White Identity Development

Helms (1995) offers a somewhat different model of White identity development. Rather than suggesting a series of independent attitude statuses, as do Rowe et al., she envisions a developmental process (defined by a series of stages or statuses) through which Whites can move to recognize and abandon their privilege. According to Helms's model, each status or stage is supported by its own unique pattern of psychological defense and means of data processing. The first stage, *contact status*, begins with the individual's internalization of the majority culture's view of People of Color as well as the advantages of privilege. Whites at this level of awareness have developed a defense Helms calls obliviousness to keep these issues out of consciousness. The second stage, *disintegration status*, involves "disorientation and anxiety provoked by unresolved racial moral dilemmas that force one to choose between own-group loyalty and humanism" (p. 185). It is supported by the defenses of suppression and ambivalence. *Reintegration status*, the next stage, is defined by an idealization of one's racial group and a concurrent rejection and intolerance for other groups. It depends on the defenses of selective perception and negative outgroup distortion for its evolution. The fourth stage, *pseudoindependence status*, involves an "intellectualized commitment to one's own socioracial group and deceptive tolerance of other groups" (p. 185). It is grounded in the processes of reshaping reality and selective perception. A person functioning in the *immersion/emersion status,* fifth along the continuum, is searching for a personal understanding of racism as well as insight into how he or she benefits from it. As a part of this process, which has as its psychological base hypervigilance and reshaping, there is an effort to redefine one's Whiteness. The final stage, *autonomy status,* involves "informed positive socioracial-group commitment, use of internal standards for self-definition, capacity to relinquish the privileges of racism" (p. 185). It is supported by the psychological process of flexibility and complexity.

Helms's model parallels the kind of identity development model for People of Color introduced in Chapter 6. The goals of identity development in each group are, however, different. For People of Color, they involve a cumulative process of "surmounting internalized racism in its various manifestations," while for Whites, it has to do with the "abandonment of entitlement" (p. 184). What they do share is a process wherein individuals (People of Color and Whites) shed their internalized racial attitudes and social conditioning and replace these with greater openness and appreciation for one's racial and cultural self as well as cultural differences.

Identity Development in the Classroom

Ponterotto (1988), drawing parallels with the earlier work of both Helms (1985) and Cross (1971), describes "the racial identity and consciousness development process" of White participants in a multicultural learning environment, an educational setting similar to that in which many readers may find themselves. Ponterotto identifies four stages through which most students proceed: (a) preexposure, (b) exposure, (c) zealot-defensive, and (d) integration. In the *preexposure* stage, the student "has given little thought to multicultural issues or to his or her role as a White person in a racist and oppressive society" (p. 151). In the second stage, *exposure,* students are routinely confronted with minority individuals and issues. They are exposed to the realities of racism and the mistreatment of People of Color, examine their own cultural values and how they pervade society, and discover how the "mistreatment extends into the counseling process" and how "the counseling profession is ethnocentrically biased and subtly racist" (p. 152). These realizations tend to stimulate both anger and guilt: anger because they had been taught that counseling was "value free and truly fair and objective" and guilt because holding such assumptions probably led them to perpetuate this subtle racism in their own right. In the *zealot-defensive* stage, students tend to react in one of two ways: either overidentifying with ethnic minorities and the issues they are studying or distancing themselves from them. The former tend to develop a strong "pro-minority perspective," (p. 152) and through it, are able to manage and resolve some of the guilt feelings. The latter, on the other hand, tend to take the criticism very personally and by way of defense withdraw from the topic, becoming "passive recipients" (p. 153) of multicultural information. In the real world, such a reaction leads to avoidance of interracial contact and escape into same-race associations. In classes, however, where students are a "captive audience," there is greater likelihood that the defensive feelings will be processed and worked through as the class proceeds. In the last stage, *integration*, the extreme reactions of the previous stage tend to decrease in intensity. Zealous reactions subside, and those students become more balanced in their views. Defensiveness is slowly transformed, and students tend to acquire a "renewed interest, respect, and appreciation for cultural differences" (p. 153). Ponterotto is, however, quick to point out that there is no guarantee that all students will pass through all four stages, and some can remain stuck in any of the stages.

White providers are encouraged to assess their own reactions to the concept of privilege and to locate their current level of development in each of the foregoing models of racial attitude. To what extent is one aware of the existence of White privilege in his or her life? This is an important question because culturally different non-White clients view and relate to a White provider in light of his or her having that privilege. As suggested in earlier chapters, one cannot help but be a magnet for the feelings of culturally different clients about White dominant culture and how it has treated them and those they love. What one can do is struggle to fully grasp the meaning and ramifications of one's White privilege and then communicate that awareness to non-White clients. Trust cannot truly evolve when two people live in perceptually different worlds. A key aspect of unacknowledged White privilege is its invisibility to Whites and its very obvious visibility to People of Color. To the extent that White providers can acknowledge the centrality of race to a non-White client and at the same time grasp the nature of their own attitude toward racial differences, the cultural distance between them can dramatically be reduced.

White Ethnics

Who are the White ethnics? Put most simply, they are national immigrant groups of Eastern and Southern European descent who share a somewhat common experience of immigration to the United States. They include the Irish, various ethnic groups making up the Russian republic, Spaniards, Portuguese, Italians, Poles, Greeks, Armenians, and Jews. All brought with them long histories of oppression and racial hatred in their native lands, were met with suspicion and rejection as newly arrived immigrants, and for a generation or two were exploited as cheap labor. Today, there still remain strong pockets of intact traditional culture within each of these communities, although many descendants have taken the path of complete and irreversible assimilation. Ironically, because of their darker physical features, they were considered non-White by Western Europeans and doubly rejected because religiously most were not Protestant. In America, however, their skin color and physical features "paled" in comparison to the non-Whites who were already here. As their economic and social positions improved, they increasingly identified themselves as White to set themselves apart from the People of Color with whom they often competed for jobs and other economic resources. This dynamic is well described by Ignatiev (1995). Their new "Whiteness" allowed members of these groups to more easily assimilate, and as they did so, they took on the racial attitudes and prejudices of the dominant culture to which they aspired.

As clients, White ethnics, especially those who have been in the United States for several generations, generally feel comfortable with European American providers. Some have assimilated so fully into majority culture, in fact, that they are culturally indistinguishable from other White clients. Most, however, still retain some cultural connection to the past, and in approaching these individuals, helping professionals should be aware of four important points. First, although White ethnics may be seen and treated as White by society at large, they do not necessarily perceive or identify themselves as members of the majority. More typically, there is the sense that, "I am not White; I am Irish (or Italian or Jewish)." Nor may they identify culturally with the dominant Northern European worldview. Thus, it is important to be able to assess what a client's connection is to traditional ethnic culture and what traditional beliefs, values, and behaviors still remain intact. If White ethnic clients do retain significant elements of traditional culture, providers must become familiar with the content of their culture.

Second, such assessments should not be made merely on external characteristics. Like People of Color, White ethnics differ widely on assimilation and acculturation. As suggested earlier, some have so fully assimilated and intermarried that there is little if any cultural material remaining beyond surface artifacts like family names, food preferences, and the like. Others are still very traditional, although they may have for convenience taken on some of the outward trappings of majority culture. Only through careful interviewing can an accurate assessment be made. In this regard, it is important to realize that external markers of culture disappear more quickly than internal ones. Thus, cultural artifacts such as values and worldview, psychological temperament, and family dynamics are more resistant to change and disappear more slowly.

Third, the cultural identity of White ethnics may be conflicted in much the same manner as was described for People of Color. This is true even for those who at first glance may appear highly assimilated. On a similar note, it is important to realize that, even if an individual has been spared the direct experience of racial hatred and discrimination, its emotional consequences can be passed on from previous generations through family dynamics.

Fourth, the fact that White ethnics can so easily assimilate into American culture, thus seemingly escaping their collective past, creates a somewhat different identity picture. In comparison to People of Color, who are reminded constantly of their ethnicity, White ethnics can bury their conflicts much deeper and further out of awareness. But again, as in the case of People of Color, the rejection of such an important part of identity as one's ethnicity cannot help but cause deep inner conflicts that eventually affect behavior. Thus, it is not uncommon to find instances of identity rejection and self-hatred among White ethnics.

Some Personal Reflections on White Ethnicity

As an American Jew, I am personally familiar with each of these dynamics. The following excerpt from Diller (1978) describes some of my own struggles and conflicts around ethnic identity as a Jew and White ethnic:

> The rejection of my Jewish past seemed almost a natural consequence of growing up. In spite of the fact that my early years were spent in a moderately religious and culturally-infused home, I slowly slipped away from my Jewish roots. The reason was not so much the content of those early experiences, but rather the quality. My memories of that world are mainly joyless and uneventful, an endless succession of unexplained rules, illogical demands, and invocations of the wrath of the "All Mighty" in order to get me to behave properly. The cultural remnants I retained from it were few—a smattering of Yiddish and the fragmented memories of being chased out of a dilapidated and run-down Galitzianer "shul" by grizzled old men, and a few years later fighting a schoolmate who called me a "dirty Jew." All resulted in an indifference to a world which I did not understand and which no one took the time to explain.
>
> My turning away was not met with hysterical protests or emotional scenes as is so often the case; it just happened. The silence of those around me reflected neither a lack of caring for me nor a de-valuing of those things Jewish, but rather a belief in the inevitability of assimilation. For my part, I experienced a sense of relief and freedom, as if a millstone, an impediment to my open experiencing of the world, had been removed. The superstition, blind faith and dogma with which I equated Judaism had no place in my adolescent understanding of how one should relate to the world. As was typical of my generation, I traded family and cultural ties for independence, and religion and faith for intellectual concerns and rationality. Having stripped away the past, I felt ready to commence the journey toward self-definiton. Self-discovery, I believed, could only begin anew, having washed away the old.
>
> In the years that followed I pursued many avenues as potential sources of fulfillment. I earned a Ph.D. in psychology; became a college teacher; involved myself in psychotherapy and encounter group work; became a social activist; experimented with drugs and the Hippy lifestyle; and studied and practiced various forms of Eastern discipline. Although I learned much from each, none by itself held any lasting satisfaction or fulfillment. Each seemed slightly hollow and incomplete, incapable of totally satisfying my identity needs. And never, during that entire period, did I give even the slightest thought to my own cultural heritage as a potential end-point to my search. Later the reasons for this became painfully clear.

The impetus to re-explore and re-discover my Jewishness came while visiting a favorite uncle. During my visit, I learned that he had of late become exceedingly interested in his own Jewish past . . . I was shocked. My uncle was a college professor, an intellectual, a scholar. He had always stood apart in my mind, had always been different from my other relatives. He too, I felt, had transcended a limiting past and had spent his life openly and rationally interacting with his world. Why would such a man suddenly turn to Judaism or to any religion for that matter?

We talked, and he told me of his growing concern about how to raise his children. He had realized how unfair it would be to cut them off from a birthright which they might find valuable later in life . . . More personally, as he grew older he realized more and more that something was missing from his life, that some dimension was lacking. He found himself thinking of the world of his childhood with greater frequency, of the teeming and bustling world of the Jewish ghetto with its push-carts, animated Yiddish and close sense of family and neighborhood. In these nostalgic memories he sensed the presence of something meaningful, something which filled the void in his present world. For these reasons, he was seeking to re-establish contact with his Jewish past.

The shock and confusion which my uncle's disclosure set off in me remained long after our visit had ended. I found myself thinking of it repeatedly, trying to make sense out of the great dissonance which existed for me between my old image of him and his new-found interest. Finally, several months later I decided to pick up a few of the books he had suggested and see for myself what he had found in them. With this, the process of rediscovery began.

The sense of shock I had experienced with my uncle was to become a frequent visitor as I sought to learn more about my Jewish past. I was surprised to meet rabbis who did not fit into old stereotypes, and men and women who could verbalize their beliefs in terms I could understand, people who made the Jewish lifestyle and experience come alive for me. I was surprised to discover the breadth and richness of Jewish culture and how much was available within my own heritage.

Approximately a year into my exploration, a single event occurred which brought to awareness a previously unsuspected reaction to my own Jewishness, unconscious feelings which for many years had been actively at work within me. One morning, while walking across campus, I looked down at the bundle of books I was carrying and saw on top a book entitled *The American Jew*. Unconsciously, I reached down with the other hand and turned it over so that the word "Jew" could not be seen. Seconds later I realized what I had done. Was I really that ashamed of being a Jew? Slowly my confusion turned to anger: anger at myself for hiding and being ashamed of what I was, and anger at a society which would allow, and even encourage, this to happen. For a moment I truly experienced the hatred and resentment which was so much a part of the lives of my Black and Chicano friends. For the first time, I understood the fascination and attraction their liberation movement had always held for me.

From this event, a new gestalt of understanding emerged. I had learned to feel ashamed of, to degrade and discount my own heritage. As a result of this awareness many of my past reactions began to make sense: why I had repeatedly been surprised and shocked at the richness of the Jewish experience; why I had never considered Judaism as a potential source of answers to my existential searchings; and why I had been so repelled when my uncle showed an interest in his own Jewish past. This experience was one of the most powerful in my life.

In the fiction of Phillip Roth, an author often maligned by his own Jewish community for some of his honest and human portraits of the American Jew, I discovered yet another little-realized aspect of my Jewishness—a conflicting allegiance to two different cultures and ways of life. I felt particularly touched and at one with the hero of his short story "Eli the Fanatic." Eli is a lawyer who is given the task of modernizing several Old World Jews recently relocated in his suburban community. It is feared that their immigrant appearance and actions will offend the Gentile community and disrupt the hard-won positive relationship between the Jews and their neighbors. After Eli succeeds in getting one of the old Jews to trade his dirty and worn out gabardines for a more modern business suit, something snaps within the lawyer. He becomes obsessed with the old clothes and eventually feels compelled to put them on. So dressed, he wanders about suburbia dazed and confused, ending up at the maternity ward of the local hospital where he gazes at his new-born child through the glass of the nursery. In Eli's conflict I saw many of my own symbolically echoed: the value I place on group identity, exclusiveness and pride versus that of universal humanism; my deep feelings of sympathy for the State of Israel and my revulsion at its militancy; my desire to remain open and learn from those different from me versus my periodic need to surround myself with fellow Jews.

As I explored the long history of the Jews, I found my very sense of personal existence and place in time being radically altered. I discovered an old and fascinating world which took hold of me and transported me back into time . . . Seeing myself symbolically extended so far back into time and becoming a part of such a wide array of movements, experiences and events were both a source of great comfort and of disorientation. I had never before thought of my roots extending further back in time than two generations, beyond grandparents and great-grandparents I barely remembered.

While traveling in Europe, this sense of timelessness and oneness with my past became a permanent part of me. I sat in the oldest synagogue in Europe on Yom Kippur eve and watched hundreds of candles project strange and eerie shadows on an ancient pulpit and congregation. Leaving the sanctuary and the walled courtyard which protected it, I could not help but shudder when I thought of the purpose of those gates and walls. I grew nervous and edgy whenever I rode trains through Germany. I could not relax until we crossed the border into Denmark, where I somehow sensed a friendliness and safety. I experienced a strange pride and expansiveness as I entered an art museum in Nice dedicated solely to the work of a single Jew—Marc Chagall. And I visited Dachau and was suffocated by its restored barracks, barbed-wire, manicured landscape and smell of ashes. As I watched a group of Italian tourists descend upon it like Disneyland, littering and posing for pictures in front of the ovens, I knew deep within me that it could all happen again. It was then I experienced my Jewishness with an intensity and certainty I have never known before. (pp. xv–xx)

Such experiences and feelings, although different in content from group to group, are typical of what White ethnics face emotionally in their efforts to find their cultural place in America.

The Nature of White Ethnic Identity

Like People of Color, White ethnics have struggled with acculturation and its damaging effects on ethnic identity. Like the majority of American Jews, my own descent is Eastern and Central European in origin. And in a manner similar to other White ethnics, Jewish identity became highly fragmented in America. With the exception of a relatively small group of Orthodox Jews who continue to practice a traditional Jewish lifestyle, most Jews have actively transformed themselves to better fit into American society. Many have adjusted their religious practices to more closely parallel Christianity, attending services only once a week and on certain special holidays. Others have become predominantly secular, transforming their Jewishness into a set of ethical beliefs, a sense of peoplehood, the burden of 2000 years of oppression, or merely cultural artifacts like Jewish food or rituals to be enjoyed on a "pick and choose" basis. Thus for many, ethnic identity has been relegated to a peripheral or at most secondary position in their lives. There is, finally, a growing population of individuals of Jewish descent who today know nothing of their heritage and feel little connection with it. At present, intermarriage rates among Jews average around 50%, in some regions as high as 80%. It is nothing short of ironic that here in America, where Jews, like other White ethnics, have experienced more material and social success and been more able to assimilate than ever before, there is a greater danger of disappearing as a group than ever before in history.

A cultural legacy of literacy, achievement orientation and hard work combined with their light-colored skin allowed Jews to quickly climb the socioeconomic ladder, primarily via professionalism and business. Like other White ethnic groups, they willingly took on the privilege of Whiteness and its attendant racism, but at the same time retained a strong sense of social justice. Many, in fact, actively supported and identified with the plight of African Americans and their movement for civil rights. But the connection has not been mutual, and since the 1980s Jewish–African American relations have reached an all-time low. In many ways, this tension epitomizes the psychological plight of Jewish and White ethnicity in America. Its essence is well captured by Memmi (1965), when he described Jews as both the oppressor and oppressed at the same time. For many African Americans, Jews have become a symbol of White oppression and privilege. They are seen and experienced as very White. Most Jews, on the other hand, perceive themselves not as White, but as Jewish. Although certainly a part of this has to do with the invisibility of White privilege, it is equally fed by the experience of feeling culturally different from America's Northern European majority, not to mention a collective history of oppression, continuing anti-Semitism (though it differs in intensity and pervasiveness from that which existed in Europe), and anti-Israel sentiment.

White Ethnic Culture

Human service providers working with White ethnics should become aware of their group's unique cultural values and worldview. Just as there is enormous diversity in cultural content across communities of Color, so too do White ethnics differ culturally from each other and from mainstream American culture. It is perhaps even more compelling to want to assume that White ethnics possess the same cultural patterns and traits as other majority Whites, since they bear such a close physical resemblance. But this is just not the case, and White ethnic cultures, like those of the communities of Color, are each unique unto themselves.

By way of example, Herz and Rosen (1982) point to four central values that define and infuse Jewish culture (and much of the discussion that follows is drawn from their work). These central values include centrality of the family, suffering as a shared value, intellectual achievement and financial success, and the verbal expression of feelings. Jewish social existence is organized around these values, and the Jewish psyche is socialized to support and internalize them.

Jewish tradition is highly family-centered. Unmarried men and women and childless couples are seen as incomplete; intermarriage and divorce are looked down upon and viewed as violations of family togetherness. Sex and family roles are fairly rigid and remain so throughout life both within the primary and extended family. High expectations are placed on children as well as adults, and socialization is accomplished through the threat of withdrawal of love and the engendering of guilt. The basic building block of Jewish life is, thus, the family as opposed to the individual, and there are strong pressures for family members to place the well-being of the family and the community before personal needs. Strong boundaries around the family protect Jewish ethnicity. Movement away from ethnicity is experienced and reacted to as rejection of the family. Within the family itself, relations are very close, often with unclear boundaries. Children are afforded higher status than in most other groups. They are expected to give their parents pleasure by way of their accomplishments and to remain within the family complex throughout life. Traditionally, the sexes tend to be segregated, yet there exist within the Jewish family very strong ties and conflicts between fathers and daughters and mothers and sons. Owing to these complex interactions, Jewish men are often described as distant and dependent, and Jewish women as intrusive and controlling.

Jews tend to view suffering as a basic part of life. Jewish history has so often been characterized by persecution and oppression that the expectation of suffering, attitudes of cynicism and pessimism, and even paranoia have become a central aspect of the family's ethos. Suffering also serves as a shared basis for group belonging, as does the experience of slavery for African Americans. In other words, it is seen as an intrinsic part of Jewish history. Suffering is seen as something that is visited upon the Jew from outside as opposed to being a punishment for one's sins. Dwelling on suffering and life's negatives often has the consequence of eclipsing the experience of happiness and pleasure, and it is not uncommon for Jews to find it difficult to enjoy life without concurrently accomplishing something. Similarly, the focus on suffering is probably related to a high incidence of hypochondriasis among Jews. Such patterns are especially evident in families of Nazi Holocaust survivors in which parental suffering overwhelms and incapacitates children and where feelings of loss are too strong to talk about.

Jews also place a high value on intellectual achievement and financial success. Historically, religious learning and scholarship were the primary sources of prestige and status in the Jewish world. A man learned and all other aspects of family endeavor served to support that learning. As Jews assimilated into the Gentile world, non-Jewish standards of success including money, professional status, and secular educational accomplishment grew increasingly important. The support of intellectual achievement within the family made success in these new secular activities easily transferable. With assimilation, a growing conflict emerged between family and success. Especially for men, becoming successful meant less time available in the home for family activities and interaction. As an oppressed minority, Jews also tended to push harder to succeed and prove themselves equal to or better than majority group members.

Within the family itself, there is enormous pressure on children and spouses to achieve. In exchange for their special status and treatment, children are expected to perform, often at unrealistically high levels. The perfectionistic demands of the family can easily create a sense of failure irrespective of one's actual accomplishments. Such demands and their attendant sense of failure can also lead to competition among family members and the devaluing of each other to bolster self-esteem. This cycle of unrealistic demands, failure, and mutual criticism leaves family members wounded emotionally and permanently poised against attack. Also related to success is the high value placed on helping others and taking care of one's own. Traditionally, success is viewed as carrying with it an obligation of charity and generosity. Doing good deeds and giving to those in need are considered highly meritorious.

Finally, verbal expression is highly prized in the Jewish world. The ability to articulate thoughts and feelings and a passion for ideas are encouraged and rewarded within the family. All members including children are expected to express themselves verbally, and it is not unusual for the intensity of interaction to escalate as passions rise. Jewish couples tend to deal with conflict openly and directly. They increasingly seek verbal resolution and understanding as arguments and disagreements intensify. Of course, external circumstances can do much to alter such family value patterns. For example, in the well-known silence of Holocaust survivors and their offspring, verbal expressiveness has been limited by the trauma of their experience.

The characteristics of heightened self-expression, achievement orientation, and adroit verbal skills often fuse in North American Jewish families to predispose its members to initiate verbal attacks when threatened. Aggressive language is used to express anger. Complaining, nagging, and criticism are means of controlling the behavior of others and at the same time venting frustration. Anger tends to be carefully controlled in the Jewish psyche and expressed only verbally or indirectly in action, but seldom spilling over into overt violence. It is important to realize that inherent in these seemingly aggressive acts is a component of caring which can make such interaction extremely confusing. Also relevant here, given Jews' long history as an oppressed people, is the possibility that some anger reactions may derive from a dynamic of identification with an oppressor.

Mental Health Issues

Jews, like other White ethnics, exhibit their own unique patterns of help seeking, attitudes, and behaviors in relation to mental health issues. Generally, Jews tend to seek treatment earlier than other ethnic groups and to present with less severe neurotic symptoms. They tend to be more accepting of emotional symptoms and less so regarding symptoms of disordered thought. In general, they exhibit a low incidence of alcohol and drug problems. They are comfortable seeking mainstream professional treatment and prefer psychotherapy (with its emphasis on verbalizing feelings, shared suffering, talking and insight as a means of resolution, and reliance on authoritative expertise) as opposed to shorter term solutions. Families tend to seek help for aspects of their chidren's behavior, especially poor academic performance, lack of achievement, and problems in separation and leaving home. When marital therapy is sought, it is usually presented in terms of communication problems that classically translate into the husband being too distant and unaffectionate and the wife either sexually frigid or withholding. Problems with extended family, in-laws, and dealing with elderly parents are also frequent sources of difficulty. Counselors unfamiliar with Jewish culture may initially have problems dealing with a family's resistances to changing patterns of enmeshment, engaging distant Jewish men, dealing with demanding and assertive Jewish women, or misreading the use of verbal aggression.

White Ethnic Identity Conflicts and Ethnotherapy

White ethnics often report difficulties in group identity development. By way of giving the reader a better sense of what these issues look like for clients and how they might be worked with clinically, I have paraphrased excerpts from sessions of an ethnotherapy group with Jews. The term *ethnotherapy* was coined by Cobbs (1972) to describe a therapeutic method developed to explore and change negative attitudes about race and ethnicity. In her research on Jewish identity and mental health, Klein (1980) found that of the 120 young Jewish adults from the San Francisco Bay Area tested approximately 15% could be classified as positive identifiers, 15% as negative identifiers, and 70% as ambivalent identifiers. These numbers are rather shocking and indicative of the extent of identity problems that still exist among White ethnics. What these statistics seem to show is that ethnic identity conflicts are slow to disappear, even with significant reductions in hostility and intergroup hatred. Rather, they are passed on from generation to generation as part of family dynamics. In the paraphrased session below, taken from a training film developed by Klein (1981), participants were asked to participate in an exercise which she called "I Am a Jew." Group members take turns (and as much time as needed) standing in front of the group and repeating the phase: "My name is Jerry Diller, and I am a Jew." They keep repeating it until feelings, memories, or images begin to flow.

> "My name is Beverly, and I am a Jew. I am a Jew. I am a Jew. The more I say it, the more nervous I get. I am a Jew. I am a Jew. It gives me the chills. It's not a strong word. It's too short, and I have to stand real tall. But it's not enough. It's as if someone is going to shake me. I realize that I've never let anyone insult me as a Jew. My trick is that I make it known from the beginning, so they wouldn't dare make any anti-Semitic remarks in front of me. But I know deep down that I am really afraid. Afraid that someone is going to come in and destroy me."

> "My name is Marlene, and I am a Jew. I am a Jew. I am a Jew. I want to tell my father. I am a Jew. My father grew up in a wealthy home in New Jersey. He always felt self-righteous about it. Always felt better than my mother, and she was the Jewish one. She and my grandmother spoke Yiddish to each other. It was because of her that I grew up in a Jewish home which my father never respected. As a child, I remember my mother cooking kippered herring, and my father complaining about the smell. I remember his comments. And I am ashamed of being a Jew. Especially with men. Dad, I am a Jew. And I am going to be a Jew if you like it or not. I am a Jew. Just like my mother. I am a Jew. I wouldn't care if I was Chinese. I just want to like what I am."

> "My name is George and, believe it or not, I am a Jew. I am a Jew. I am a Jew. Oy, am I a Jew. I am a dirty, #$%@& Jew. I am a Jew. I am a Commie, pinko, Jew. I am just beginning to get some of those feelings again. There was a lot about being a Jew in my childhood. I never felt that I was a good Jew. I can see myself having stones thrown at me as a kid, because I was dressed in regular clothes. It was Easter and all the Catholic kids were dressed in their best clothes. I was called a dirty Jew a lot. We fought the Italian kids a lot. That is just how it was. I want to keep saying it. I am a Jew. I am a Jew. (Very loudly). I am a Jew. Can you hear me out there?"

According to Klein (1980), such experiences and the opportunity to explore personal feelings about ethnic identity and belonging are highly therapeutic and "overwhelmingly positive." Her postgroup research showed increases in self-esteem and ethnic identification and a decrease in social alienation. By way of summary, Klein (1981) suggests, "For minority group members group pride and self pride are inextricably bound. Struggling with and resolving conflicts in Jewish identity release tremendous energy formerly stifled by ambivalence and disaffiliation. This energy can be a potent source of self acceptance and acceptance of one's own kind."

References

Aboud, F. (1987). The development of ethnic self-identification and attitudes. In J. S. Phinney & M. J. Rotheram (Eds.), *Children's ethnic socialization: Pluralism and development* (pp. 32–55). Newbury Park, CA: Sage.

Aboud, F. (1988). *Children and prejudice.* Oxford: Blackwell.

Aboud, F., & Doyle, A. B. (1993). The early development of ethnic identity and attitudes. In M. E. Bernal & G. P. Knight (Eds.), *Ethnic identity: 1. Formation and transmission among Hispanics and other minorities* (pp. 46–59). Albany: State University of New York Press.

Adorno, T. W., Frankel-Brunswik, E., Levinson, D. J., & Sanford, R. N. (1950). *The authoritarian personality.* New York: Harper & Row.

Allport, G. W. (1954). *The nature of prejudice.* New York: Doubleday.

Anderson, J. A., & Adams, M. (1992). Acknowledging the learning styles of diverse student populations: Implications for instructional design. In L. L. B. Borders & N. Van Note Chism (Eds.), *Teaching for diversity* (pp. 5–18). San Francisco: Jossey-Bass.

Atkinson, D. R. (1983). Ethnic similarity in counseling psychology: A review of research. *The Counseling Psychologist, 11*(3), 79–92.

Atkinson, D. R., Brown, M. T., Casas, J. M., & Zane, N. W. S. (1996). Achieving ethnic parity in counseling psychology. *The Counseling Psychologist, 24*(2), 230–258.

Atkinson, D. R., Casas, J. M., & Wampold, B. (1981). The categorization of ethnic stereotypes by university counselors. *Hispanic Journal of Behavioral Sciences, 3*, 75–82.

Atkinson, D. R., Morten, G., & Sue, D. W. (1993). *Counseling American minorities; A cross-cultural perspective* (4th ed.). Dubuque, IA: William C. Brown.

Atkinson, D. R., Whitely, S., & Gin, R. H. (1990, March). Asian-American acculturation and preferences for help providers. *Journal of College Student Development, 31,* 155–161.

Austin, G. A., Prendergast, M. L., & Lee, H. (1989). Substance abuse among Asian American youth. *Prevention Research Update No. 5* (pp. 1–13) Portland, OR: Northwest Regional Educational Laboratory.

Bay Area Association of Black Psychologists (1972). Position statement on use of IQ and ability tests. In R. L. Jones (Ed.), *Black psychology* (pp. 92–94). New York: Harper & Row.

Bennett, M. B. (1993). Towards ethnorelativism: A developmental model of intercultural sensitivity. In R. M. Paige (Ed.), *Education for the intercultural experience* (pp. 1–51). Yarmouth, ME: Intercultural Press.

Bernal, M., & Castro, F. (1994). Are clinical psychologists prepared for service and research with ethnic minorities? *American Psychologist, 49,* 797–805.

Bernard, B. (1991, April). *Moving toward a "just and vital culture": Multiculturalism in our schools.* Portland, OR: Northwest Regional Educational Laboratory.

Boyd, N. (1977). *Perceptions of Black families in therapy.* Unpublished doctoral dissertation, Teacher's College, Columbia University, New York.

Boyd, N. (1982). Family therapy with Black families. In E. E. Jones & S. J. Korchin (Eds.), *Minority mental health* (pp. 227–249). New York: Praeger.

Braginsky, B., & Braginsky, D. (1974). *Methods of madness: A critique.* New York: Holt, Rinehart & Winston.

Broverman, I. K., Broverman, D. M., Clarkson, F. E., Rosenkrantz, P. S., & Vogel, S. R. (1970). Sex-role stereotypes and clinical judgments of mental health. *Journal of Consulting and Clinical Psychology, 34*(1), 1–7.

Brown, M. T., & Landrum-Brown, J. (1995). Counselor supervision: Cross-cultural perspectives. In J. P. Ponterotto, J. M. Casas, L. A. Suzuki, & C. M. Alexander (Eds.), *Handbook of multicultural counseling* (pp. 263–287). Thousand Oaks, CA: Sage.

Burroughs, M. (1968). *What shall I tell my children who are Black?* Chicago: M.A.A.H. Press.

Carillo, C. (1982). Changing norms of Hispanic families: Implications for treatment. In E. E. Jones & S. J. Korchin (Eds.), *Minority mental health* (pp. 250–266). New York: Praeger.

Casas, J. M., & Pytluk, S. D. (1995). Hispanic identity development: Implications for research and practice. In J. P. Ponterotto, J. M. Casas, L. A. Suzuki, & C. M. Alexander (Eds.), *Handbook of multicultural counseling* (pp. 155–180). Thousand Oaks, CA: Sage.

Churchill, W. (1994). *Indians are us? Culture and genocide in Native North America.* Monroe, MA: Common Courage Press.

Clark, C. (1972). Black studies or the study of Black people. In R. L. Jones (Ed.), *Black psychology* (pp. 3–17). New York: Harper & Row.

Clark, K. B. (1963). *Prejudice and your child.* Boston: Beacon Press.

Clark, K., & Clark, M. (1947). Racial identification and preference in Negro children. In T. H. Newcomb & E. L. Hartley (Eds.), *Readings in social psychology* (pp. 169–178). New York: Henry Holt.

Cobbs, P. (1972). Ethnotherapy in groups. In L. Solomon & B. Berzon (Eds.), *New Perspectives on encounter groups* (pp. 383–403). San Francisco: Jossey-Bass.

Collett, J., & Serrano, B. (1992). Stirring it up: The inclusive classroom. In L. L. B. Borders & N. Van Note Chism (Eds.), *Teaching for diversity* (pp. 35–48). San Francisco: Jossey-Bass.

Costello, R. M. (1977). Construction and cross validation of an MMPI Black–White scale. *Journal of Personality Assessment, 41,* 515–519.

Cross, T. L. (1988, Summer). Services to minority populations: What does it mean to be a culturally competent professional? *Focal Point.* Portland, OR: Research and Training Center, Portland State University.

Cross, T. L., Bazron, B. J., Dennis, K. W., & Isaacs, M. R. (1989). *Towards a culturally competent system of care.* Washington, DC: Georgetown University Child Development Center.

Cross, W. E. (1995). The psychology of Nigrescence: Revising the Cross model. In J. P. Ponterotto, J. M. Casas, L. A. Suzuki, & C. M. Alexander (Eds.), *Handbook of multicultural counseling* (pp. 93–122). Thousand Oaks, CA: Sage.

Cross, W. E. (1971). The Negro-to-Black conversion experience: Toward a psychology of Black liberation. *Black World, 20*(9), 13–27.

Curry, N. E., & Johnson, C. N. (1990). *Beyond self-esteem: Developing a genuine sense of human value.* Washington, DC: National Association for the Education of Young Children.

Daly, A., Jennings, J., Beckett, J. O., & Leashore, B. R. (1995). Effective coping strategies of African Americans. *Social Work, 40,* 240–248.

Dana, R. H. (1988). Culturally diverse groups and MMPI interpretation. *Professional Psychology, 19*(5), 490–495.

D'Andrea, M. (1992). The violence of our silence. *Guidepost, 35*(4), 31.

D'Andrea, M., & Daniels, J. (1995). Promoting multiculturism and organizational change in the counseling profession: A case study. In J. P. Ponterotto, J. M. Casas, L. A. Suzuki, & C. M. Alexander (Eds.), *Handbook of multicultural counseling* (pp. 17–33). Thousand Oaks, CA: Sage.

Devore, W., & Schlesinger, E. G. (1981). *Ethnic sensitive social work practice.* St. Louis: C. V. Mosby.

Diamond, S. (1987). *In search of the primitive: A critique of civilization.* New Brunswick, NJ: Transaction.

Diller, J. V. (Ed.) (1978). *Ancient roots and modern meanings: A contemporary reader in Jewish identity.* New York: Bloch.

Diller, J. V. (1991). *Freud's Jewish identity: A case study in the impact of ethnicity.* Cranbury, NJ: Fairleigh Dickinson University Press.

Diller, J. V. (1997). *Informal interviews about self-esteem and racism with People of Color raised outside of the United States.* Unpublished notes, Conference on Race and Ethnicity in Higher Education, Orlando, FL.

Dollard, J. (1938). Hostility and fear in social life. *Social Forces, 17,* 15-26.

Draguns, J. G. (1981). Dilemmas and choices in cross-cultural counseling: The universal versus the culturally distinct. In P. B. Pedersen, J. G. Draguns, W. L. Lonner, & J. E. Trimble (Eds.), *Counseling across cultures* (pp. 3–22). Honolulu: University of Hawaii Press.

Duran, E., & Duran, B. (1995). *Native American postcolonial psychology.* Albany: State University of New York Press.

Erikson, E. (1968). *Identity, youth and crisis.* New York: Norton.

Falicov, C. J. (1986). Cross-cultural marriages. In N. Jacobson & A. Gurman (Eds.), *Clinical handbook of marital therapy* (pp. 429–450). New York: Guilford Press.

Fleming, C. M. (1992). American Indians and Alaska natives: Changing societies past and present. In M. A. Orlandi (Ed.), *Cultural competence for evaluators: A guide for alcohol and other drug abuse prevention practitioners working with ethnic/racial communities* (pp. 147–171). Rockville, MD: U.S. Department of Health and Human Services.

Freedman, D. G. (1979, January). Ethnic differences in babies. *Human Nature,* 36–43.

Fogelman, E. (1991). Mourning without graves. In A. Medene (Ed.), *Storms and rainbows: The many faces of death* (pp. 25–43). Washington, DC: Lewis Press.

Gallimore, R., Boggs, J., & Jordan, C. (1974). *Culture, behaviorism and education: A study of Hawaiian-Americans.* Beverly Hills, CA: Sage.

Garcia Coll, C. T. (1990). Development outcome of minority infants: A process-oriented look into our beginnings. *Child Development, 61,* 270–289.

Gaw, A. C. (1993). *Culture, ethnicity and mental illness.* Washington, DC: American Psychiatric Press.

Goodman, M. E. (1952). *Race awareness in young children.* London: Collier.

Gordon, M. (1964). *Assimilation in American life.* New York: Oxford University Press.

Graham, J. R. (1987). *The MMPI: A practical guide* (2nd ed.). New York: Oxford University Press.

Grant, D., & Haynes, D. (1995). A developmental framework for cultural competence training with children. *Social Work in Education, 17,* 171–182.

Green, J. W. (1982). *Cultural awareness in the human services.* Englewood Cliffs, NJ: Prentice Hall.

Grieger, I., & Ponterotto, J. G. (1995). A framework for assessment in multicultural counseling. In J. P. Ponterotto, J. M. Casas, L. A. Suzuki, & C. M. Alexander (Eds.), *Handbook of multicultural counseling* (pp. 357–374). Thousand Oaks, CA: Sage.

Grier, W., & Cobbs, P. (1968). *Black rage.* New York: Basic Books.

Grinberg, L., & Grinberg, R. (1989). *Psychoanalytic perspectives on migration and exile.* New Haven, CT: Yale University Press.

Group for the Advancement of Psychiatry, Committee on Cultural Psychiatry. (1984). *Suicide and ethnicity in the United States.* Series No. 128. New York: Brunner/Mazel.

Gushue, G. V., & Sciarra, D. T. (1995). Culture and families: A multicultural approach. In J. P. Ponterotto, J. M. Casas, L. A. Suzuki, & C. M. Alexander

(Eds.), *Handbook of multicultural counseling* (pp. 586–606). Thousand Oaks, CA: Sage.

Hacker, A. (1992). *Two nations: Black and white, separate, hostile, unequal.* New York: Ballantine.

Hale-Benson, J. (1986). *Black children: Their roots, culture and learning style.* Baltimore, MD: Johns Hopkins University Press.

Hampden-Turner, C. (1974). *From poverty to dignity: A strategy for poor Americans.* Garden City, NY: Anchor Press.

Hardiman, R., & Jackson, B. W. (1992). Racial identity development: Understanding racial dynamics in college classrooms and on campus. In M. Adams (Ed.), *Promoting diversity in college classrooms: Innovative responses for the curriculum, faculty and institutions* (pp. 21–37). San Francisco: Jossey-Bass.

Hardy, K. V., & Laszloffy, T. A. (1995). The cultural genogram: Key to training culturally competent family therapists. *Journal of Marital and Family Therapy, 21*(3), 227–237.

Hauser, S. T., & Kasendorf, E. (1983). *Black and White identity formation.* Halabar, FL: Kreiger.

Healey, J. F. (1995). *Race, ethnicity, gender, and class: The sociology of group conflict and change.* Thousand Oaks, CA: Forge Press.

Helms, J. E. (1985). Cultural identity in the treatment process. In P. Pedersen (Ed.), *Handbook of cross-cultural counseling and therapy.* Westport, CT: Greenwood Press.

Helms, J. E. (1990). An overview of Black racial identity theory. In J. E. Helms (Ed.), *Black and White racial identity: Theory, research and practice* (pp. 9–32). Westport, CT: Greenwood Press.

Helms, J. E. (1995). An update of Helms's White and People of Color racial identity models. In J. P. Ponterotto, J. M. Casas, L. A. Suzuki, & C. M. Alexander (Eds.), *Handbook of multicultural counseling* (pp. 181–198). Thousand Oaks, CA: Sage.

Herz, F. M., & Rosen, E. J. (1982). Jewish families. In M. McGoldrick, J. F. Pearce, & J. Giordano (Eds.), *Ethnicity and family therapy.* New York: Guilford Press.

Hill, R. (1972). *The strengths of Black families.* New York: National Urban League.

Hines, P. M., & Boyd-Franklin, N. (1982). Black families. In M. McGoldrick, J. K. Pearce, & J. Giordano (Eds.), *Ethnicity and Family Therapy* (pp. 84-107). New York: Guilford Press.

Ho, D. R. (1994). Asian American perspectives. In. J. U. Gordon (Ed.), *Managing multiculturalism in substance abuse services* (pp. 72–98). Thousand Oaks, CA: Sage.

Ho, M. (1987). *Family therapy with ethnic minorities.* Newbury Park, CA: Sage.

Hollingshead, A. B., & Redlich, F. C. (1958). *Social class and mental illness.* New York: Wiley.

Holtzman, W. H., Diaz-Guerrero, R., & Swartz, J. D. (1975). *Personality: Development in two cultures.* Austin: University of Texas Press.

Hoopes, D. S. (1972). *Reader in intercultural communication* (Vols. 1 & 2). Pittsburgh, PA: Regional Council for International Education.

Hsu, F. (1949). Suppression vs. repression: A limited psychological interpretation of four cultures. *Psychiatry, 12*, 223–242.

Hudson Institute. (1988, September). *Opportunity 2000: Creative affirmative action strategies for a changing workforce.* Washington, DC: Employment Standards Administration, U.S. Department of Labor.

Ignatiev, N. (1995). *How the Irish became White.* New York: Routledge.

Jacobs, J. H. (1977). *Black/White interracial families: Marital process and identity development in young children.* Unpublished doctoral dissertation, The Wright Institute, Berkeley, CA.

Jacobs, J. H. (1992). Identity development in biracial children. In M. P. P. Root (Ed.), *Racially mixed people in America* (pp. 190–206). Newbury Park, CA: Sage.

Jensen, A. R. (1972). *Genetics and education.* New York: Harper & Row.

Jewell, D. P. (1965). A case of a "psychotic" Navaho Indian male. *Human Organization, 11*(1), 32–36.

Jones, A., & Seagull, A. A. (1983). Dimensions of the relationship between the Black client and the White therapist: A theoretical overview. In D. R. Atkinson, G. Morten, & D. W. Sue (Eds.), *Counseling American minorities: A cross-cultural perspective* (2nd ed., pp. 156–166). Dubuque, IA: William C. Brown.

Jones, E. E., & Korchin, S. J. (1982). Minority mental health: Perspectives. In E. E. Jones & S. J. Korchin (Eds.), *Minority mental health* (pp. 3–36). New York: Praeger.

Jones, J. M. (1972). *Prejudice and racism.* Reading, MA: Addison-Wesley.

Jones, R. L. (1972). *Black psychology.* New York: Harper & Row.

Jung, C. G. (1934). On the present situation of psychotherapy. In *The collected works of C. G. Jung (1953–1979)* (Vol. 10, pp. 157–173). Princeton, NJ: Princeton University Press.

Kagen, S., & Madsen, M. (1972). Experimental analysis of cooperation and competition of Anglo-American and Mexican-American children. *Developmental Psychology, 6*, 49–59.

Kardiner, A., & Ovesey, L. (1951). *The mark of oppression.* Cleveland, OH: World Press.

Kendall, F. E. (1997, June). *Understanding white privilege.* Paper presented at the National Conference on Race and Ethnicity in Higher Education, Orlando, FL.

Kerwin, C., & Ponterotto, J. G. (1995). Biracial identity development: Theory and research. In J. P. Ponterotto, J. M. Casas, L. A. Suzuki, & C. M. Alexander (Eds.), *Handbook of multicultural counseling* (pp. 199–217). Thousand Oaks, CA: Sage.

Kich, G. K. (1992). The development process of asserting a biracial, bicultural identity. In M. P. P. Root (Ed.), *Racially mixed people in America* (pp. 304–317). Newbury Park, CA: Sage.

Kim, U., & Berry, J. W. (1993). *Indigenous psychologies.* Newbury Park, CA: Sage.

Kivel, P. (1996). *Uprooting racism: How White people can work for racial justice.* Gabriola Island, BC: New Society Publishers.

Klein, J. (1980). *Jewish identity and self-esteem: Healing wounds through ethnotherapy.* New York: Institute on Pluralism and Group Identity.

Klor de Alva, J. J. (1988). Telling Hispanics apart: Latin sociocultural diversity. In E. Acosta-Belen & B. R. Sjostrom (Eds.), *The Hispanic experience in the United States* (pp. 107–136). New York: Praeger.

Kohout, J., & Pion, G. (1990). Participation of ethnic minorities in psychology: Where do we stand today? In G. Stricker, E. Davis-Russell, E. Bourg, E. Duran, W. R. Hammond, J. McHolland, K. Polite, & B. E. Vaughn (Eds.), *Towards ethnic diversification in psychology education and training* (pp. 105–111). Washington, DC: American Psychological Association.

Kohout, J., & Wicherski, M. (1993). *Characteristics of graduate departments of psychology:1991–1992.* Washington, DC: American Psychological Association.

Kramer, M., Rosen, B., & Willis, E. (1973). Definitions and distributions of mental disorders in a racist society. In C. V. Willie, B. Kramer, & B. Brown (Eds.), *Racism and mental health* (pp. 353–340). Pittsburgh: University of Pittsburgh Press.

Kroeber, A. L. (1948). *Anthropology: Race, language, culture, psychology, prehistory.* London: Harrap.

Kroeber, A. L., & Kluckhohm, C. (1952). *Culture: A critical review of concepts and definitions.* Cambridge, MA: Papers of the Peabody Museum No. 47.

Kuhn, T. S. (1970). *The structure of scientific revolutions.* Chicago: University of Chicago Press.

Kunjufu, J. (1984). *Countering the conspiracy to destroy Black boys.* Chicago: Afro-Am Publishing.

Landau, J. (1982). Therapy with families in cultural transition. In M. McGoldrick, J. K. Pearce, & J. Giordano (Eds.), *Ethnicity and family therapy* (pp. 552–572). New York: Guilford Press.

Larsen, J. (1976, October). *Dysfunction in the evangelical family: Treatment considerations.* Paper presented at the meeting of the American Association of Marriage and Family Therapists, Philadelphia.

Lee, C. C., & Armstrong, K. L. (1995). Indigenous models of mental health intervention: Lessons from traditional healers. In J. P. Ponterotto, J. M. Casas, L. A. Suzuki, & C. M. Alexander (Eds.), *Handbook of multicultural counseling* (pp. 441–456). Thousand Oaks, CA: Sage.

Legters, L. H. (1988). The American genocide. *Policy Studies Journal, 16*(4), 768–777.

Lewin, K. (1948). *Resolving social conflicts: Selected papers on group dynamics.* New York: Harper & Row.

Linton, R. (1945). *The cultural background of personality.* New York: Appleton-Century-Crofts.

Lum, D. (1986). *Social work practice and People of Color: A process-stage approach.* Monterey, CA: Brooks/Cole.

Lum, R. G. (1982). Mental health attitudes and opinions of Chinese. In E. E. Jones & S. J. Korchin (Eds.), *Minority mental health* (pp. 165–189). New York: Praeger.

Manson, S., & Trimble, J. (1982). American Indians and Alaska Native communities: Past efforts, future inquiries. In L. Snowden (Ed.), *Reaching the underserved: Mental health needs of neglected populations* (pp. 143–163). Beverly Hills, CA: Sage.

Marin, G. (1992). Issues in the measurement of acculturation among Hispanics. In K. F. Geisinger (Ed.), *Psychological testing of Hispanics* (pp. 235–252). Washington, DC: American Psychological Association.

McAdoo, H. P. (1985). Racial attitude and self-concept of young Black children over time. In H. P. McAdoo & J. L. McAdoo (Eds.), *Black children: Social, educational, and parental environments* (pp. 213–242). Newbury Park, CA: Sage.

McDougall, W. (1977). *Is America safe for democracy?* New York: Ayer.

McGoldrick, M. (1982). Normal families: An ethnic perspective. In F. Walsh (Ed.), *Normal family processes* (pp. 399–424). New York: Guilford Press.

McIntosh, P. (1989, July/August). White privilege: Unpacking the invisible knapsack. *Peace & Freedom*, pp. 10–12.

Meadow, A. (1982). Psychopathology, psychotherapy, and the Mexican-American patient. In E. E. Jones & S. J. Korchin (Eds.), *Minority mental health* (pp. 331–361). New York: Praeger.

Memmi, A. (1965). *Dominated man: Notes towards a portrait*. Boston: Beacon Press.

Memmi, A. (1966). *The liberation of the Jew*. New York: Grossman.

Minuchin, S. (1974). *Families and family therapy*. Cambridge, MA: Harvard University Press.

Minuchin, S., Montalvo, B., Guerney, G., Rosman, B., & Schumer, F. (1967). *Families of the slums*. New York: Basic Books.

Mosby, D. P. (1972). Towards a new specialty of Black psychology. In R. L. Jones (Ed.), *Black psychology* (pp. 33–42). New York: Harper & Row.

Moynihan, D. P. (1965, March). *The Negro family: The case for national action*. Washington, DC: Office of Policy Planning and Research, U.S. Department of Labor.

Myers, H. F. (1982). Stress, ethnicity, and social class: A model for research with Black populations. In E. E. Jones & S. J. Korchin (Eds.), *Minority mental health* (118–148). New York: Praeger.

Nobles, W. W. (1972). African philosophy: Foundations for Black psychology. In R. L. Jones (Ed.), *Black psychology* (pp. 18–32). New York: Harper & Row.

Norton, D. G. (1983). Black families life patterns, the development of self and cognitive development of Black children. In G. J. Powell, J. Yamamoto, A. Romero, & A. Morales (Eds.), *The psychosocial development of minority children* (pp. 181–193). New York: Brunner/Mazel.

Obgu, J. U. (1978). *Minority education and caste: The American system in cross-cultural perspective*. New York: Academic Press.

Oetting, E. R., & Beauvais, F. (1990). Orthogonal cultural identity theory: The cultural identification in minority adolescents. *International Journal of Addiction, 25*, 655–685.

Parham, T. (1992). *The White researcher in multicultural counseling, revisited—Discussions and suggestions*. Paper presented at the annual meeting of the American Psychological Association, Washington, DC. Quoted in D'Andrea, M., & Daniels, J. (1995). Promoting multiculturism and organizational change in the counseling profession: A case study. In J. P. Ponterotto, J. M. Casas, L. A. Suzuki, & C. M. Alexander (Eds.), *Handbook of multicultural counseling* (pp. 17–33). Thousand Oaks, CA: Sage.

Pearl, A., & Reismann, F. (1965). *New careers for the poor: Nonprofessionals in human service.* New York: Free Press.

Perkins, M. (1994, March 17). Guess who's coming to church? Confronting Christians' fear of interracial marriage. *Christianity Today,* pp. 30–33.

Petersen, P. B., Draguns, J. G., Lonner, W. J., & Trimble, J. E. (1989). *Counseling across culture.* Honolulu: University of Hawaii Press.

Pinderhughes, E. (1982). Afro-American families and the victim system. In M. McGoldrick, J. K. Pearce & J. Giordano (Eds.), *Ethnicity and family therapy* (p. 108–122). New York: Guilford Press.

Pinderhughes, E. (1989). *Understanding race, ethnicity, and power: The key to efficacy in clinical practice.* New York: Free Press.

Ponterotto, J. G. (1988). Racial consciousness development among White counselor trainees: A stage model. *Journal of Multicultural Counseling and Development, 16,* 146–156.

Ponterotto, J. P., Casas, J. M., Suzuki, L. A., & Alexander, C. M. (Eds.). (1995). *Handbook of multicultural counseling.* Thousand Oaks, CA: Sage.

Poussaint, A. F. (1972). *Why Blacks kill Blacks.* New York: Emerson Hall.

Powell, G. J. (1973). The self-concept in White and Black children. In C. V. Willie, B. Kramer, & B. Brown (Eds.), *Racism and mental health* (pp. 299-318). Pittsburgh: University of Pittsburgh Press.

Powell, G. J., Yamamoto, J., Romero, A., & Morales, A. (1983). *The psychosocial development of minority children.* New York: Brunner/Mazel.

Proshansky, H., & Newton, P. (1968). The meaning and nature of Negro self-identity. In M. Deutsch, I. Katz, & A. Jensen (Eds.), *Social class, race and psychological development.* New York: Holt, Rinehart & Winston.

Reynolds, C. R., & Kaiser, S. M. (1990). Test bias in psychological assessment. In T. B. Gutkin & C. R. Reynolds (Eds.), *The handbook of school psychology* (pp. 487–525). New York: Wiley.

Rokeach, M. (1960). *Beliefs, attitudes, and values.* New York: Basic Books.

Rosenberg, M. (1979). *Conceiving the self.* New York: Basic Books.

Rosenhan, D. L. (1975). On being sane in insane places. In D. L. Rosenhan & P. London (Eds.), *Theory and research in abnormal psychology* (pp. 254–270). New York: Holt, Rinehart & Winston.

Rosenthal, D. (1976). *Experimenter effects in behavioral research.* New York: Halsted Press.

Rosenthal, R., & Jacobson, L. (1968). *Pygmalion in the classroom: Teacher expectations and pupils' intellectual development.* New York: Holt, Rinehart & Winston.

Rowe, W., Behrens, J. T., & Leach, M. M. (1995). Racial/ethnic identity and social consciousness: Looking back and looking forward. In J. P. Ponterotto, J. M. Casas, L. A. Suzuki, & C. M. Alexander (Eds.), *Handbook of multicultural counseling* (pp. 218–235). Thousand Oaks, CA: Sage.

Russo, N. R., Olmedo, E. L., Stapp, J., & Fulcher, R. (1981). Women and minorities in psychology. *American Psychologist, 36,* 1315–1363.

Saeki, C., & Borow, H. (1985). Counseling and psychotherapy: East and west. In P. B. Pedersen (Ed.), *Handbook of cross-cultural counseling and therapy.* Westport, CT: Greenwood Press.

Scanzoni, J. N. (1971). *The Black family in modern society*. Chicago: University of Chicago Press.

Scarr, S. (1993). Biological and cultural diversity: The legacy of Darwin for development. *Child Development, 64*, 1333–1353.

Seifer, R., Sameroff, A., Barrett, L., & Krafchuk, E. (1994). Infant temperament measured by multiple observations and mother report. *Child Development, 65*, 1478–1490.

Smolowe, J. (1993, November). Intermarried . . . with children. *Time, 142*(21), pp. 64–65.

Snowden, L., & Todman, P. A. (1982). The psychological assessment of Blacks: New and needed developments. In E. E. Jones & S. J. Korchin (Eds.), *Minority mental health* (pp. 227–249). New York: Praeger.

Soriano, F. I. (1994). The Latino perspective: A sociocultural portrait. In J. U. Gordon (Ed.), *Managing multiculturalism in substance abuse services* (pp. 117–147). Thousand Oaks, CA: Sage.

Spenser, M. B., & Markstrom-Adams, C. (1990). Identity processes among racial and ethnic minority children in America. *Child Development, 61*, 290–310.

Stack, C. (1975). *All our kin: Strategies for survival in a Black community*. New York: Harper & Row.

Stonequist, E. V. (1961). *The marginal man: A study in personality and culture conflict*. New York: Russell & Russell.

Sue, D. W., Arredondo, A., & McDavis, R. J. (1992). Multicultural counseling competencies and standards: A call to the profession. *Journal of Counseling and Development, 70*, 477–486.

Sue, S., & McKinney, H. (1975). Asian Americans in the community mental health care system. *American Journal of Orthopsychiatry, 45*, 111–118.

Sue, S., McKinney, H., Allen, D., & Hall, J. (1974). Delivery of community health services to Black and White clients. *Journal of Consulting Psychology, 42*, 794–801.

Sue, S. W., & Sue, D. (1990). *Counseling the culturally different: Theory and practice* (2nd ed.). New York: Wiley.

Sue, S., & Zane, N. (1987). The role of culture and cultural techniques in psychotherapy: A critique and reformulation. *American Psychologist, 42*, 37–45.

Suzuki, L. A., & Kugler, J. F. (1995). Intellectual and personality assessment: Multicultural perspectives. In J. P. Ponterotto, J. M. Casas, L. A. Suzuki, & C. M. Alexander (Eds.), *Handbook of multicultural counseling* (pp. 493–515). Thousand Oaks, CA: Sage.

Takaki, R. (1993). *A different mirror: A history of multicultural America*. Boston: Little, Brown.

Thompson, C. (1949). The Thompson modification of the Thematic Apperception Test. *Journal of Projective Techniques, 13*, 469–478.

Thornton, M. C., Chatters, L. M., Taylor, R. J., & Allen, W. (1990). Sociodemographic and environmental correlates of racial socialization by Black parents. *Child Development, 61*, 401–409.

Tong, B. R. (1981). *On the confusion of psychopathology with culture: Iatrogenesis in* the *"treatment" of Chinese Americans.* Unpublished manuscript, The Wright Institute, Berkeley, CA.

Torrey, E. F. (1986). *Witch doctors and psychiatrists: The common roots of psychotherapy and its future.* New York: Harper & Row.

Trawick-Smith, J. W. (1997). *Early childhood development: A multicultural perspective.* Upper Saddle River, NJ: Prentice Hall.

Trawick-Smith, J. W., & Lisi, P. (1994). Infusing multicultural perspectives in an early childhood development course: Effect on the knowledge and attitudes of inservice teachers. *Journal of Early Childhood Teacher Education, 15,* 8–12.

Turner, J. R. (1985). *Differential treatment and ethnicity.* Unpublished notes, The Wright Institute, Berkeley, CA.

Valentine, C. A. (1971). Deficit, difference, and bicultural models of Afro-American behavior. *Harvard Educational Review, 41,* 135–157.

Vontress, C. E. (1981). Racial and ethnic barriers in counseling. In P. B. Pedersen, J. G. Draguns, W. L. Lonner, & J. E. Trimble (Eds.), *Counseling across cultures* (rev. ed., pp. 87-107). Honolulu: University of Hawaii Press.

Walpold, B., Casas, J. M., & Atkinson, D. R. (1982). Ethnic bias in counseling: An information-processing approach. *Journal of Counseling Psychology, 28,* 489–503.

Wechsler, H., Solomon, L., & Kramer, B. (1970). *Social psychology and mental health.* New York: Holt, Rinehart & Winston.

Weinstein, G., & Mellen, D. (1997). Anti-Semitism curriculum design. In M. Adams, L. A. Bell, & P. Griffin (Eds.), *Teaching for diversity and social justice* (pp. 170–197). New York: Routledge.

White, J. (1972). Towards a Black psychology. In R. Jones (Ed.), *Black psychology* (pp. 43–50). New York: Harper & Row.

Wijeyesinghe, C. L., Griffin, P., & Love, B. (1997). Racism curriculum design. In M. Adams, L. A. Bell, & P. Griffin (Eds.), *Teaching for diversity and social justice* (pp. 82–109). New York: Routledge.

Williams, J. E., & Morland, J. K. (1976). *Race, color and the young child.* Chapel Hill: University of North Carolina Press.

Williams, R. M. (1947). The reduction of intergroup tensions. *Social Science Council Bulletin, 59,* 119–127.

Wolkind, S., & Rutter, M. (1985). *Sociocultural factors in child and adolescent psychiatry.* Boston: Blackwell Scientific.

Wylie, R. C. (1961). *The self-concept.* Lincoln: University of Nebraska Press.

Yamamoto, J., Jones, O., & Palley, N. (1968). Cultural problems in psychiatric therapy. *Archives of General Psychiatry, 19,* 45–49.

Yellow Horse Brave Heart, M. (1995). *The return to the sacred path: Healing from historical trauma and historical unresolved grief among the Lakota.* Unpublished doctoral dissertation, Smith College School of Social Work, Northampton, MA.

York, S. (1991). *Roots and wings: Affirming culture in early childhood programs.* St Paul, MN: Redleaf Press.

Index